Pursuing a Heart of Wisdom is  workers. This book holds up th dark places of our sinful hearts. A parents and youth today, John Kwasny combines the word of God with practical insight to illumine the path to wisdom (Psalm 119:105). This book will work to strengthen your ministry of discipleship by providing a measure of confidence as you help God's people walk with Christ in the midst of the daily struggle with our fallen nature.

Stephen T. Estock
Coordinator, Committee on Discipleship Ministries (CDM),
Presbyterian Church in America

Wow! Dr. Kwasny has provided us with a much needed resource. Many parents and youth workers desire to disciple their students but are paralyzed when problems arise. *Pursuing a Heart of Wisdom* not only provides us with practical tools but also trains us in the theological foundation needed to broach these hard topics with our students! Dr. Kwasny is thoughtfully clear in his words and faithful to Scripture in his counsel, but more importantly, he takes us to our resting place that is only found in the Great Counselor, the person and work of Jesus Christ. Whether a parent, youth worker, or counselor, this resource fills a needed gap in our ministry to teenagers!

Sonny and Morgan Walker
Biblical Counselors and Director of Student Ministries,
First Presbyterian Church of Rome, Georgia

Youthworkers and parents are being required in this rapidly-changing culture to navigate and hack their way through an increasingly dense jungle of complicated issues. But, in this pastoral, readable book by Dr. John Kwasny, we're offered a guide who directs us with compassion, practical help and thoughtful, biblical counsel. Having done scores of both parents' seminars and youthworker seminars over the years, I can promise that in this book, parents and youthworkers will find the thoughtful, thorough guide we need—no dodging hard questions, no ducking controversial topics, no easy answers. And how refreshing to read a book that invites us to reframe these discussions using the biblical language of wisdom, not by shrinking down the complexity of real psychological problems, but by focusing on the sufficiency of biblical insight.

Duffy Robbins
Author and Speaker,
Professor of Christian Ministry, Grove City College, Grove City,
Pennsylvania

There are few people who are as qualified as John Kwasny to write this kind of guide for those who counsel and disciple teenagers. John writes as someone who knows teenagers well, having raised teens himself and also counseling them over his many years in the church. Whether you need an overall orientation to counseling teens or need help dealing with the details of particular issues, this book offers quality biblical wisdom that you will not find anywhere else. I am especially thankful for how practical this guide is, being rich with case studies, questions to ask, and "pointers" for counselors. Most of all, I am thankful that he is tackling very difficult, complex issues in a way that never compromises the gospel of Jesus Christ.

Chase Maxey
Executive Director and Counselor
Biblical Counseling & Training Ministries

It is not often I get the privilege to read a book deeply committed to a thoughtful, biblical approach to counseling teens. It is for the parent, the youth worker, the caring adult who wants to think well and wisely about the culture of our young people. If you want to understand the struggles teens are facing, the importance of a strong theological perspective and godly influences in their lives, read this book.

Julie Lowe
Counselor and Play Therapist,
Faculty Member at CCEF

PURSUING
A HEART
OF WISDOM

COUNSELING
TEENAGERS BIBLICALLY

JOHN C. KWASNY

CHRISTIAN
FOCUS

Copyright © John C. Kwasny 2019

paperback ISBN 978-1-5271-0386-3
epub ISBN 978-1-5271-0437-2
mobi ISBN 978-1-5271-0438-9

10 9 8 7 6 5 4 3 2 1

First published in 2019
by
Christian Focus Publications Ltd,
Geanies House, Fearn, Ross-shire,
IV20 1TW, Great Britain.
www.christianfocus.com

with

Reformed Youth Ministries,
P.O. Box 697,
Cookeville,
Tennessee, 38503

Cover and Interior Design
by Pete Barnsley (Creativehoot.com)

Printed and bound
by Bell & Bain, Glasgow

CONTENTS

Dedicated to the Youth Ministry of
Pear Orchard Presbyterian Church (PCA)

Foreword

When I first got involved in youth ministry, I had no idea what I was signing up for. But, I guess that's how most professions are in life. We have an idea of what it is we might be doing, but once we become engaged in the day-to-day work, we're enlightened to our initial naiveté. For many, youth ministry is synonymous with fun and games. Without a doubt, having fun is a part of youth ministry, if it isn't fun—in many ways—you probably should consider rethinking some of what you're doing.

That said, it wasn't long after I began serving in student ministry when I realized that ministry to youth was not all fun. My eyes were quickly opened to the dangers, sadness, and general brokenness in the lives of students and families. A student pulling a knife on their parent, couples engaging in oral sex, students exploring their sexuality in ways opposed to Scripture, death, depression, anxiety, eating disorders, addiction—you name it; those serving in student ministry will see it.

Truth be told, youth workers often find themselves on the front lines of cultural trends. That is, they may see things that senior pastors—those who are more 'seasoned' in ministry—have not even dealt with. More often than not, it seems that those serving in student ministry are fresh out of college and are faced with issues they may feel ill-equipped to deal with. To be sure, there are those times when student ministry workers need to point students to pastors and counselors who have more experience in a given area. That said, are youth workers ever able to assist students with their problems?

As Christians, we believe in a sovereign God who is reigning and ruling over all creation. We believe that He orchestrates the providences of each and every individual we come across. And, in His good providence, He often has you—the youth worker or parent or grandparent or volunteer or mentor—in the lives of these students to help point them to truth.

To borrow a phrase from Paul David Tripp, we need to see that we can be an instrument in the Redeemer's hand—bringing the gospel to bear in the lives of broken students and families.[1] Ministry (and life for that matter) is often designed to bring us to the end of ourselves. It exposes our helplessness and need for Jesus. What I discovered in youth ministry was that God consistently exposed my inadequacies to do the actual ministry He was calling me to. It's through our weaknesses that His strength and power are clearly displayed.

One of the greatest graces God gifts to the church are our sisters and brothers in the faith. He places wise pastors, counselors, teachers, and experts in our path. Those who not only have great wisdom, but have a heart to pass it on to others—not hoard it like it's theirs to keep. John Kwasny is one of those graces God bestowed in my life.

As I encountered the unthinkable in youth ministry, I would often find myself sitting in John's office. Too many times to count, John graciously answered my inquiries about issues with students and families. Rare was the time when John had the door closed or was unable to respond to my questions.

While John is not omniscient—he wouldn't claim that either—I often found myself amazed at his answers. What left me bewildered and often in despair, was something he already had an

---

1   Tripp, Paul David, *Instruments in the Redeemer's Hands: People in Need of Change Helping People in Need of Change* (P&R Publishing: 2002).

answer to. Through his decades of counseling, he was imparting wisdom the Lord imparted to him.

Before you move along too quickly, pause to think about what you're holding in your hands. This is decades of wisdom and experience. Scenarios that John has dealt with first-hand. Topics he has taught in seminary classes and spoken on in seminars. This is a valuable tool for those serving in youth ministry or for those parents and grandparents discipling the next generation.

The names and the stories that follow are changed to protect those who sat in the counseling chair, but the content that lies ahead is as real as it gets—these are not hypotheticals. Much of the material is weighty enough on its own but knowing that young hearts and minds are dealing with these issues, adds a level of sobriety that's staggering.

Before I close this out, one more word on wisdom. Wisdom is contained in the pages ahead and some of that wisdom is understanding that we will not all be experts in everything. While all of us are given gifts by God, He does not gift us in the same way and chooses to bestow a certain gift to one person while giving a different gift to another. Therefore, we all need to know our limitations in certain areas of counseling and reach out to those who can help us. Sometimes the greatest way we can counsel others is by finding those who are better equipped to counsel those we care most about. John gives wisdom in this area as well.

While it's important to point out this aspect of wisdom, I also want to guard from downplaying the significance of relationship. Christians know that we are created in the image of a triune God, so we are hard-wired for relationships. When we apply this to the church and home, we know they thrive in meaningful relationships. Although you might not have a certain area of expertise, know that God has made many youth workers and parents *experts* in their students and children. If you have years with a specific student or child, God can use that significantly in the realm of counseling.

Our heartbeat at Reformed Youth Ministries (RYM) is passing the faith on to the next generation. What John has given us in, *Pursing a Heart of Wisdom*, is a must-own resource for anyone who shares RYM's passion. While RYM knows there are a variety of views on counseling, we trust that anyone will see the value of this resource no matter where you land on the counseling spectrum. It's the prayer of RYM that God would use this to help you ease the pain and suffering in many student's lives and, by doing so, give them a small taste of the restoration to come.

John Perritt
January 2019

Introduction

'My son, if your heart is wise, my heart too will be glad' (Prov. 23:15). A healthy body. A strong mind. A good academic record. Success in every extra-curricular activity. A bright future. Out of all the qualities and successes adults desire to see in the lives of teens, a wise and understanding heart should be at the top of the list. Grounded in the fear of the Lord (Prov. 9:10), godly wisdom is essential to navigate the minefield of the teenage years. Far too often, it is assumed by many that adolescents are destined to be foolish—hopefully, outgrowing such foolishness by adulthood. Sadly, many teens are left to themselves during these years, dealing with the temptations and the struggles of their hearts and minds all on their own. Yet, all through the Book of Proverbs, young people are taught to gain wisdom through listening to and obeying their parents and other wise adults. If teenagers are to listen and learn wisdom, then parents and other mature adults are to speak wisdom and live wisely before them! To put it in today's terms, all teens need Biblical counseling in order to pursue a heart of wisdom—and God calls parents and youth ministry leaders to offer them Biblical counseling.

FOR PARENTS

Do teenagers really want help from their own parents? Some would argue that teens would rather talk to a good friend, another adult, or maybe even a professional when they are experiencing problems. While there may be some truth to that assessment, it begs the question: Why don't more teens ask for counsel from their parents? Some may foolishly believe that their parents are out-of-touch with the modern teenage experience when they actually have much wisdom to offer. Others may have tried to get help from parents, only to be neglected or outright rejected. Still other teens might have received some poor counseling that led them in the wrong direction. Finally, there are certainly teens and parents who have a broken relationship, not allowing for Biblical counseling to be spoken or heard. If any of these are obstacles to your parent-teen counseling process, then they deserve to be overcome. Parent, you should never just assume that your teen does not want to hear from you. Whether he or she seeks your counsel or not, work from the belief that he or she definitely needs your wisdom. Your child has been given to you! A major aspect of the training and discipline process is the giving and receiving of Biblical wisdom.

Not only do you, as a Christian parent, have wisdom that your teenager requires; there are several other reasons you are his or her best Biblical counselor. For one thing, there are no other adults on earth who know your teenager as well as you do. You have probably lived with your teenager his or her entire life, have walked through all the stages of development so far, and observed most problems firsthand. Furthermore, you have been on the battlefield of parenting for many years, striving to train and discipline your teen to the best of your ability. You may not have always been successful—and you certainly have made many mistakes—but God continues to call you to raise your teenager in the fear and admonition of the Lord (Eph. 6:4). And, ultimately, no other person in this world loves your teenager as much as you do. Even when you have been frustrated and exhausted in your parenting—and maybe angry and afraid too—the God-given love of a parent for a child is present. Hopefully, that knowledge of and love for your teen will translate into the compassionate giving of wisdom for their problems.

Built on a foundation of a loving parent-teen relationship, it is incumbent that the Christian parent learn some of the basic principles of Biblical counseling. Beginning by embracing Biblical presuppositions, a parent must become grounded in: (1) Who God is, (2) Who the teenager is, (3) Where teenage problems come from, and (4) How to solve those problems Biblically. From Biblical presuppositions, a basic understanding of the counseling process will help the parent to effectively listen, evaluate, and offer wisdom. Learning basic questions to ask your teenager as well as essential Biblical principles of common teenage problems is also a part of the process. As a parent desiring to help your teenager, God's Word is necessary to shape your understanding of counseling presuppositions, process, and problem-solving. This book will get you started in the effort to guide your teen to pursue wisdom and Biblically solve problems. Where you may need the help of other Biblical counselors at some point, your teenager needs you first and foremost. And, even when other counselors are involved from time to time, your counseling must continue throughout all the teenage years.

FOR YOUTH MINISTRY WORKERS

Youth Ministry is an essential aspect of the work of the local church, as well as the overall discipleship of teenagers. Unfortunately, whether they have been earned or not, unflattering stereotypes of youth ministry have existed for years: The church youth group is just a place for good, clean, fun. The youth group is heavy on entertainment, but light on serious Christian education. Youth ministry workers act more like the teens than actual adults. Unfortunately, even parents can think this way about their church's youth ministry! But the truth is that our teens need their youth group to be a place where they can grow as disciples of Jesus Christ. And, connected to that discipleship ministry is the necessary work of Biblical counseling. The teenagers in your youth ministry—even the 'good' ones—have problems. They need to learn how God's Word applies to daily life, and to all of their struggles and sin. They need older, mature adults in their lives to show them compassion, listen to them, and offer wise instruction.

Often times, teenagers will seek you first when they are experiencing problems. At other times, parents will talk to you about their teenagers. There will be particular instances when you will need to keep conversations with your teens confidential; at other times, parents will need to be included. Unfortunately, you may discover that some parents are giving bad counsel or just ignoring the teen's problem altogether. In any event, remember that your role in helping teenagers is to come alongside and assist parents with their task of raising their own children. Even if parents are contributing to the teenager's problem, you must still counsel teens to honor and obey them—learning to relate to them in a godly way. Of course, the best case scenario is when you are able to fully partner with parents, working together to help the teen pursue a heart of wisdom. When parents and youth ministry workers are committed to God, to Biblical counseling, and to the teenager, there is a great opportunity that the teenager will thrive and grow through any problem.

So, if you are a youth ministry leader or worker, this book is also for you. It will give you the foundations of Biblical counseling, including proper presuppositions, a Biblical process, and principles for common problems. Coupled with the teaching and overall discipleship occurring in your youth ministry, this information is intended to begin to equip you as a Biblical counselor. Additionally, it will be helpful to seek the guidance and wisdom of pastors and other Biblical counselors as you begin to counsel your teens. At times, there will be problems that are beyond your current knowledge and skill level that will require referral to pastors, Biblical counselors, or even medical professionals. When that is the case, it is vital that you continue to walk with him or her during this time. Your relationship and example is an important part of the Biblical counseling process, even when formal counseling has stopped. Recognize that Biblical counseling is an essential task of the youth ministry worker, as it is part and parcel of the overall discipleship process. Your desire should always be to see each teen walking with Christ, and in all wisdom and righteousness.

It can be a frightening thing when first hearing or seeing a teenager in distress, or engaged in outright sinful rebellion. It can also be just as scary to have to sit down and offer wise counsel to that teen. Yet, God calls mature believers to offer truth and wisdom to the next generation, and not hide the greatness of God from them (Ps. 73). Counseling teenagers Biblically takes courage, compassion, and grace. Only when we are dependent on the Great Counselor, the Holy Spirit, will we be able to act in faith and speak the truth in love. Children have always needed parents and other mature adults to train, love, and guide them through the minefield of the teen years. Take the time and learn from God's Word in order to grow as a Biblical counselor for the glory of God and the good of your teen!

Part 1
Preparing to Counsel Teens Biblically

1.
Planting Firmly in Biblical Presuppositions

'All teenagers lie.' 'Teens are just animals with clothes on.' 'Adolescence is a time of incredibly unpredictable hormonal change.' 'Young people are just fools.' 'The core problem with teens today is low self-esteem.' These, and the hundreds of other things you believe about teenagers are 'presuppositions'—foundational beliefs that fit together to form your overall understanding of youth. Every time you interact with a teenager, your thoughts, words, and actions emerge from a set of basic foundational beliefs. Some of your beliefs come from your own experiences. Others have settled in your hearts and minds from the influence of the unique culture around you. Hopefully, most have come to be a part of your 'operating system' as you have grown in your knowledge of God, His Word, and His world. As Christians, we are responsible to think only from a Christian worldview—believing the truth about our teens, their problems, and the Biblical solutions to those problems.

So, to wisely counsel the teenager in your life, it's essential to ensure that your presuppositions are actually aligned with God's Word. In other words, operating from Biblical presuppositions is the first step to becoming a Biblical counselor! Fundamentally, it is your presuppositions which define what sort of counselor you are, and what counseling you will offer. For example, if you believe that teenagers are little more than hormonally driven, socialized animals, then your counsel will probably center only on controlling their creature impulses. Or, if your fundamental view of God is one where He created the world, but then left it for human beings to run it on their own, then your counsel for a teen will focus primarily on human responsibility. When foundational views of God and people are faulty or deficient, the counsel that emerges from them will miss the mark as well. If you examine much of the advice given to teenagers today, including counsel given by some Christians, you will quickly learn that the main problem is that their underlying presuppositions are not Biblical.

Therefore, before we can dive in and rightly understand the specific problem that our teenagers are experiencing, we must dig deep to our root systems and make sure we are firmly grounded in the Word of God. When counseling teens, it is essential that we are planted firmly in Biblical presuppositions concerning (1) God; (2) the teenager; (3) how the problems of teenagers develop; and, (4) the solutions to those problems. These four fundamental areas combined will lead to the right process of handling the problems of youth, grounded in Biblical principles of each particular problem. To put it another way, the truer we are to Biblical orthodoxy, the more Biblical our practice of counseling teens will be. Only then will we be able to call on our teens to pursue wisdom in all of life.

ABOUT GOD

Hopefully, as a Christian parent or youth ministry worker, you recognize how a wrong view of God will send your counseling down the wrong path. The atheist may counsel their teenager to deal with the fact that life is random and religion is just an emotional crutch. The deist who doesn't believe in a God who is personally involved with His creation would probably tell his teen that he alone has wrecked his life, and God expects him to fix it. The pantheist who believes 'all is in God and God is in all' will potentially expose her teenager to some sort of new age philosophy of life, or just tell her to 'go with the flow.'[1] Every counselor has a set of beliefs of God and those views always trickle down into their counseling process and practice. As Christians, our presuppositions about God must be true and accurate in order for us to lead our teens into all truth. So, let's briefly summarize a Biblical view of God that will deeply influence our counseling of teenagers.

God exists. 'In the beginning, God ...' (Gen. 1:1). The fundamental truth that there is a God in Heaven and He does all that pleases Him (Ps. 115:3) dictates how we look at all of our problems in this life. God is eternal—He has always existed and will exist forever (1 Tim. 1:17). There has never been, or ever will be, a time when human beings exist without God also existing. People are never ultimately alone, or independent of God. Yet we also know that this God is not the same God that all other anti-Christian religions profess to worship. The true and only God is one God in three persons—the Father, the Son, and the Holy Spirit (2 Cor. 13:14). All three persons are co-equal in power, being, and glory. God is always at work in this world, and in the lives of God's people. When addressing any problem of youth, we begin and end with the reality of the existence of God.

God is Creator. Genesis 1 not only teaches us that God exists, but also that He created all things, visible and invisible, apart from sin (Gen. 1:1-31). This world did not just randomly explode on its own from some immense cocktail of cosmic gasses. Human beings did not evolve from lower lifeforms, and thus retain some sort of animal-like qualities. God created all things out of nothing (Heb. 11:3), by the Word of His power. Also included in the understanding of God as Creator is that He is wholly distinct from His creatures. He is the Divine Maker and Designer; we are not. His creative power formed and fashioned every last teenager in this world. If we do not believe

---

1   Even though 'go with the flow' is now a colloquial phrase that communicates something like 'relax' or 'chill out', its original meaning was to somehow get into the flow of existence since we are all God and God is in all.

God is the Creator of the universe, then there will be absolutely no meaning in this life. Without intelligent design by the one, true God—where will we turn to solve our problems? If God has not created all things and all people, then all we will be able to offer our teens is man-centered counsel with no lasting hope.

God is sovereign. God is before all things, and in Him all things hold together (Col. 1:17). He can do all things consistent with His nature, which means no purpose of His can be thwarted (Job 42:2). God did not just create the world and then leave it to human beings to run on their own. He did not give people unbounded free will that can somehow end up overriding God's sovereign will. If these things about God are true, what difference does the belief that God is totally in control of our lives make to our counsel of teenagers? To begin with, it means that we are not in control of our lives. Every problem teenagers experience is known by God. Every situation, every direction, every outcome falls under the sovereign rule of the King of the universe. To deny the sovereignty of God is to greatly diminish His power, His glory, and His love for His people. If we in any way attempt to share a God who is limited in His ultimate control of His world with our teens, our counsel will end up giving humans too much power and control.

God is holy, just, and righteous. For many semi-religious people, their beliefs about God typically end with the fact that He exists and He might have had a hand in the creation of this world. It is a huge leap for most modern people to embrace a God who is in total control of all things. Yet, a belief that is just as challenging is the recognition that God is completely holy, just, and righteous (Ps. 7:11; Ps. 145:17; Rev. 4:8). The holiness of God pervades the Scriptures, from Genesis to Revelation. It can rightly be understood as the supreme attribute of God, subsuming all others within it. So why is it so hard to believe in a holy God? A holy God means there is an ultimate standard of morality and perfection. Within that holiness, a righteous and just God demands that His creatures also pursue righteousness and justice. In other words, we cannot truly believe in a holy God without it impacting the way we live. His perfection only shows us how imperfect we are. That fact on its own creates great difficulties for all of us, including our teenagers. But if we do not counsel from a foundational view that God is holy, righteous, and just we will deny that there is objective truth and a moral standard in this world.

God is loving, gracious, and kind. If the counsel given to our teenagers focuses only on the holiness of God to the utter neglect of His merciful love, consider how that will impact our counseling. Most likely, your teen will end up with a skewed sense of God and their law-based duty to Him. Thankfully, we know that God's love and compassion for His people is not only a reality, but is an extension of His holiness and righteousness (1 John 4:7-8; Ps. 63:3; Matt. 20:34). It's too tempting for us to conceive of God as either holy or loving, and thereby emphasizing in our counseling either the law of God OR the grace of God as if they excluded one another. Rightly believing in the love, grace, and kindness of God firmly alongside His holiness and righteousness will enable you to offer true Biblical counseling. Does your teenager need to grasp the holiness of God and His law? Definitely. Does he or she also need to know the love of God for sinners? Most definitely. A God of love, grace, and mercy must always be on full display in our counseling.

God is personal. A last foundational belief about God that greatly impacts our counseling of teenagers is the fact that God intimately enters into the world of His people. He is not only transcendent, but immanent (Jer. 23:23-24). He does not just keep His distance, harshly handing out judgment for our sins and missteps. Jesus is Immanuel, God with us (Matt. 1:23). The Holy Spirit proceeded from the Father and the Son to reside within God's people (1 Cor. 3:16). God never leaves nor forsakes all who are His adopted children (Heb. 13:5-6). How radically life-giving it makes our counseling when we show our teenagers that God is near, and that a relationship with God is possible in Christ. To only portray to our teens a God who is distant, angry, demanding and foreboding is putting a stumbling block between them and the Savior. Christianity alone is a religion based on a real relationship with the God of the universe. Knowing a God who first knows me rounds out a fully-orbed God that is detailed for us in His Word.

ABOUT TEENAGERS

The psychologist G. Stanley Hall is credited with beginning the formal study of adolescence in the early 1900s.[2] He formed his view of teenagers by combining the implications of Darwin's evolutionary theory and Freud's psychodynamic view of the person. These theories of the human being led him to understand adolescence as a transitional time of 'storm and stress,' where the teen has yet to 'evolve' into an adult. Accordingly, Hall believed that the teenage years were primarily characterized by conflicts with parents, mood disruptions, and risky behavior. Does that sound accurate, by your own experience? It certainly describes many of today's teens. But the more important question is: Is this the complete truth? Without a Biblical understanding of humanity, Hall and other researchers in teenage behavior can only give us limited assistance to counsel our teens. Thankfully, God's Word is sufficient to properly construct a more complete view of the teenager, built on a right view of God.

Teens are made in the image of God. The crowning achievement of God's creation was making man in His own image (Gen. 1:26-27). So does that go for our teens too? Or, are we to only see adults as image-bearers, but children and youth as somewhat less-than-human? Hopefully, you truly believe that God's image is imprinted on all human beings—because this truth will greatly impact your counseling. Understanding that teens are made in the image of God means they bear His communicable attributes, even in their immature state. By the grace of God, teenagers can grow in knowledge and understanding.

---

2   https://en.wikipedia.org/wiki/G._Stanley_Hall

They can show love and compassion to others. They can even operate from hearts of mercy and grace. So, whether you are counseling a teenager who is a Christian, or not a Christian, he or she is not merely driven by animal impulses or raging hormones. As image-bearers, all teenagers are unique creations of God and must be treated as such.

Teens are sinners. If all have sinned and fall short of the glory of God (Rom. 3:23), that certainly includes teenagers. Most of us have little difficulty believing this fact, right? Unfortunately, it can be tempting to look at the problems of adolescence only through the lens of the goodness of man. Particularly, we reveal a denial of the truth that teens are sinners by making a variety of excuses for teenage behavior or by simply recognizing the depth and impact of their sin. This is not to say that all of the problems our teenagers are experiencing are due solely to their own sinful hearts and minds! As will be discussed later, sin is only part of the problem. Yet, if we in any way deny that teens are sinners—and capable of being great sinners at that—we will not help them towards the Biblical change that is required. Since Adam our first parent fell into sin, our teens reap the consequences of total depravity as well.

Teens are body and soul. God formed man from the dust of the ground and breathed in him the breath of life (Gen. 2:7). Human beings are both body and soul, internal and external, material and immaterial. Teenagers have bodies that are not fully developed, brains that are still maturing, and body chemistry that is still in flux. To not recognize teens as bodies and souls will keep us from recognizing the influence of their bodies on their souls. But the fundamental error on the other side of the coin is to only see teenagers as a mass of chemicals and hormones! They are not just biological machines devoid of soul. As Anthony Hoekema, a professor of systematic theology, writes, 'Though the Bible does see man as a whole, it also recognizes that the human being has two sides: physical and nonphysical. He has a physical body, but he also has a personality. He has a mind with which he thinks but also a brain which is part of his body, and without which he cannot think. Man is one person who can, however, be looked at from two sides.'[3]

Teens are accountable and responsible. A right view of the human being also includes that we are all without excuse before God for our behavior (Rom. 1:20). Just as there are none righteous, no person can claim not to be responsible for his sin (Rom. 3:10). All people, including teenagers, are accountable for their own sins. To deny man's responsibility is to reject the truth of the authority, justice, and righteousness of God. He alone has judged us all to be sinners as a perfectly holy God—and we must all give an account to Him for our actions (Rom. 14:12). If God holds all His creature responsible and accountable, then so must all human authorities hold teenagers responsible and accountable. This Biblical presupposition ensures that we won't look to excuse the behavior, words, or thinking of our teenagers—as we work towards solution. We will also direct their hearts and minds to the God to whom they are accountable and responsible.

Teens are sufferers. Sin in the hearts of our teenagers produces all sorts of suffering. Their bodies will also cause them pain and suffering at times. Then, there's the suffering that comes from the fallen world and the sins of others. On top of all that, we have the great adversary of our souls, Satan, who constantly attempts to bring suffering into our lives. In order to understand our teenagers Biblically, it is vital to have compassion for them as sufferers as well as sinners. Even if your teen has brought some of the suffering on himself, he will still need to be seen as a sufferer. Thankfully, the Scripture is full of God responding to the suffering of His people (see the Books of Exodus, Judges). A right view of God as merciful and gracious is reflected to our teenagers when we empathize with whatever suffering has entered their lives. Human suffering comes in all sorts of forms, including diseases, disabilities, and disorders. Recognizing the acute or chronic trials and tribulations

---

3   Anthony Hoekema (1986), *Created in God's Image,* (Grand Rapids: Eerdmans), p. 217.

that are part and parcel of adolescence will only increase our ability to help.

Teens are restorable. Finally, a Biblical view of the teenager culminates in the great hope of the gospel—that restoration is possible in Christ (Rom. 5:10). Even the most troubled teen with the most complicated of problems can be redeemed by God and reconciled to Christ. This truth also means that solutions can be found to their problems in Christ Jesus. When we recognize the power of God to transform, to save, and to sanctify our teens, then we are able to offer them hope. Without this foundational belief deep in our hearts, we can only help our teens survive their problems and not truly overcome them. Only in Christ will true heart change and lasting behavior change be possible! As counselors and parents, a right view of the human being keeps us utterly dependent on the work of God's Spirit in the life of all of our teenagers.

ABOUT PROBLEMS

The second half of this book will provide counseling help for fifteen common problems of the teenage years. Biblical principles and solutions will be discussed with the primary goal of true Biblical change and Christ-centered growth. Obviously, each problem will be somewhat unique in how it develops, its particular causes and contributing factors, and how it is solved. But before we can get there, it's essential that we understand and firmly hold on to the Biblical presupposition on how ALL of our mental, emotional, spiritual, and relational problems develop. This knowledge will keep us tethered to God's Word, with the opportunity to wisely counsel our teens. Clearly, theories abound when it comes to the question of where our problems originate and how they progress. While there are elements of truth in some psychological theories that have been developed over the years, a basic Biblical formulation of how our problems develop is foundational. God's Word is a treasure trove of truth that leads us to a right understanding of teenage problems, built on a knowledge of God and the human being.

All things external. Just as the process of interpreting any written text requires an understanding of context, the best place to start to understand the problems of teenagers is with the 'external context' of their day-to-day lives. First and foremost, there is Satan, a roaring lion seeking to devour our young people (1 Pet. 5:8). He is the Father of Lies, working to deceive their hearts and minds (John 8:44). On top of that, there is the influence of a Satan-influenced world that is calling on our teens to be conformed to its philosophy and empty deceit (Col. 2:8; Rom. 12:2). The anti-Christian propaganda of secular institutions and the seduction of so much electronic entertainment and social media is difficult for teenagers to resist. Additionally, our teens can often succumb to environmental problems that exist because we live in a fallen world—toxins, chemicals, drugs, unhealthy food, etc. A final set of external problems in the lives of our teens are due to the sins of others—parents, family members, friends, enemies, strangers, etc. The prevalence of all sorts of abuse, neglect, bullying, and other violent actions can also produce or contribute to the mental, emotional, spiritual, and relational problems of our teens. A Biblical understanding of problems includes all things that occur outside of self.

Our physical bodies. Then there are problems that develop within the individual teen. As previously mentioned, teenagers are body and soul, material and immaterial, physical and non-physical. The tricky thing is discerning what problems may originate with a body issue and which ones are only partially influenced by our bodies. Clearly, there will be times when we need some expert medical help to diagnose a body dysfunction or disease. But it is important to remember that even medical professionals rely on theories about the etiology of mental and emotional problems which may or may not be entirely valid. Even so, it must be part of our presuppositions concerning the development of problems to recognize the influence of the body on most of the problems of teens. Immature body chemistry, fluctuating hormones, and developing brain functioning can have a role in problem development. Additionally, we have to evaluate the impact of particular diseases, disabilities, and injuries. As amazing a creation as our bodies are, the effects of sin means we have to address body issues when dealing with the souls of our teens.

The heart level. Addressing the error that all of our problems are external to the human being, Jesus said: 'For from within, out of the heart of man, come evil thoughts, sexual immorality, theft, murder, adultery, coveting, wickedness, deceit, sensuality, envy, slander, pride, foolishness. All these evil things come from within, and they defile a person.' (Mark 7:21-23). Many of the problems of adolescence begin in the heart, producing behavioral, emotional, and mental problems. The human heart, Biblically speaking, is our inner self, the location of faith and belief, the center of our attitudes and deepest thoughts. Our hearts are the locus of faith and worship. And, unfortunately, our hearts are idol factories that keep us from the right worship of God.[4] So it makes sense that our problems often originate here—sometimes as a response to things external to us, or to issues in our bodies. The ultimate problem of teenagers is that their hearts are deceitful, sinful, and impossible to cleanse (Ps. 51:10; Prov. 20:9).

The doing level. So, what happens to the problems that begin on the heart level? Imagine the heart level as the basement of a house. If a fire is burning in the basement, sooner or later the smoke and flames will make it up to the next level—the first floor of the house. This level in your teenager's 'house' can be described as the 'doing level.' The doing level includes a person's actions, thoughts, and words—all the things that encompass the basics of human behavior. According to Matthew 7:15-20 and Luke 6:43-45, this level can be properly thought of as the 'fruit of our hearts.' From the overflow of our hearts, words come out of our mouths (Luke 6:45). We think a particular way and do certain things due to the essential operating system in our hearts. So if our

---

4   Timothy Keller (2009), *Counterfeit Gods,* (New York: Dutton), p. xxiii.

teens are experiencing a heart idol problem (the fire in the basement), it will typically produce wrong, unhealthy or sinful words, thoughts, and actions. The doing level is most often where teenage problems will be observed.

The feeling level. Staying with our analogy, the top floor of the 'house' of our teenager's internal life can be thought of as a person's feeling level. Our feelings, or emotions, are responses made about our environment or ourselves that trigger body chemistry. While we have all sorts of descriptive labels for our feelings, they really just fall into two categories—bad feelings or good feelings. If you think about it, feelings are often the prime indicators of issues that are going on at the doing level and the heart level. In other words, heart problems can produce problems of behavior as well as troubling emotional responses. The feeling level rounds out the three 'floors' that work together to manifest a particular teenager problem. All must be considered when counseling our teenagers and working towards solution, which is the subject of our final set of Biblical presuppositions.

ABOUT SOLUTIONS

So, how do we go about making sure the solutions we offer our teens are grounded in Biblical truth? The Bible doesn't give us a singular prescription for each of the many problems our young people experience. For example, we don't read a passage of Scripture that reads: 'Struggling with depression? Just trust God more and you will be fine.' Or, 'Have OCD? Just stop obsessing so much!' Looking to God's Word to give us simplistic steps to fix all our problems is a wrong-headed attempt to transform the living and powerful Holy Scriptures into a mere self-help book. What we actually do gain from the inspired Word of God is the fundamental truth that people can change, as well as principles that can be applied in order for change to occur. Holding on to this Biblical reality doesn't mean that change is easy or that anything and everything about our teens can or will change. There are certainly problems that they may struggle with for quite a long time. But, without the seminal belief that our teens can change, we will end up in a deficient view of solutions to problems. Therefore, within the overall goal of Biblical change, we can think through how to accomplish it—by the power of the Holy Spirit and the grace and love of God.

Salvation and sanctification. Can a non-believing teen find solutions to their emotional, mental, and relational problems? Yes, and no. Yes, God's common grace can enable a non-Christian teenager to stop drinking too much or learn some anger management techniques. But, no, unbelievers cannot achieve real Biblical change that is only found in Christ. The more important question is: Do we truly desire to see the problems of our teenagers solved outside of a relationship with Christ? To put it even more bluntly: What good is it for teens to become less anxious, better adjusted mentally and emotionally—with few problems in their lives—yet still on their way to hell? To be clear, the opportunity for some level of change in the lives of non-Christians can certainly be used by God to draw them into saving faith. But what we need to always remember is that the ultimate change we are seeking for our teens is redemption in Jesus Christ! That alone is the end as well as the beginning of all other solutions. Our primary problem is spiritual—separation from God—which makes the primary solution salvation in Christ.

When our teenagers are saved by the grace of God, they have become new creations. The old has passed away, the new has come (2 Cor. 5:17). Yet, a right theology of salvation recognizes that all of our problems don't fade into oblivion from that point forward. God's Word teaches us the Spirit-led process of sanctification for every true believing teenager (Gal. 2:20; 1 Thess. 4:3). So, in one sense, sanctification by the indwelling work of the Spirit and the power of God enables our teens to solve many of their problems. Yet, from another vantage point, the problems themselves will be used by God to sanctify them as well! Again, we truly want our teens to experience real solutions to emotional, mental, and spiritual problems. But we also never want to espouse an understanding of Christianity that includes perfectionism or total health, happiness and prosperity in this life. In other words, we hold in tension that growing in Christ means the removal of some problems, as well as the need for others to remain. God has the higher goal of holiness for teenagers, not simply a problem-free existence.

Body side. If we believe that body state contributes to the problems in teenagers, then we would be remiss to not offer body-based solutions. This is where we will need competent medical help for our teens, where necessary. Yet, there are also solutions to the body side that a parent or Biblical counselor can communicate to our teens. A healthy diet is a good place to begin, since this is not typical practice of all our adolescents. What our teens put into their bodies can have an impact on their behavior, attitudes, and thinking. How about the lack of physical exercise (couch-potato-ness) that can characterize a majority of our teens? A change of physical fitness has proven to help mental and emotional fitness. Then, we must not neglect the glaring deficiency of sleep that can be part and parcel of the teenage world. Helping with sleep habits, as well as proper balance of work and rest, is also part of the Biblical counseling of teens. When we understand that teens are going through tremendous physiological changes, we would be remiss if we don't factor this in to our counseling.

Feeling level. If our emotions are indicators of problems that are occurring at the doing level and heart level of our teens, then it is essential that we pay attention to them. To deny the expressed feelings of teenagers is to ignore a significant element of their overall change. Some teens may have great difficulty sharing what they are truly feeling. Others may believe that their feelings don't matter. Still others may be so driven by their feelings that they are unwilling to look at their behavior, thoughts, and heart attitudes. And there are also those teens that are working overtime to numb their feelings as much as possible. Each and every problem that needs to be solved in the lives of teenagers will have an emotional component. At the minimum, teens will have any of a variety of bad feelings that will expose the fact that there is a deeper problem. In that way, feelings often act as a 'check engine' light that requires we look under the hood of our hearts!

Doing level. This is the level of the 'house' of inner life where our teens can actually begin to experience real Biblical change. Sinful actions can be replaced with right behavior. Unrighteous, unhealthy words can be reduced as new patterns of speech can begin. Faulty thinking, and the believing of lies, can be changed and transformed into a renewed mind. So, whatever problem is occurring in the life of our teen will always have a 'doing' aspect. A change in behavior, words, and thinking is possible by the work of the Holy Spirit (Gal. 5:22-23). But it is vital to remember that solutions can never end at this level, or we will end up in mere behaviorism or moralism. And, that sort of behavior change will often be short-lasting and not enduring. For example, while it is wonderful for our teens who are abusing alcohol to stop drinking altogether, that will be incomplete and insufficient change if we don't get to the heart of the problem. This goes for all teenage problems, which leads us to our last section.

Heart level. When we are justified by faith and have a relationship with Christ as Savior and Lord, our heart has been fundamentally and eternally changed. Christians have had their heart of stone transformed into a heart of flesh, enlivened by the Spirit of God (Ezek. 36:26). Then, the overall orientation of the heart of a Christian gradually becomes one that is serving God rather than serving self. So what sort of ongoing heart change do we require after salvation? For one thing, idols of the heart still exist, even in the heart of sincere believers. Our teens can still struggle with hearts of anger, discontentment, laziness, pride, anxiety, shame, etc. Biblical change occurs when they learn to destroy the idols of their heart and constantly return to the right worship of God. As God's Spirit and His Word do their joint work in hearts, change will be reflected on the doing and feeling levels as well.

Being planted firmly in Biblical presuppositions is essential as we seek to understand and solve the problems of youth. As counselors and parents, our counsel is defined by our presuppositions—our foundational beliefs about God, the human being, how problems develop, and how problems are solved. When guided by Scripture, we know that our highest goal in whatever we do—including helping the teenagers before us—is to glorify God (1 Cor. 10:31). From there, we seek to be an instrument in the hand of our Savior to be used in the overall discipleship of our teens. What greater task do we have as counselors to youth than to point them to Jesus, walk with them as fellow disciples of Christ, and pursue wisdom in the solutions to their problems? From these foundational presuppositions, we can then seek a Biblical process of Biblical counseling which will further aid us as parents and youth ministry workers.

2.
Practicing a Biblical Counseling Process

Thinking Biblically about God, teenagers, and their problems leads us forward to the practice of Biblical counseling. So how do we go about offering right counsel—Biblical wisdom—to address the significant struggles in the lives of our young people? A helping process is more than simply lecturing teens about the problem itself. It's vastly different than coming up with a punishment in an attempt to curb the behavior. Biblical counseling is a gospel-driven, Christ-centered series of conversations between parent and child, counselor and counselee, leader and student. It is the essential work of relational dialogue that seeks true Biblical change, growth in grace, repentance and faith, knowledge and wisdom. While advanced training as a Biblical counselor would be extremely useful, there is a basic process of counseling teens that can be utilized by any parent or youth worker. It's a process driven by the love of Christ for the teenager, as well as the desire to be used by God as an instrument of change. Built upon Biblical presuppositions, an efficient Biblical process of counseling will give a great opportunity for Biblical change and solution.

An easy way to conceive of the process of Biblical counseling is as that of a CIRCLE, not simply a series of steps. Picture four chairs spaced equally around a round table. The counselor 'sits' in the imaginary first chair, then moves around the circle, chair by chair, in conversations with the teenager. As the process goes on, the counselor rotates back and forth between chairs, backwards and forwards around the table. As long as the problem persists, the process circle spins round and round. Here are the four parts of the Biblical counseling process:

- Listening
- Evaluation
- Confrontation
- Education

Again, these are not steps, but different components of the entire process. Biblical counselors continually listen, evaluate, confront, and educate—moving towards solution and change. Each 'chair' in the process is necessary for a well-rounded approach to whatever problem our teenager is facing. In the end, the counselor occupies all four chairs at the same time! So let's briefly describe each part of the process.

LEADING WITH LISTENING

What would counseling be without listening? Unfortunately, it's tempting to be slow to listen and quick to speak when it comes to dealing with teenagers. Add to that the fact that many adolescents either don't talk much to the adults in their lives or enjoy speaking about what's going on in their hearts. So, the listening 'chair' is often a challenging one that should never be neglected or minimized. It's vital to lead the counseling process with listening, and by listening. Our listening must be active and purposeful. It must lead our teenagers forward to solution. We must direct the counseling conversation by our listening and through our listening. If we don't do a thorough job with our listening, then our teenagers will not talk, or say very little. And if we are not intentional in our questions, as well as our responses to what we hear, there will be little progress. Leading with listening keeps us from doing all the talking, turning counseling into a lecture, or only engaging in monologue instead of a dialogue. So, let's think about some of the basic principles of listening as Biblical counselors and parents.

Listen long. 'The purpose in a man's heart is like deep water, but a man of understanding will draw it out' (Prov. 20:5). Whether or not you view your teenagers as 'deep,' it will take time to draw out his or her feelings, thoughts, and heart attitudes. Biblical listening is like dropping a bucket down, again and again, into the deep well of a heart and bringing it to the surface. Be willing to listen long when it is tempting to listen short. Another way to think about this listening principle is: Don't jump to conclusions! We can often hear just a few pieces of the story and fill in the blanks ourselves. Then, we can end up assuming and presuming we have our teen figured out. The longer we listen, the more we learn about what is going on in their heads and hearts. Listening long also communicates something very important: that we actually care to know the person who is before us. How often do our teens say to us: 'You don't understand!' Sometimes they are responding that way because we aren't spending enough time in the listening chair, and we've bounced prematurely into the next part of the process.

Ask open questions. The use of closed questions will only receive short, focused answers—usually yes or no answers. They sound like this: 'Did you use drugs tonight?' 'Are you depressed?' 'Did that make your angry?' While you will need to ask a certain amount of closed questions in order to understand what is going on, you will have to get comfortable asking more open questions in the end. Open questions will elicit longer, and much more reflective answers. They will tell you more about the teenager's story and show you more of his or her mind and heart. Open questions look like this: 'Tell me about when you started feeling this way.' 'Why do you think you did that, or thought like that?' 'What did you do next?' 'How does that make you feel?' Remember that you are actually wanting your teen to talk; and you are leading him or her to talk about certain things. Open questions are fundamental to keep the conversation going in a healthy direction.

Listen to gather information. You are not just listening to an interesting (or scary) story when you are counseling your teen. And, as much as you are demonstrating love and compassion by listening long and hearing their whole story, that isn't the end of the matter either. We listen to our teenagers in order to gather information. In a way, when we are sitting in the listening chair, we are putting our detective hats on, piecing together bits of data in order to understand. Without knowledge and information, we won't be of much help in getting to the heart of the matter. So you will always be asking yourself the question: 'What information am I still lacking that will help me to understand, in order to offer help?' That question will keep you leading in your listening. No, this is not meant to look like a police interrogation. We do not seek to know information in order to indict or convict, but to help and to seek wisdom together with your teenager.

Clarify and summarize. As you are listening to your teenager, there will be things that you will have a hard time understanding. Always be willing to say: 'I don't understand,' or 'I missed what you just said.' If your teen isn't making sense, it's a mistake just to assume and to fill in blanks with your own presumptions. Learn to ask good clarifying questions that will help you to better understand. Even if you think you have a good idea what's going on, it is worth asking for clarification to hear it once again. Your teenager may tell you something different than the first time. Another technique that enables productive listening is stopping often to summarize. Examples of summarization are: 'What I heard you say is (blank)... Is that right?' 'You have given me a lot of information. Let me try to help you by taking a moment to summarize.' This gives your teen the opportunity to say: 'No, that's not exactly what I'm saying' or 'Yes, that's about right.' Clarifying and summarizing not only helps you to listen well; it communicates to the teenager that you are actually listening.

Note non-verbals. Several years ago, one of my favorite television dramas was called 'Lie to Me.' [1] The lead character of the crime drama

---

1   *Lie to Me,* TV show, (2009-2011).

was an expert on reading the non-verbals of people in order to conclude whether they were lying or telling the truth. It was utterly fascinating to learn all the ways people communicate without saying a word. This reminds us, that when we are counseling teens, we must pay attention to their non-verbals and their body language. We are to watch what their eyes are saying, what their posture is communicating, and what their gestures tell us about themselves. Non-verbals can either confirm that what they are saying is accurate and true, or give us a vital hint that they may not be telling the whole truth. As a parent or youth worker, you have probably been noting non-verbals in your own teens for a while. Don't neglect to factor them in to your understanding!

Listen to the heart. In a similar way as a medical doctor uses a stethoscope to listen to how the heart is beating, the Biblical counselor is ultimately listening for what is going on in the heart of the teenager. We are not just listening for factual information, but also for how the state of the innermost self is 'sounding.' So, for what exactly should you be listening? Most importantly, you need to learn the teen's view of God and self. How does he or she understand God in the midst of this problem? Is there anger towards God—or is there apathy, despair, or even rebellion against Him? You will also be listening for idols of the heart that make the problem more complex and stubborn. Seek to understand the level of hope your teen currently has as well. Is he or she hopeful that change can happen, or are they stuck in hopelessness? Finally, you are listening for the overall desire and motivation for change. Is the teen just waiting on God to fix things, or more active in striving to seek Biblical change in conjunction with the Spirit? The more we listen to our teens, the more we will see their hearts. As we read earlier, 'Out of the abundance of the heart, the mouth speaks' (Luke 6:45).

EFFECTIVE EVALUATION

As you are listening to the heart and mind of your teenager, the next 'chair' in the counseling process is evaluation. In reality, you will be occupying both the listening chair and the evaluating chair at the same time. Remember, we are listening in order to evaluate, not as an end to itself. And notice that we are using the word 'evaluate' rather than 'diagnose.' What you will be engaged in is not a medical or psychiatric process, where some sort of official diagnosis is required. Certainly, the teenager may be coming to you already diagnosed by a medical, psychological, or educational professional. The label or diagnostic category may be helpful to some extent, but it will only tell you so much. With all the information on the internet and social media, your teenager may also have self-diagnosed or applied a psychological label of some sort. Ultimately, as Biblical counselors, effective evaluation is much broader and robust than simply attempting to affix a diagnostic label on someone. Evaluation that is wise and Biblical considers modern diagnoses and labels, but is not necessarily bound to them.[2] Effective evaluation follows particular Biblical principles, pointing to real heart change.

Apply the levels of problems. The feeling level, the doing level, and the heart level paradigm can be used as the framework for your evaluation of most teen problems. For example, if your teen comes to you saying she is depressed, you can mentally put 'depressive feelings' at the feeling level. Then you will know how to evaluate what she is thinking, doing, and saying—actions located at the doing level which are producing problems at the feeling level. After that, as you are listening for the heart, you may hear self-pity, anger, anxiety, or a myriad of other things expressed. Or, a second example is a teen who is thoroughly addicted to pornography. At the doing level, he is viewing porn and thinking obsessively about porn. But what's at the heart level with this addiction? And, what emotions occur at the feeling level

2   Michael R. Emlet (2017), *Descriptions and Prescriptions,* (Greensboro, NC: New Growth Press), p. 37.

as a result? Or finally, you are counseling a teen with a generalized anxiety disorder. Anxiety can be properly located on the doing level, but anxious thoughts or the actions that result from it are fueled by an anxious heart as well. Applying the three levels of internal problems reminds us that we are not focused on just simple diagnostic labels, and better moves us forward to solution. It reminds us that change must occur on all levels, and each level impacts the other.

Use Biblical terminology. Again, just to be clear, diagnostic categories and labels can be very useful. If a teen comes to you diagnosed with Bipolar Disorder, it will give you a lot of information about what he or she is experiencing. But at the same time, a diagnosis like Bipolar may tempt you or the teen to believe that the Bible has nothing to say about the problem—since that term is not found anywhere in Scripture. Yet, the Bible does have much to say to us about depression—and Bipolar Disorder is a specific form of depression. Or, what if a teenager tells you he has ADHD? Attention-Deficit Hyperactivity Disorder is not described in the Bible, right? But we certainly have Biblical principles about some of the unwise behavior that can accompany ADHD as well as the concept of developing a renewed mind with clear thinking. The point is that effective evaluation makes use of Biblical categories to gain better understanding, whenever possible. Certainly, the Scriptures do not discuss in detail every single sort of human problem, just like we don't see every type of disease or disability mentioned. More importantly, the Bible is very efficient when it comes to teaching us the foundational issues that are operative in any and every problem in this life. So, use Biblical terminology when evaluating teenage problems, looking for how different problems often have the same heart origins.

Distinguish sin and suffering. As discussed in the previous chapter, your teenager is a sinner *and* a sufferer. As a fallen creature with a sinful nature, some of the problem he is experiencing comes from his own sinfulness. As a fallen creature living in a fallen world, he is also suffering from the sin of others, a weak or unhealthy body, and the effects of the environment. Sometimes, the sin aspect of the problem will be prominent and obvious. Your teen is experimenting with illegal drugs. Or, your teen is sinfully bitter against his friends. Yet, sin does not occur in a vacuum. Your drug-addicted teen could have been preyed upon by an older teen, and responded out of a longing to fit in and be accepted. Your other teenager may have been wrongfully used and hurt by his friends. As much as we need to call sin what it is, we must not ignore the fact that sin comes in all sorts of suffering contexts. Your evaluation will not be effective if you diminish the sin; or, if you don't understand the suffering that has preceded from or resulted in the sinful behavior.

Use the Ephesians 4 conceptualization. Another effective way to evaluate particular teen problems is to follow the apostle Paul's problem framework as found primarily in Ephesians 4. Paul teaches that, as Christians, we have put off the old self, are being renewed in our minds, and have put on the new self (Eph. 4:22-24). In the last section of the chapter, Paul actually gives some examples which illustrate this process. The problem of lying requires that we put off falsehood, understand that we are members of one another, and put on the truth (Eph. 4:25). When a teen has an anger issue, Paul writes that he is to put off sinful anger, think through how he is giving the devil a foothold in his life, and then put on righteous anger (Eph. 4:26-27). Finally, if your teen is a thief, she is to put off stealing, think more about sharing, and put on hard work and develop a giving heart. Using this conceptualization, the Biblical counselor will be asking these evaluative questions: 'What things need to be put off (stopped)?' 'What things need to be put on (started)?' 'How does thinking need to be changed?' The Ephesians 4 framework can be found throughout the New Testament epistles, and can be applied to many of the typical problems of our teens.

Determine a direction. The last element of an effective evaluation transitions the Biblical counselor to the last two 'chairs' of the counseling process. Remember, evaluation is intended to move us forward to Biblical change and solutions. So that means we have to determine a direction—a path of Christ-centered growth, wisdom, and maturity. Clearly, each particular problem will require its own unique direction—which is what the second part of this book will be all about. The way forward may also mean the help of other professionals. Yet, the direction of Biblical counseling will always include certain gospel-driven aspects, whatever the problem. Our teens will always need to be pointed to Christ, learn to be more dependent on His Spirit, and how to glorify God in all things. They will also need to mature in relationships with other people. Ultimately, we will always want them to think wisely and Biblically about whatever they are experiencing in this life. In other words, there will always be different secondary areas to address for each problem, but the overall primary direction is always the same. That direction is determined by God, and not us or our teens.

COMPASSIONATE CONFRONTATION

If you are a parent of a teenager, you have almost certainly been involved in a confrontation or two with him or her. If you are a youth ministry worker, the same goes for you. But this is not the sort of confrontation we have in mind for this third 'chair' of an effective Biblical counseling process. This sort of confrontation that occurs in a counseling context is more akin to a 'clash of ideas or opinions,' where the conflict is between the ways of looking at things rather than between opposing rivals. Confrontation takes place as the counselor sees wrong patterns of thinking, behaving, etc. that need to be challenged before change can occur. Confrontation in Biblical counseling is motivated by compassion and the desire to see the teenager freed, rather than remaining in bondage. This fact doesn't mean counseling will always involve a hostile sort of clash, or yelling and screaming! Compassionate confrontation is all about holding up the light of truth to penetrate the dark places in the hearts and minds of our teenagers. So, let's consider some of the elements of this next essential part of the process.

Allow self-confrontation. The idea of self-confrontation sounds sort of cruelly schizophrenic, doesn't it? Do we really expect our teens to confront themselves with the truth? Yes! This stage of counseling is so much more productive when the counselee is illuminated by the Spirit and the Word, and comes to the right conclusion about his problem. For example, your teenager has come to you about his long-standing depression. As you talk about it in depth, he looks at you and says: 'Wait a minute. I'm not depressed. I'm just really, really angry at God! Could all this anger inside my heart be making me depressed?' Bingo! If you are leading the counseling process well—listening and beginning to effectively evaluate—you will also give the teenager some time for reflection. If your teen actually begins to think deeply about his problem, it can become crystal clear what is really going on. This sort of confrontation won't always happen; and, often times your teen will only have partial realizations about the truth. During this time, we need to pray that our teens learn how to self-confront as an essential skill of their lifetime sanctification.

Confront lovingly. As loving Christians, why do we need to use the adjective 'compassion' when describing the confrontation aspect of the counseling process? Unfortunately, even as lovers of Christ, our own frustration, surprise, or zeal can tempt us to confront far too forcefully and unlovingly. Speaking the truth in love (Eph. 4:15) is the Biblical standard that must drive all of our confronting in counseling. Telling your teenager the truth, without love, is harsh and overbearing. Loving your teenager, without speaking the truth, can be self-serving and manipulative. A Biblical confrontation is difficult enough for anyone to hear (and handle) without the additional humiliation that comes when it is not delivered in love. For many of us, confronting in love is easier said than done. As a parent or youth counselor, it is easy to get lost in our own anger or anxiety about the particular problem of our teen. So, with much prayer, we must exercise self-control of our own emotions as we confront lovingly.

Confront firmly and clearly. At the same time, the counsel we offer our teens must never be fuzzy or vague. Biblical truth is robust, rich, and piercing to the soul. We must not water any of our instruction down, or minimize the problem in any way. Your teen hasn't just been 'shading the truth'—he's been lying and deceiving others. Being angry at God is not acceptable because God is a 'big boy and can handle it'—it is unrighteous and sinful. Anxiety can certainly be described as a human struggle, but it doesn't make the teen any less un-trusting of the Lord. Now, this doesn't mean you are pointing a condemning finger in the face of your teen and declaring: 'Sinner!' The clarity and firmness of the confrontation is necessary because it actually gives hope. Knowing the truth about our problems and how to solve them is the only way to freedom. If, out of misguided compassion, we don't tell the whole truth about what we are seeing in our teen's life, then we only give false hope. We will talk more about how compassionate confrontation gives hope in a moment.

Confront timely. You have listened long and listened well to your teenager. You have thought through what the problem is and how change can be achieved. So when exactly is the best time to speak the truth in love to your teen—especially a rather hard truth? This is where some good Spirit-led discernment comes into play. Will confronting too soon cause your teen to 'shut down' and possibly shut you out? Then, it may be better to wait. Or, will your teen think you actually condone and approve of his behavior since you haven't said anything about it? You may have waited too long. The key principle here is to recognize that we can either confront too soon out of our emotion and passion, or wait too long because we're afraid of our teen's response. Timeliness is a wisdom issue, so you should be praying for it as you are counseling. Remember that, in the end, you are counseling out of compassion for your teen, not simply to shame or condemn him or her.

Build hope. It may appear that any form of confrontation in counseling will only send a message of defeat to teens. After all, facing our problems can be very humiliating. But the truth is that confronting wrong thinking, doing, and heart attitudes in a loving and compassionate way should actually *increase* hopefulness. How exactly does confrontation build hope? Bringing light into dark places of our hearts and minds offers relief and freedom. Knowing exactly what we are dealing with in our lives offers opportunity to change. Biblical confrontation infuses hope when it's most needed. It brings clarity as it begins the process of Biblical change. Without hope, the teenager will have little motivation or energy to actually address the problems at hand. True hope will be in the love and power of God in their lives, not in themselves, or someone else. Compassionate confrontation ultimately produces hope as it points to the fact that the problem is never bigger than God!

EDIFYING EDUCATION

The last 'chair' around the counseling process circle is *education*. The etymological root of the word helps us to see why it is an essential part of the process. The root *educere* means 'to lead out of.' Education is always an authoritative activity, leading a person out of ignorance and foolishness into knowledge and wisdom. That's exactly what our teenagers need! Just as they require an academic education in order to pursue a calling or career, our teens need to be spiritually educated in order to find solution to their problems. The sort of education that occurs in a counseling process always seeks to edify—building up and strengthening the teenager. Education isn't simply telling a teen what to do or to just 'stop it.' Education that is edifying is the work of leading the teenager out of the darkness into the light of Christ, from immaturity to maturity, and from foolishness to wisdom. If we truly want our teens to have the opportunity to grow in grace, we will make sure to teach them and to train them—leading them into the school of Christ.

Shape the content creatively. We all learn differently, due to our intellectual abilities, personalities, experiences, etc. So while the truth is the same truth for all of our teens, each individual needs to have that truth content shaped for his or her needs. For example, if your teen is an athlete, you may find yourself using sports analogies to help describe the problem and its solution. Or, many of our teens relate to the various elements of the pop culture, which means scenes from their favorite movies or television shows can be very useful in the education process. Just as good teachers in any arena strive to use examples and illustrations to advance learning, so must you when counseling your teen. If you just lecture your teenager, or talk down to your young person, he or she will not be receptive to the truth. Educational communication is both a skill and an art—and that is true in Biblical counseling as well. Be creative in telling the truth so that your listener can hear and understand!

Be a coach. Why do competitors at all levels and types of sports need coaches? Why can't athletes just learn the skills of the particular game at an early age and then compete on their own? Well, for one thing, coaches keep their athletes focused, reminding them by constant repetition and reinforcement so that their skills become second nature. Coaches are teachers and trainers, both giving knowledge as well as reviewing what is already known. In the same way, Biblical counseling has this sort of coaching component to it. Teenagers, like all human beings, need to be constantly reminded, re-focused, and encouraged as they learn and change. Sometimes, we can act as though people should simply hear the truth, obey, and immediately change. Again, that's akin to thinking an NFL quarterback only requires a class in high school about football, needing no further practice. Being a Biblical counseling 'coach' to your teen recognizes the fact that practice, practice, practice is required to experience Biblical change. It allows you to exhort, encourage, challenge—in firmness and love—with the tenacity and persistence our teenagers need from us.

Be patient. If you are a parent of a teenager, you already know how much patience is required, especially in the midst of great sin and suffering, trials and temptation. The counseling process demands the utmost of patience—something that can be in short supply when we are helping others. Patience is a fruit of the Spirit (Gal. 5:23), and it is tethered to the knowledge that we are not the Holy Spirit! Patient educators and coaches are willing to say and teach the same things over and over again until the student and athlete are fully trained. Don't expect your teen to learn quickly—it takes time, most of the time. Certainly, there are some problems that demand a rapid change of direction. Yet, your teen is still developing emotionally, mentally, physically, and spiritually—which can be a slow process. As discouraging as it can be to see little change, it forces us to trust in God's sovereign plan for our teens in all things.

Teach to trust. Here is yet another opportunity for you to remind yourself of the ultimate goals of Biblical counseling: to glorify God and to sanctify your teenager! Of all the things our teens need to learn in the midst of any problem, they will always need to learn to trust more deeply in God. They will need to trust that God loves them. They need to trust that God provides the resources for change. They need to trust that God will save and sanctify them through all situations of life. They need to trust that God will forgive their sins when they confess and repent of them. If we do not teach them to trust more completely in God, they may be tempted to trust in other people or in themselves. In other words, if we simply help teens to solve their problems with little or no reference to their need of a Savior and Deliverer, then we enable self-reliance and self-centeredness. Beyond all of the counsel, confrontation, and education we may offer, the underlying flow of our helping is to teach them to trust and love God more! This is the only way to long-term hope and change.

Teach in Christ. The final component of this last 'chair' of our Biblical counseling process emanates from these words of the apostle Paul:

But that is not the way you learned Christ!—assuming that you have heard about him and were taught in him, as the truth is in Jesus, to put off your old self, which belongs to your former manner of life and is corrupt through deceitful desires, and to be renewed in the spirit of your minds, and to put on the new self, created after the likeness of God in true righteousness and holiness (Eph. 4:20-24).

Over and over again in his epistles, Paul uses the phrase 'in Christ' to demonstrate what real change and transformation is, at its core. When we teach our teens 'in Christ,' we are acknowledging that this is their essential identity as believers. So what about teens who are not Christians? While they are not currently in Christ, we are still pointing them to Christ in every conversation. We should be careful to not forget to talk about Christ when we are teaching about change. And that also means that you, as parent or youth worker, are operating 'in Christ' as the counselor! As Paul says, the only real truth is always in Jesus! We will revisit this essential truth in our next chapter.

Again, these components of the counseling process circle are not steps in a linear agenda. Listening leads to evaluating. Effective evaluation leads to compassionate confrontation and edifying education. But, in real process with real teenagers, the process is not so one-directional. You will listen for a while, begin to evaluate, and then return to the listening 'chair' again. As you are evaluating, you may jump directly to your education 'chair' to teach a necessary truth about the problem. Depending on how your teen responds to your compassionate confrontation, you may have to go back to 'square one' for more listening and evaluating. Hopefully, you get the picture. A good counseling process encourages precision and thoroughness, so we don't just resort to bad habits of presumption, lecturing, and condemning. Practicing a Biblical counseling process communicates that we care deeply about our teenager and desire to see real and lasting Biblical change in his or her life.

3.
Partnering Together in Community

To whom do teenagers go when they are experiencing mental, emotional, spiritual, and relational problems? In our modern age of individualized and virtual technology, many teens wade into social media to chat, or share their struggles in a group text with their friends. Others may go directly to mental health websites, ending up with a smattering of both truth and error about their problems. Still others end up talking to psychotherapists, psychologists, or psychiatrists. So, how many teenagers actually seek out their parents for help? Or their local church youth pastors? While we certainly know God can use any people or resources to help our teens in their struggles, our goal should be to ensure that they have parents and the local church available to them as well.

Unfortunately, there are a variety of barriers that keep teens from receiving help from either parents or youth ministry leaders. Parents can seem out of touch, more willing to condemn than love, or simply disinterested in the struggles of their youth. The local church may appear judgmental and only filled with people who don't have any struggles. Friends can often be perceived to be more caring and compassionate than parents and the church, as well as more 'safe' and confidential. And, of course, we all know that everything written on medical/self-help websites is true, right? So, it should not surprise us if a teenager doesn't seek wise counsel from his or her parent, or the church. What it should do is motivate parents and youth ministry workers to overcome any and every obstacle to the process of real change.

But, what if your teens do come to you? What happens when a teen actually asks for help from parents or youth ministry leaders? Are you communicating that you are willing, able, and prepared to offer Biblical counsel? Understandably, you may feel ill-equipped and untrained, depending on the problem. Yet, you should never be unwilling or uncaring. Teenagers not only need their parents and church ministry leaders to help them deal with their problems—they need to know that they actually love them in the midst of the problems! In other words, teenagers need the closest adults in their lives to reflect the love and the grace of the Father, the Son, and the Holy Spirit to them. They need to be received and welcomed in their struggles. More than that, they need to be pursued and sought after, even when they act like they don't want or need help. To truly achieve Biblical change in their lives, our teens need the vital partnership of home and church, working in conjunction with the Spirit and the Word of God. While there may be other helpers that can be effective, it is the parent and the 'covenant parents' of the local church that are most vital.

PARENTS PARTNERING WITH THE CHURCH

Biblical counseling begins at home. The Proverbs are filled with wisdom that connect mothers and fathers to the spiritual lives of their teenagers. 'Hear, my son, your father's instruction, and forsake not your mother's teaching ...' (Prov. 1:8). 'My son, do not forget my teaching, but let your heart keep my commandments ...' (Prov. 3:1). 'Hear, my son, and accept my words, that the years of your life may be many' (Prov. 4:10). 'A wise son makes a glad father, but a foolish son is a sorrow to his mother' (Prov. 10:1). God's Word and common sense tells us of the absolute necessity of parents teaching, training, and counseling their own children in all wisdom. Often times, the typical problems of youth can be fueled by either the unwillingness of parents to effectively train their children in Biblical wisdom, or the refusal of teens to listen to and obey their parents. In a Christian home, the normal and regular process of problem solving comes from parents giving wise counsel to their teenagers, and youth receiving and applying it.

The principle of 'Biblical counseling begins at home' puts a heavy responsibility on the shoulder of parents when it comes to the passing on of wisdom. For one thing, they have to actually teach Biblical wisdom! When our teens are experiencing problems, they need to hear more from their parents than mere opinions or worldly speculations. The 'teaching,' 'commandments,' and the 'words' described in the Book of Proverbs are the teaching of Scripture, the commandments of Christ, and the Word of God. So when our teens are struggling with diverse problems, they need Biblical truth from the lips of their parents. They require the proper application of Scripture to their problems. They need parents who teach Biblical wisdom as well as ones who are living wisely in front of them. Why do the Proverbs say that wise teens give parents great joy? Because they are walking together with Christ, on the same spiritual path with one another. When parents lead well in wisdom, they then have much to offer their teenagers—words of life and hope.

What if the teenager refuses to talk to his or her parents about the problem? Well, this scenario is one reason parents need to partner with the local church. But just because teens won't talk doesn't mean parents cannot offer Biblical counseling. No, parents shouldn't be encouraged to harass their teenagers or threaten them in any way. But our teenagers do need parents to be persistent, and pursue them in their pain and sinfulness. So parents must consistently demonstrate that they want to be part of the process. They need to communicate that they're not going anywhere. Even when teens are the most resistant and rebellious, Biblical counseling still begins at home. It is a sanctifying process for parents to patiently await the best and wisest opportunities to help their teenagers.

Don't parent solo. Sadly, there are many single parents who know the reality of having to raise children on their own. Many do a wonderful job in spite of the challenges; but others struggle mightily, especially when teenage problems emerge. How much better is it when a teenager has both a mother and a father involved in his or her spiritual training and Biblical counseling! While one parent may certainly do a better job at handling a particular problem (or problems in general) than the other, mothers *and* fathers are necessary to the process of Biblical counseling. Having both parental perspectives at work in the life of the teen will go a long way to change and maturity. After all, the Proverbs speak of the instruction and wisdom of moms and dads, not one over the other. So, hopefully, you are not forced to handle the problems of your teenager alone. Work together as a team!

But let's take this principle one step further. Even if a teen has two parents involved in his or her life, is that enough when problems arise? At times, yes—possibly when a particular problem is in its early stage. Or, maybe if the depression, anxiety, or anger problem is limited to a very specific situation. Yet, the more serious or chronic the issue is, the more counselors and helpers that will be necessary. As Proverbs 11:14 says, 'Where there is no guidance, a people falls, but in an abundance of counselors there is safety.' Now, we should understand that this proverb cannot be speaking of any and every sort of counselor out there; instead, only Biblical counselors will provide our teens with spiritual safety. So parents are responsible to enlist only those who will give godly truth to their teens. Parents are not to put their children at risk by seeking counselors who will give them worldly wisdom that is in opposition to the truth of the gospel. Christian parents must make sure they are fully informed of the views of any counselor that are included in the process of helping their teen.

Most importantly, parents should make full use of their churches—especially their youth ministry leaders. Now, why is it essential to seek their help? What if they aren't trained or competent to give them Biblical counsel? First, I am assuming the presence of youth pastors or ministry workers who are willing and able. Hopefully, this book on Biblical counseling teens will be of help in that effort. But even more importantly, those ministering to the youth in the church should be committed to teaching teenagers God's truth, loving them with the love of Christ, and discipling them with the help of the Spirit. They are called to be Biblical counselors as those who are called to the gospel ministry. Hopefully, your teen already has a relationship with the youth pastor. Maybe he has gone to him for counsel already. Or, you may need to lead in the process of working together with your youth directors to help your teen. This brings us to the next aspect of this important partnership.

Teens in the church. If a teenager has a medical issue that won't resolve on its own, an appointment with a physician would be required. If the problem gets worse or doesn't respond to the treatment protocol, then time in the hospital may be necessary. But when healing finally comes, will the teen remain in the hospital indefinitely, or check in with the doctor week in and week out? Probably not! Most likely, the teenager would love to never have to see the doctor much in the future or have a long hospital stay ever again. Now, hopefully, parents don't treat youth pastors or ministry workers like they are medical doctors—only needed when their teenagers have a problem. And even though it is proper to understand the local church as a type of hospital for the spiritually sick, we should not view it as an institution we only participate in when we have personal problems which need solutions. The church's youth ministry, as well as the overall church community itself, is meant to be not only the routine hospital for spiritual problems, but also the regular, nourishing family of God!

With that analogy in mind, what we don't want to communicate to our youth is that they only need the church when they are experiencing problems. This would be akin to the belief that we only require a relationship with Jesus when we are in crisis or simply want something from Him! When parents are truly partnering with the local church for the counseling and discipleship of their teens, they will also teach their teens to fully participate in the local body of Christ, week in and week out. As much as the family is absolutely vital to a teen's growth in grace, so is the wider family of God, manifested in the local church. Unfortunately, when a teen is struggling with a particular issue, he or she may be inclined to create some distance from the church, youth ministry workers, and even Christian friends. Parents must advocate for their teens to stay connected to the church, and even require it at times—as much as they are able. When teens lose contact with the local body of Christ—just like when they distance themselves from their own families—they will miss out on a lifeline for their souls.

But you may be thinking: What if the real problem with my teenager is that he or she is in rebellion against God and has rejected Christ and His Church? To somehow 'force' this teenager to attend worship or the youth ministry programming at this point would possibly be counter-productive, if not nearly impossible to implement. In this particular circumstance, the better way to approach a teenager is to view involvement in the church community as the best *result* of Biblical change rather than the primary *cause* of it. As the Holy Spirit does His work in the heart of a teen, He will also draw him or her into a relationship with God's people. So when a teenager rebels against Christ and refuses to connect to the body of Christ, Christian parents are temporarily without the church as an important partner. Yet, the parent must never stop pointing the teen to Jesus and His people, encouraging the only relationship that will produce true heart change. Prayerfully, as Biblical change begins, the teenager will seek out and desire to be a full part of the family of God.

THE CHURCH PARTNERING WITH PARENTS

In the best case scenario, teenagers with problems have Christian parents who can offer godly counsel and a local church youth ministry that is also competent in offering Biblical counseling. Unfortunately, there are youth ministries more interested in only providing clean entertainment and social activities rather than necessary discipleship, sound teaching, and Biblical counseling. Then, there are also youth directors and ministry workers who really want to help teens with their problems, yet are either untrained or more steeped in a secular psychological worldview than a Biblical counseling model. These situations need to change in order for the local church to be the best sort of partner for parents in the problems youth face today. When there is a commitment to true Biblical discipleship of youth, then the youth ministry can either lead in the process with parents, or simply come alongside parents who are also offering godly counsel to their own teens.

Leading in the process. There are times when a troubled teen will go directly to his or her youth pastor, seeking wisdom and help. Or, maybe a youth ministry worker hears about a particular problem and seeks out the teenager. In both cases, this is an opportunity for the local church to take the lead in Biblical counseling. After a first meeting with the teenager, it may become apparent that the problem is too complex for youth ministry staff to handle well. Maybe someone on the pastoral staff will be called in, or a referral to a local Biblical counselor will need to be made. Yet, in a majority of cases, youth pastors and workers will be able to go a long way to helping the teen with the problem at hand. The willingness for the church to lead in the counseling process connects individual Biblical counseling to the overall discipleship culture of the church. In other words, when the local church is committed to discipling teenagers through all the youth ministry programming, this should also include the commitment to offer Biblical counseling to youth as well.

Another place for the church to lead as the primary partner in Biblical counseling is when parents are either non-Christians or are offering little or no counsel to their own teens. There are teens in our churches who are the only Christians in their homes, and others who come from severely broken homes. Unfortunately, these teens operate like spiritual orphans, needing the church to be their spiritual, covenant parents. Being raised by non-Christian parents may also be contributing to the problem they are experiencing, or at the very least, not helping the matter very much. Even if teens have Christian parents, they may not be giving them the best counsel—or have their heads in the sand regarding their teens. Again, these are opportunities for the church to take the lead. Youth pastors and workers can step in and provide Biblical care and counsel—not to supplant or undermine parents, but to follow Christ in the care of His people. As has already been said, this is less than optimal, but it may be the only starting place.

Leading in the Biblical counseling of teenagers means that youth ministry workers must be welcoming and accepting. It's one thing to welcome teenagers into the youth ministry who are spiritually mature, sweet, or just quiet and obedient. But embracing youth who are in pain, or struggling in their sin, is much more challenging. Welcoming these teens doesn't mean ignoring their problems or condoning their sin. It means opening our hearts of compassion to them, while offering Biblical exhortation, confrontation, and counseling. Additionally, teenagers who are struggling need to be accepted by the youth ministry—as sinners made in the image of God, and in need of change. Accepting them doesn't mean a total tolerance of their sin or foolish choices. Instead, the church is to accept them in the sense that they will take them as they are, and seek to help and care for them as much as possible, by the grace of God. The local church leads in welcoming our teens to Jesus as the compassionate lover of their souls!

Pointing to parents. Another essential principle that the local church must always abide by when counseling teenagers is that parents must never be ignored. After all, God has given children to their parents first, not to the youth ministry or the local church! So even if parents are non-Christians or are not engaging in Biblical parenting, the hearts of teenagers still must be pointed to their parents. This may mean that a teenager will need to be counseled to reconcile with his or her parents. Or, he or she will be called upon to honor and obey his or her parents, in whatever the situation. Youth ministry workers in the church should always work to do what they can to strengthen the relationship between teens and their parents. When dealing with a problem, teenagers must always be counseled to seek out the help of their parents first. In this way, the priority of the family is routinely honored by the local church. Remember: Biblical counseling begins at home!

Pointing the hearts and minds of our teenagers to their parents also means that we refuse to undermine parents in our counseling. Teens must honor and respect their parents even when their parents are acting or living less-than-respectably! Youth ministry counselors should never intimate that they are 'on the teenager's side' opposed to the 'parents' side.' Now, this gets challenging when Biblical counselors are told stories about parents who are significantly in error in their parenting or lifestyle choices. In these cases, teens need to be called upon to obey Christ first, even if they may have to go against what their parents are telling them. Even this has to be done with respect and honor, not with an ungodly or prideful spirit. Again, we want to strengthen the bonds between parents and their teens, not weaken them. Youth ministry workers must act with wisdom with the goal of not subverting the God-given authority of parents.

Working with parents. The other significant posture of the youth ministry of the local church is one of coming alongside parents—all who want to partner with the church to help their teens. Taking time to talk with parents to get their perspective about the problem is essential for the counseling process—and vice versa. On one hand, youth ministry counselors will seek to encourage parents to help their own teenagers. On the other hand, parents can give input that will allow the youth ministry workers to better counsel the teen. In the end, the ideal situation is where both youth ministry workers and parents have a similar perspective on the problem, and the Biblical process of change that is necessary. Having a heart-to-heart dialogue, where both sets of helpers trust each other, is the chief goal.

What, then, is the typical procedure when teenagers come to the youth ministry worker first with their particular problem? When and how should their parents become involved? The short answer is: As soon as possible! Parents who really want to know what's going on in the lives of their teens do not typically like to have important information withheld from them. And, if the problem increases in risk to the teen (drug use, sexual activity, suicidal ideations, etc.), it becomes even more imperative to be extremely quick to talk to parents. In answer to the 'how' question of involving parents, a good practice is for the youth ministry worker to direct the teen to talk to his or her parents first. Something may be said like, 'I'll give you twenty-four hours to tell your parents about the problem. If you are unable to talk to them by then, I will need to talk to them with you.' While that may sound threatening, it is simply making the statement of the importance of partnering with parents. It doesn't allow the teenager to think he or she can deal with a problem without the knowledge of parents.

Which then begs this question: As a church-based Biblical counselor, when should we extend confidentiality to a teenager? Typically, this question is asked in the fear that not keeping confidentiality will potentially prevent a teen from seeking counseling from the church. This is an understandable concern, and may actually happen. But while we have a responsibility to keep a teen's information private and secure, we also have a duty to their parents. So the rule of thumb is to never promise confidentiality or allow the teenager to simply assume you will keep everything confidential. You are not a lawyer or a doctor—you are a Biblical counselor/youth ministry worker. What you want the teen before you to do is to trust that you will wisely share information only when necessary. And, you want them to embrace your partnership with their parents as well. If the teenager won't seek counseling with you, that is his or her choice. The key exception to this rule is if the teen is being, or has been, abused or neglected by the parents. If that is the case, then confidentiality will still be broken—as you enlist the help of elders, child protective services, civil authorities, etc. Other than that tragic situation, seek to have a relationship with the teenager where you are not 'put on an island' as the only one that is involved in the problem.

PARTNERING TOGETHER IN THE GOSPEL

The apostle Paul wrote to the church at Philippi: 'I thank my God in all my remembrance of you ... because of your partnership in the gospel from the first day until now' (Phil. 1:3,5). When parents and youth ministry workers partner to offer Biblical counseling to a teenager, they are also being called to look to a much greater partnership—a partnership in the gospel. This commitment of both church and home comes from the realization that our teens need the gospel more than anything else in this life. They need the gospel for salvation. They need the gospel for true heart change. They need the gospel for their sanctification. They need the gospel for their identity in Christ. They need the gospel for their joy, peace, and hope. They need the gospel for all of their relationships. All Biblical counselors—parents and youth ministry workers alike—should submit themselves to the gospel as the power of God at work in the lives of our teens.

Keeping the focus on our partnership together in the gospel puts all the problems of our teenagers into necessary perspective. While we will always want to help our teens solve their problems, we want so much more than that. If sinking into a depression ultimately propels them to call out to Christ for salvation, then we should be grateful for that particular problem. If falling into sexual sin and ending up with an unwanted pregnancy is used by God in our teen's life to discipline and sanctify her, then we should praise the Lord for this problem as well. Sure, we would all love to have the teens in our families or in our church go through the vital teenage years without any serious mental, emotional, or relational problems. Not only is this unrealistic, but it also denies God's sovereign and gracious purposes for suffering, trials, and temptations in their lives. How often does real growth and change happen when everything is going smoothly? While the problems of teenagers will break our hearts, parents and youth ministry workers must always look in hope to the power of the gospel and the work of the Spirit! Only then will we keep our role in helping to solve the problems of youth in the right context.

Part 2
Biblical Counseling Principles for Typical Teenage Problems

4.
Anger and Bitterness

'Fathers, do not provoke your children to anger, but bring them up in the discipline and instruction of the Lord' (Eph. 6:4). In one sentence, the apostle Paul teaches us several important truths about anger. The emotional response of anger is something that is provoked out of our hearts by people and situations. Parents can sinfully provoke or tempt their teenagers to respond in anger. And, Biblical training, instruction, and discipline are essentials for the prevention of and solution to anger in our teenagers. Paul's inerrant counsel to parents is just the beginning of what God's Word has to say about anger, and its more stubborn cohort, bitterness. While it is often assumed that explosive expressions of anger, and all sorts of other angst, is just normative during the teenage years, that doesn't mean it is somehow healthy or acceptable. Sinful anger and bitterness are part of the human condition, which require that they be handled Biblically.

Opening PORTRAITS

- Andy is a 14-year-old who typically appears as a pretty easy-going teen. Yet, when he is teased or told 'no' too many times by his parents, his veins nearly pop out of his neck and his fists clench. Just recently he punched a hole in his bedroom wall when he was grounded from video games for a month.

- 17-year-old Beverly says she never gets angry, even after years of friends rejecting her and being on the outside of her youth group. Instead, she is just 'hurt' and will never make the mistake again of trusting another person.
- Carl, a 16-year-old, is often sarcastic, cynical, and downright moody. He talks a lot about life being unfair, people being 'idiots,' and God not being very good at His 'job.' When Carl is confronted, he claims to only be joking.

Typical PROBLEMS

1. Sinful Anger

People use a variety of words and idioms to describe the expression of anger. 'You make my blood boil.' 'You are such a hothead.' 'I'm doing the slow burn.' Rather than looking at them as different types of anger problems, it's more helpful to view them as a variety of *intensities* on two different *directional* spectrums: anger directed **outward** and anger directed **inward.** All forms of anger typically emerge when an essential goal of ours is blocked. Here are descriptions of the two anger spectrums:

1a. Externalized Anger (blowing up). Since this type of anger is outwardly expressed, this anger spectrum is the most obvious to us. It is also referred to as 'ventilation,' as angry words are said (or yelled) and angry actions are on display (hitting, punching, etc.) It appears to be the most violent of all expressions of anger, at least in the moment. On the 'low' intensity end of the spectrum, we use terms like:

- Annoyance
- Exasperation
- Indignation
- Irritation
- Mad

Then, on the 'high' intensity side of externalized anger, we have terms such as:

Temper tantrum

Rage

Wrath

Infuriation

Whether anger is externalized at a lower intensity or a much higher intensity, it can do great damage to other people, property, or self. Blowing up, or venting anger, is a teenage problem that must be solved.

1b. Internalized Anger (stuffing down). The much more socially acceptable forms of anger expression occur on the 'internalization' spectrum. Rather than blowing up, the teenager stuffs all his anger deep down inside. Another descriptive term for this anger response is 'clamming up.' On this spectrum, the teen could have a low level of anger turned inward, or a more intense anger that he or she is attempting to stuff down. Some of the typical terms used for this sort of anger (in order of intensity) are:

- Disappointment
- Hurt
- Annoyance
- 'Stewing'
- Resentment

While some may argue that internalizations of anger are not sinful, but are actually demonstrations of restraint or even self-control, this spectrum is still problematic. For one thing, they can be expressions of unforgiveness. Stuffing down anger can also lead to other problems, most notably depression, passive-aggressivenes, and relationship issues.

2. Bitterness

In one sense, bitterness can be understood as occurring at the furthest extreme of the 'internalized anger' spectrum—just above resentment. When a teen makes a routine practice of stuffing down his anger, then, in the end, it will become bitterness. Bitterness is long-term anger, which cripples the heart and soul. As described in Hebrews 12:15, it is a chronic attitude that takes root in the heart, causing relational divisions.

Yet, if we only see bitterness from this vantage point, then it would appear that teens who externalize their anger never suffer from bitterness. That is not the case. Even when a person blows up in anger and seemingly 'vents' it all out, bitterness can still ensue. That means sinful anger and bitterness can both be present whether a person typically externalizes anger or most often internalizes anger.

Bitterness occurs when there is unforgiveness present in the heart or unresolved anger which becomes long standing. It is also produced in the heart when relationships are not reconciled. Bitterness also produces more complicated problems like depression, as well as physical health issues. Ultimately, it can create distance in all relationships, including his or her relationship with God.

Evaluation PERSONALIZATION

For each teenage problem, good questions must be asked in order to evaluate comprehensively. We are always evaluating a person, not simply diagnosing a problem. Each teenager you counsel will have unique variables in their lives that will impact the problem and solution. For the problems of anger and bitterness, here are the personal issues we need to listen for and evaluate:

Anger pattern

1. Is the anger more externalized or internalized?
2. Is it on the lower end of the intensity spectrum, or the higher end?
3. Is it a chronic anger problem, or more specific to a current crisis (a blocked goal)?
4. How long has he or she been struggling with an anger problem?

Presence of violence

1. Are there violent words expressed in anger? Corrupt, foul language used?
2. Does the teen hit or destroy things in anger?
3. Is there physical violence, or threats of violence against another person?
4. Is there violence against self, or suicidal thoughts?
5. Has there been any criminal behavior?

Presence of bitterness

1. Has the anger become long-standing?
2. Is there a particular person the teen is bitter towards?
3. Is there a particular situation or circumstance he is she is bitter about?

Physical factors

1. Is the teen experiencing any physical health issues that relate to the anger problem?
2. Does the teen have any intellectual or physical disabilities?
3. Would a medical evaluation be helpful?
4. What is the status of the teen's eating, exercise, and sleeping habits?

Relational issues

1. Is the anger targeted to a certain person, or group of people?
2. Who are his or her closest friends? Are they angry/bitter teens too?
3. Does he or she have Christian friends?
4. How does he or she relate to parents and siblings?
5. What about enemies?
6. Is he or she more social or withdrawn?

Understanding of forgiveness

1. Who does the teen have trouble forgiving?
2. Does he or she have a Biblical understanding of forgiveness? Of grace?
3. Does he or she need to seek someone else's forgiveness?

Cover up

1. Is the anger more of a secondary emotion, covering up deeper issues?
2. Is there underlying guilt or shame?
3. Is there deeper fear or anxiety?
4. Are there secret sins that need to be exposed?

Relationship with God

1. Is the teen angry with God?
2. What about his or her devotional life? Prayer and Bible study?
3. What is the teen's basic understanding of God?
4. What about the role of the Holy Spirit in spiritual maturity?

Righteous anger

1. Has the teen been sinned against, and is righteously angry?
2. What part of the anger is righteous?
3. Has righteous anger turned into sinful anger?

Other related problems

1. Is there any drug or alcohol use involved?
2. What about depression? Anxiety?
3. Are there any other related problems?

Biblical PRINCIPLES

After listening and evaluating, the Biblical counseling process moves forward to compassionate confrontation and edifying education. In order to offer wise counsel that gets to the heart of the matter, Biblical principles of the problem must be understood and applied. It's just too easy to merely communicate our own opinions and experiences rather than the life-giving truth of God! So the following principles should operate as 'hooks' for your thoughts on the subject. They will keep you on the rails of Biblical truth, which the Holy Spirit can then use to bring heart change into the life of your teenager. Theories and ideas abound about how to solve the problems of anger and bitterness. Keep your focus on applying Biblical principles to the unique experience of the teen who is before you.

Acknowledge it

The starting point for just about any problem is for a person to actually acknowledge there is a problem. This is certainly true for anger! You've probably heard people say things like, 'I don't get angry; I just get revenge.' Or, like in our opening portrait of Beverly, 'I'm not angry; I'm just hurt.' There are plenty of different words and idioms teenagers can use that either minimize or attempt to ignore the fact that they are actually angry. Do not allow your teen to deny it, but simply and clearly admit: 'I am angry!' Anger is not to be vented, stuffed, minimized or ignored. Only when it is acknowledged, can a Biblical course of action be taken. Only when your teen admits what particular situation or person is leading him or her to anger, can we gain understanding of what to do next.

In Ephesians 4:26-27, we read these words about anger: 'Be angry and do not sin; do not let the sun go down on your anger, and give no opportunity to the devil.' The apostle Paul is not simply commanding us to be angry. More importantly, he is communicating that our anger does not need to become sinful. In other words, we all get angry, but Christians do not have to allow anger to lead to sinful thoughts, words, and actions. So rather than believing (like Beverly) that ALL anger is sinful and so I must deny or downplay the fact that I'm angry—a right understating of Scripture shows that we can be angry and not sin in it!

Acknowledging anger will move the teen to address the issue that is fueling the anger in the first place.

Redirect it

One of the main problems with our anger is that it often fails to accomplish God's purposes—succeeding only in creating other problems. When Carl, our cynical 16-year old, witnesses a good friend being bullied at school, this evokes anger in his heart. But, if Carl sinfully ventilates it by slashing the bully's car tires, some people may cheer, but this will only create further problems for Carl. If Carl chooses to simply stuff down his anger and gets resentful about how unfair the world is, he may just end up getting depressed. Instead, Carl needs to learn to redirect his anger to solve the actual problem which provoked his anger in the first place. Since God has given him a strong sense of justice, he must use his anger to pursue any and all righteous means of justice! If Carl didn't get angry about the suffering of his friend in the first place, he would have no motivation to help and make things right. Sinfully externalizing or internalizing will defeat the purpose of his anger.

So, when you are counseling your teen about their anger, it won't help to just say, 'Stop getting so angry!' When he or she is angry about an injustice being done—to self or someone else—communicating 'stop it' is akin to saying, 'Don't care so much.' Again, here's the key: Anger that is rooted in a response to injustice needs to be redirected. Blowing up or clamming up is a misuse of our anger. It directs our anger toward all the wrong things, which ends up enabling us to avoid the actual issues. Sometimes, your teen may simply be afraid to confront the problem. At other times it may feel like there is nothing that can be done. But the truth is, God wants His people to use anger that is rooted in a sense of justice to deal with the injustices in our lives and the lives of other people! Think about the actions that Carl can take in his anger. He can pray for the bully. He can report the bullying to the authorities. He can certainly defend his friend and confront the bully, if God gives him the right opportunity and words. In the end, Carl can even end up being an anti-bullying advocate in his school! And this will keep Carl's anger from turning into cynicism, apathy, and bitterness—as he trusts more fully in God in the process.

Re-focus it

When the sinful anger in the heart of a teen is more self-centered rather than solely rooted in a response to the injustices of this world, we have a different Biblical principle in play. Andy, our 14-year old, is a good example for us here. While he thinks being teased or being told 'no' by his parents is a great injustice, it really isn't. Andy is suffering from having his eyes on the wrong objects of his delight. To put it another way: He is seeking to find his joy in the wrong places, and is regularly disappointed. Andy believes that having his own way will make him happy and allow him to shed all his discontentedness. He also thinks that he must always be admired and respected, so that's why any teasing or joking hurts his pride and evokes his wrath. Our delights are often in all the wrong things: our sports teams, our hobbies, our relationships, our jobs, etc. All of these easily become idols that demand our total worship and allegiance.

As it is in Andy's case, anger erupts when some obstacle gets in the way of a delight or an idol, proving that it holds too much sway in our lives. Our anger calls us to re-focus on a much higher and better object of delight! As Christians we know that our delight is to always be in the Lord (Ps. 37:4). When we delight in Him, we can then truly enjoy our lesser delights, as well as put them in perspective. How do we teach Andy this truth, practically speaking? Instead of using his anger to attempt to get his own way, it should act as a 'check engine' light that forces him to admit he is seeking his joy in the wrong things. How much more delightful would it be if he simply submitted to his parents and obeyed them 'in the Lord?' When he is teased, he can look for ways to love his enemies, putting his joy into pleasing God and serving others (Matt. 5:44). In the end, Andy must get much less self-centered and much more God-centered. His anger exposes his heart idols, allowing him to re-focus on a better source of delight.

Don't let the sun set

Let's return to Ephesians 4 again for our next Biblical principle concerning anger: 'Be angry and do not sin; do not let the sun go down on your anger, and give no opportunity to the devil' (Eph. 4:26-27). This text is often effectively used in marriage counseling, where Christian couples are exhorted to resolve their conflicts before going to bed. So how can we apply it to the typical anger of teens? Think about Beverly again. She certainly appears to be letting day after day go by with unresolved anger towards her friends in her heart. This 'stuffed-down' anger has hardened into bitterness, creating a resolution to never allow friends to reject her again. Any righteous anger has long ago become sinful, simply based on the fact that she has let the sun go down on her anger. Because of this failing on Beverly's part, she has given opportunity for the devil to create havoc in her life.

This Biblical principle reminds us that we must deal with what is causing anger in our hearts now! Remember, the God-given emotion of anger moves us to passionately resolve the real problems in our lives or the lives of others. Unfortunately, unresolved anger in our lives, day after day, will end up controlling us instead. It gives the devil an opportunity to become lord over our hearts. So, after a hard time at a youth group event, Beverly needs to confront her angry and bitter thoughts immediately. As the Psalmist says: 'Be angry, and do not sin; ponder in your hearts on your beds, and be silent' (Ps. 4:4). Beverly can literally sit on her bed, and think about how the Lord would have her respond. She can cry out to the Lord in her pain. She should seek His comfort and find her joy in Him. She has to think through how to act and what to say. Most importantly she must forgive, refusing to remain angry and bitter at her rejecting friends the rest of her life. Our teens need to be challenged to confront the anger that resides within their hearts, meditate and think deeply about it, and sit in quietness before a sovereign and loving God.

Slow it down

Anger has a way of moving the dial of our hearts, minds, and behaviors from a standard speed to a 'flash forward, lightning' speed. Think about Andy again. When teased, his blood begins to boil and his face immediately turns beet red. Almost immediately as the 'no' is emerging from his dad's lip, his eyes flash, his fists clench, and the veins nearly pop out of his neck. Andy moves from a happy-go-lucky teen to the angry 'Hulk' in almost a split second. James recognizes this problem when he writes: 'Know this, my beloved brothers: let every person be quick to hear, slow to speak, slow to anger; for the anger of man does not produce the righteousness of God' (James 1:19-20). Many of our teens become angry way too fast. It makes them appear to be all emotion, all hormones, with little rationality. But being fast to anger typically ends in some very unrighteous activities, often with deep regrets to follow.

Growing in the grace of God means learning to take more time to become angry. Anger that is unbridled has a way of racing out of control. It moves at the speed of light. It erupts, flashes, and burns like a fire. So like switching a movie from fast-forward to slow-motion, teens like Andy have to learn to slow down the process of his anger. When teasing comments are made, or he is being picked on, Andy needs to slowly think through towards a proper response. When he is told 'no' by his parents, he needs to stop and think, even walking away slowly to process what's happening. Yes, this is easier said than done. It is a learning curve, requiring Andy to have the power of God in his heart and mind. He needs to hold on to Proverbs 14:29, 'Whoever is slow to anger has great understanding, but he who has a hasty temper exalts folly.' A teen with a quick temper is the poster-child of foolishness and immaturity. Someone like Andy must be called upon to commit to the wise slow-down of all of his anger responses, with the help of the Spirit.

Put off, put on

In Ephesians 4, the apostle Paul describes the process of 'putting off' the old man and its behaviors, and 'putting on' the new man. In other words, as Christians, we are empowered by the Spirit to be able to stop old ways of living and start new ways—by God's grace. When it comes to anger, one of the most significant behaviors to put off is revenge against those who have hurt us. Beverly could be plotting revenge against her friends who have ostracized her repeatedly. Andy may also be seeking revenge for all who have teased him. Both have to be taught to put off or put away our plans for revenge: 'Beloved, never avenge yourselves, but leave it to the wrath of God, for it is written, "Vengeance is mine, I will repay, says the Lord"' (Rom. 12:19). This instruction will probably seem so foreign to their ears, as the world, their peers, and their sinful hearts celebrate revenge and make heroes out of human avengers. It often feels like revenge is the only response that will make us feel better. Revenge is sweet, right? But God's Word tells the teen struggling with anger to put off revenge, and leave it for God, the perfect avenger.

But this Biblical principle is not just about stopping bad behavior, but also putting on God- glorifying behavior as well. If Andy or Beverly simply resist getting revenge (passively or aggressively), they will still not be experiencing real heart change for their anger. Listen to these difficult words of Jesus: 'But I say to you who hear, Love your enemies, do good to those who hate you, bless those who curse you, pray for those who abuse you' (Luke 6:27-28). To become truly free of the effects of sinful anger, Andy and Beverly need to do the impossible (without Christ) thing and love their enemies, do good to them, bless them, and pray for them. When our anger is rooted in self-righteousness mixed with a strong sense of justice, this will not only seem impossible, but feel very unfair. Yet, God's Word tells us that it is the right thing to do—not just for our enemies, but to solve the problems of an angry and bitter heart. Putting off revenge and putting on love is the Biblical process that will reconcile our relationships rather than continue to destroy them.

Uproot bitterness

In Hebrews 12:15, we learn the essential counsel on bitterness: 'See to it that no one fails to obtain the grace of God; that no "root of bitterness" springs up and causes trouble, and by it many become defiled.' Bitterness is long-term, stored-up sinful anger. It takes roots and hardens the heart, against people and even God. Think about Beverly again. Clearly, her bitterness is deeply impacting her own heart and mind. But consider what it is doing in her youth group. Instead of acting like brothers and sisters in the family of God, bitterness has sprung up and caused divisions within the group. Certainly, the other teens who are rejecting and ostracizing Beverly need to be challenged and confronted. They need to learn how to love God and other people. But Beverly's stored-up bitterness is contributing to the problem as well. It is easy to imagine that, even if the friends in her youth group repent and change their ways, Beverly still may refuse to forgive and risk reconciliation. Bitterness tries to convince us that we must protect our own hearts and not open up to people again.

Hebrews 12:15 also connects bitterness to a failure to obtain the grace of God. Bitterness is the opposite of grace, because it holds other people to very rigorous standards. Out of the pain in our teenager's heart, he or she can simply refuse to show grace and love to others. This is a demonic deception that will keep us from the grace of God, only creating further problems. Since it is connected to grace, the only solution is forgiveness, as the apostle Paul expresses it: 'Be kind to one another, tenderhearted, forgiving one another, as God in Christ forgave you' (Eph. 4:32). The very essence of God's grace is His willingness to forgive sinners in His Son, Jesus Christ. Beverly needs to know and remember how much she has been forgiven. She needs to learn to forgive those who have wronged her. Then, she will need to be challenged even further: to be kind and tenderhearted to those who have been unkind and mean-spirited. While we can certainly be sympathetic towards Beverly in her suffering, dealing with the bitterness is vital for her heart as well as her present and future relationships.

Exercise self-control

The fruit of the Holy Spirit known as self-control, or self-discipline, is absolutely necessary for just about any teenage problem (Gal. 5:23). Anger, in its outwardly explosive forms, seeks to aggressively control others. Internalized anger can also attempt to exert control over the lives of others, in more passive-aggressive ways. But, then, anger ends up controlling the angry person, keeping him or her captive and hurting. Andy may end up getting so violent in his anger, that he forces his parents to give in and give him his way. Beverly might figure out how to manipulate members of her youth group in passive-aggressive ways. Carl could easily use his negativity and pessimism to get people to feel sorry for him. For all our teenage friends: what is the cost of controlling others? Using anger to have others revolve around our desires, our needs, and our interests is a tough way to live. And, if these habits don't begin to break in the teenage years, it is will be a rough road ahead. Proverbs 25:28 puts it this way: 'A man without self-control is like a city broken into and left without walls.'

Therefore, the solution to teens using their anger to control others (and thereby being controlled by it) is growing in the fruit of the Spirit. Rather than trying to control their situations, our young people need to learn to trust in God's total control of all things. It is only God's Spirit who can give us that trust, as well as the strength, to control our anger. Teens need to learn that lacking self-control of their anger leaves them vulnerable to the work of Satan as well as being controlled by other people. Andy is allowing the teasers in his life to control him. Beverly is allowing her so-called friends to control her too. Like a city without walls, the teen without self-control is left open to invaders of any kind. If your teen is a Christian, he or she can learn to exert control by the power of the indwelling Spirit. Exercising Spirit-led self-control not only prevents long-term anger and bitterness, but potentially violent situations.

Righteous anger?

A last Biblical principle for counseling a teenager with anger and bitterness could have been the first: Check for the presence of righteous anger. As was noted earlier, Christians can be angry and not sin (Eph. 4:26). Being made in the image of God, we can emulate His righteous anger, especially when we are responding to injustice. Your teen may be righteously angry over the mistreatment of a friend. He or she may have righteous wrath over being treated unfairly or being a victim of abuse. Your teen may even be righteously angry over his or her sin! Typically, most of us tend to think all of our anger is righteous— or at least mostly righteous. But, if we are honest, most of our anger is pretty self-serving and unrighteous. Yet, it is still vital to help your teen discern if he or she is experiencing righteous anger.

Unfortunately, as sinful human beings, even our righteous anger can quickly degenerate into sinful anger. It gets tainted by our self-righteousness, unrealistic expectations, and false judgments. We can become impatient, and take matters into our sinful hands. We can make the situation all about ourselves, rather than the glory of God. So while you need to help your teenager recognize righteous anger, you also must help him or her see how even his or her righteous acts are like dirty rags (Isa. 64:6). And then, challenge him or her to work on keeping the anger righteous, following Biblical principles. In the end, only our Savior expressed righteous anger all the time, for all the right reasons. As with all human problems, they should humble us in comparison to the greatness and glory of King Jesus.

Wisdom POINTERS

If we want our teenagers to pursue hearts of wisdom, then we will have to counsel them wisely. It's one thing to operate from Biblical presuppositions, to understand an effective counseling process, and to know Biblical principles concerning a problem—but quite another to apply them all wisely. So, a Biblical analysis of each teenage problem will end with some 'wisdom pointers'—some 'do's and don'ts'—to help counsel your teen wisely. When dealing with the problems of anger and bitterness:

- Do communicate the love of Christ for sinners.
- Don't confront your teen's anger with your own anger.
- Do show true compassion for the pain the teen is experiencing.
- Don't excuse all anger as being simply a normal emotion.
- Do recognize when anger is actually righteous.
- Don't just tell a teen to 'stop it' or that Christians don't get angry.
- Do comfort a teen who has long-standing bitterness.
- Don't offer techniques which 'safely' vent out the anger.
- Do help to redirect the teen's anger to solve the real problem.
- Don't allow the teen to deny, minimize, or ignore the anger.
- Do point to the power of the Spirit to produce self-control.
- Don't ignore suicidal comments, even if said in anger.

5.
Anxiety, Fear, and Worry

The world, in its fallen state, has always been a scary place. Each generation grows up with plenty to fear because of the ongoing presence of evil. Even so, it is often tempting for adults to communicate to teenagers that they have little reason to be anxious or afraid. After all, it's not like they are living through the Great Depression, the Black Death, or a major World War, right? What is there to worry about in a time of great abundance and relative ease? Yet, the reality is that teens do struggle with real anxiety, fear, and worry. Whether it is situational (after a trauma like a school shooting) or more chronic due to a deeply held heart idol, these connected problems must be addressed Biblically. It is not enough (or realistic) to try to take away all opportunities to be anxious. They, like all Christians, must learn to grow in their trust for God, their understanding of self, and in a more mature love for God and other people. God's Word gives us important instructions concerning this common heart problem.

Opening PORTRAITS

- Daniel, a 15-year old, has been experiencing pretty severe digestive problems and migraines over the past year. Everything seems to stress him out lately—especially school. The family doctor says there is nothing physically wrong with Daniel, but he does need to learn to not become so anxious about insignificant things.

- 17-year old Emily confides in you that she is having regular panic attacks every few weeks or so. At first, she thought she was having a heart attack—until she diagnosed herself using a psychiatric website. Emily has been attending church and youth group less and less because she is afraid she may have a panic attack and be humiliated.

- Fran has always been extremely shy. Her parents just believed she would grow out of it one day. Now sixteen years old, Fran has dropped out of the youth group and never comes to Sunday School—only attending the worship service with her mother.

- Gary, a 16-year old, claims to have OCD. He proudly tells you that he is very organized and is a perfectionist. But he is concerned about becoming overly obsessed with the weather, especially since he can't leave the house if there is even a 10 per cent chance of a thunderstorm.

Typical PROBLEMS

1. Generalized Anxiety

While all people experience anxiety from time to time, generalized anxiety is a persistent and excessive worry about a variety of different things. The teenager who expresses that she is 'a worrier by nature' can probably be characterized as struggling with generalized anxiety. Another indicator of this problem is when a person is worried more days than not, over many months and even years.

2. Phobias

There are a plethora of rational things for teenagers to fear. If a walk in the woods ends up with a confrontation with a grizzly bear, we would want our young person to experience some level of fear—so he could flee! A phobia, on the other hand, is always irrational in nature, even if there seems to be a good reason to be afraid. Spiders may be scary, but arachnophobia occurs when it rises to an irrational level. Teens may develop an irrational fear about just about anything, including: a fear of heights, public speaking, crowded spaces, germs, and even storms. Phobias appear to only be solved by complete avoidance of the fear-producing thing, person, or situation.

3. Panic Attacks

Panic attacks are appropriately named, since they are often first thought to be the experience of a heart attack. Chest pains, shortness of breath, sweaty palms, a sense of terror, and feelings of weakness or dizziness are its main symptoms. Ultimately, panic attacks create sudden feelings of acute and disabling anxiety. To the sufferer, panic attacks seem to come 'out of the blue,' with little connection to a fearful situation or event. After experiencing several panic attacks, an individual can find his or her greatest fear to be the next attack.

4. Obsessive-Compulsive Disorder (OCD)

Another, more complicated form of anxiety, is commonly known as obsessive-compulsive disorder (OCD). This problem is characterized by excessive thoughts (obsessions) that lead to repetitive, often extreme, behaviors (compulsions). Common examples are: excessive handwashing due to obsessions about germs or sickness, repetitive checking things like door locks, appliances, and switches, and various forms of hoarding behavior. True OCD is more than simply needing to be organized or have everything in order—it is rooted in deep anxiety and fear.

5. Post-Traumatic Stress Disorder (PTSD)

Originally, the symptoms of post-traumatic stress disorder (PTSD) were observed primarily in soldiers returning home from war, as they experienced genuine trauma. Today, PTSD may be experienced when an individual has difficulty recovering from a wide range of terrifying events, whether he or she either experienced them or simply witnessed them. The main symptoms of PTSD may include: regular nightmares, unwanted memories of the trauma, heightened fear reactions, depression, and avoidance of situations that would bring back the memories. While it is normal to have a negative reaction to a trauma, PTSD is a chronic response that is rooted in anxiety, fear, and worry.

6. 'Stressed out'

While being 'stressed out' is not a proper diagnostic label, it is a typical way that many teens communicate their worry and anxiety. Stressors are a part of life; being stressed out is a state of allowing them to overwhelm. Teens who are not handling their stress well can develop stomach ulcers, digestive problems, migraines, or other physical symptoms. Even though it is tempting to think being stressed is normal, it is characteristic of anxious thoughts and excessive worry.

Evaluation *PERSONALIZATION*

As was said previously, there are essential questions that must be asked in order to evaluate a problem comprehensively. We are always evaluating a person made in God's image, not simply diagnosing a problem. Each teenager you counsel will have unique variables in their lives that will impact the problem, as well as a solution. For the problems of anxiety, worry, and fear, these are the personal issues you will need to listen for and evaluate:

Overall anxiety pattern

1. Is the anxiety more generalized, or is there a specific underlying fear?
2. When did the present pattern of anxiety begin?
3. Has there been any experience of panic attacks?
4. Are there obsessive thoughts or extreme compulsions?
5. Was there a traumatic event that has not been handled properly?

Physical factors

1. Is the teen experiencing any physical health issues that relate to the anxiety problem?
2. Are there any intellectual or physical disabilities of note?
3. Would a medical evaluation be helpful?
4. What is the status of the teen's eating, exercise, and sleeping habits?
5. Is the teen complaining of digestive issues or regular headaches?
6. Has the teen reported any symptoms of a panic attack?

Relational issues

1. Is the fear, worry, or anxiety connected to a specific person?
2. Is the teen experiencing social anxiety or fearful of relationships in general?
3. Has the teen withdrawn from people or become isolated?
4. Is the anxiety keeping him or her from typical social activities?

Marriage and family

1. Are there significant family problems that are contributing to teen anxiety?
2. Is the home life peaceful, or full of conflict?
3. Is the teen worried about any other family or extended family issues?

Relationship with God

1. What is the teen's basic understanding of God?
2. What about his or her devotional life? Prayer and Bible study?
3. How does the teen describe his or her trust in Jesus Christ?
4. What about the role of the Holy Spirit in spiritual maturity?

Other related problems

1. Is there any drug or alcohol use involved?
2. Is the teenager depressed?

3. Are there any other related problems?

Biblical PRINCIPLES

After listening to your teenager—and starting to do some evaluation—the Biblical counseling process moves on to compassionate confrontation and edifying education. In order to offer wise counsel that gets to the heart of the matter, Biblical principles of the problem must be understood and applied. As has been said previously, it's just too easy to merely communicate our own opinions and experiences rather than the life-giving truth of God! With that in mind, the following principles should operate as 'hooks' for your thoughts on the subject. They will keep you 'between the lines' of Biblical truth, which the Holy Spirit can then use to bring heart change into the life of your teenager. Theories and ideas abound about how to solve the problems of anxiety, fear, and worry. Keep your focus on applying Biblical principles to the unique experiences of the teen whom you are helping.

Understand the temptations

In many cases, teens have very specific situations or people that are tempting them to worry. Daniel, our 15-year old, is reporting that he is 'stressed out' about everything lately, but especially school. He is experiencing severe digestive issues and migraines as well. So what is actually tempting Daniel to be so anxious? Maybe he is worried about his grades and academic record. Or, it could be that he is being bullied, or has found himself on the outside of important relationships. He could be anxious about relating to the opposite sex. Whatever the case, Daniel needs to admit and understand what is tempting him to worry. If he has ended up being anxious about 'everything'—even insignificant things—it is still important to deal with some of the known major temptations. Our teenagers need to admit the things, people, situations, or issues that trigger an anxious response.

But understanding temptation must go beyond a simple knowledge of the basic fear source in order to pursue true heart change. Think about Daniel again. If he is stressed about his grades, what is truly creating his anxious heart? Is he fearful that he may not get into college, therefore not able to follow his desired career path? Or, are 'straight A's' deeply connected to his identity, as he has always taken great pride in his intelligence? What if he is really anxious about disappointing his parents who have regularly applied pressure to succeed? To truly get to the source of the temptation, we must ask WHY is the WHAT producing such anxiety? Clearly, not every teen worries excessively about his or her grades. *What our anxiety typically reveals is the stubborn idols of the heart—the ones that are not easily pleased or satisfied.* If Daniel locates the source of his anxiety as 'good grades,' he has not gone far enough. We must help him get a handle on the reasons behind why his academic success is so important to him.

In the teenager's world, there are so many situations that can produce anxiety. Some will be clear and obvious: relationships, friends, enemies, money, grades, etc. Others will be more difficult to pinpoint: the insecurity that comes from their parent's troubled marriage, a desire to have life go smoothly and according to plan, or a need for complete safety and security. To rightly deal with anxiety that is either specific or generalized, the starting place is to recognize that our hearts are easily tempted to worry due to many difficulties in this life. Even that admission is difficult for many teens who act like they have everything under control. As will be discussed later, it is exactly their desire to be in control which is often producing their anxiety. Recognizing our weakness and vulnerability connected to specific issues in our lives allows us to see how much we need Jesus!

Move from worry to concern

Now, in reference to Daniel, you may be thinking to yourself: 'I want my teenager to worry about his grades. He shouldn't just be apathetic about them!' This illustrates a common misconception about human worry. According to God's Word, worry is always sinful. *It is a self-focused response that reveals a lack of trust in God's care, goodness, and sovereignty over our lives.* Followers of Christ are commanded by Jesus not to worry: 'Therefore I tell you, do not be anxious about your life, what you will eat or what you will drink, nor about your body, what you will put on. Is not life more than food, and the body more than clothing?' (Matt. 6:25). Echoing these words of Christ, Paul writes: 'Do not be anxious about anything, but in everything by prayer and supplication with thanksgiving let your requests be made known to God.' (Phil. 4:6). Worry, or anxiety, is never described as righteous or good—even though it is a common experience for all human beings. So, if Daniel is truly worried about his grades, this is not an admirable trait, or one that should be encouraged. The choice for our teenage is not between worry or apathy—since both are sinful options. Worry must be dealt with Biblically.

So, that leads us to the proper understanding of the heart and mind attitude known as concern. What is concern? Isn't it synonymous with worry? A Biblical view of concern begins with recognizing the focus of concern. While worry is self-focused, concern remains centered on a deep care for others, and for the glory of God. Concern dwells on what is true and righteous, rather than what is false and misdirected. We see this term used by the apostle Paul in 2 Corinthians 11:28, where he describes his concern for all the churches (NIV). Concern may be defined in modern dictionaries as being equivalent to worry or anxiety, but that is not a Biblical sense of the distinction. Without an opportunity to be properly concerned about something or someone, then all deep caring would be considered sinful. We should not be looking for our teenagers to be apathetic or so 'chill' that nothing bothers them. There is much in this life to be righteously concerned about, without becoming sinfully worried.

With this necessary distinction in mind, let's go back to Daniel. To just tell this teen to stop worrying so much about his school grades is not enough. Again, not worrying may be interpreted as not caring—

or even being irresponsible. Daniel should be rightly concerned about the state of his grades, because they do matter when it comes to a college education and his future career. But he should become more concerned about working hard, studying well, and using his mind to learn. He should be concerned about the way he uses his God-given gifts and abilities in order to glorify God. His grades cannot be so tied to his identity that he loses his main concern in life right now—to find and grow in his identity in Jesus Christ. Teaching Daniel to be rightly concerned rather than sinfully worried will free him to rest— and maybe even enjoy the process of learning.

To summarize this essential principle: Worry always has a self-focus attached to it, while concern is grounded in a trust in God. Worry will usually produce other problems in life, such as physical health problems, panic attacks, and struggles trusting other people. If we could put worry and concern on a spectrum line, concern crosses the boundary into worry as our faith in the power and love for God diminishes. So, when our teen is tempted to worry, we must help him or her get back over that boundary line into the realm of concern. Concern allows a person to still be at peace, while worry simply produces unrest of heart and soul. Christians alone can move from worry to concern when we rest in the sovereign grace of God.

Overcome fear with love

When a teenager is stuck in an irrational fear of anything, it can reveal a lack of faith in a God who is in control. Thus, it is right to think of fear and faith as being opposites—as we grow in faith, our fears are often relieved. But, according to the apostle John, fear has another opposite—love: 'There is no fear in love, but perfect love casts out fear. For fear has to do with punishment, and whoever fears has not been perfected in love' (1 John 4:18). Fran, who has been extremely shy all of her life, may need to learn this essential principle. Her shyness could be a cover for a deeper fear of people. Her purposeful dropping out of youth group and Sunday School may expose this crippling fear, as it becomes easier just to avoid her peers. While Fran may be having trouble trusting God when it comes to relationships, her bigger challenge is to learn to love people rather than simply fear them.

Consider the various ways that fear and love stand in opposition to one another. Fear is always suspicious about personal involvement; love always looks to give to others. Fear refuses to take significant risks; love lays down its life for others. Fear is self-focused and self-protective; love is open and vulnerable. Fear builds wall between people, while love seeks to tear them down. Fear dwells on potential evil and danger; love thinks no evil at all. Fear keeps itself busy with worrying about tomorrow, while love stays occupied on today. Therefore, as John writes, love overcomes fear. When a teen is bent towards fearing other people or social situations, he or she needs to learn how to love God more, and risk loving people better as well. Too many teenage relationships are fear-based rather than based in sacrificial love. Instead of becoming captive to the fear of getting hurt, or the fear of the rejection of others, our teens must grow in a love for others in order to overcome social anxiety.

Fear God, not man

Let's expand on the necessary Biblical counselling we need to offer Fran. While it is true that she needs to grow in her love for people, she also needs to learn to fear God more. Think about these important words of Jesus:

> I tell you, my friends, do not fear those who kill the body, and after that have nothing more that they can do. But I will warn you whom to fear: fear him who, after he has killed, has authority to cast into hell. Yes, I tell you, fear him! Are not five sparrows sold for two pennies? And not one of them is forgotten before God. Why, even the hairs of your head are all numbered. Fear not; you are of more value than many sparrows. (Luke 12:4-7)

Now, it may not be of much initial comfort to Fran for you to say: 'What's the worst thing the members of your youth group can do to you? All they can do is kill you!' But the truth is that other people can do us no ultimate harm. Only God is in control of our eternal destinies. So the fear of people ends up making them more important to us than God. Fearing people gives them power and control that they really don't have.

So, coupled with learning to truly love others, we overcome our fear of people by fearing God more. Rather than seeking to be a people-pleaser, Fran and all of our teens must mature into God-pleasers. Of course, this doesn't equate to being mortally afraid of God or simply fearing His anger and wrath. Fearing God is so much more expansive, including the right worship of God, a holy reverence for His name and glory, and a devotion to obey Him in all things. The fear of other people keeps our eyes locked on to what they are doing in our lives rather than God's amazing plan and purpose for us. Certainly, people can be scary and are able to do many frightening things to us. Yet, when our fear of God grows, God becomes bigger and people become smaller. God is the only one worthy of our devotion and worship. Fran's fear problem is first about a problem of a low view of God and her inability to worship Him alone.

Seek God's Kingdom first

Both Daniel and Fran are struggling with different forms of anxiety that can be solved in various ways. Yet it is essential for them to see the bigger picture of their problems that will also redirect their hearts and minds. We return to Matthew 6 for these insights from King Jesus:

> Therefore I tell you, do not be anxious about your life, what you will eat or what you will drink, nor about your body, what you will put on. Is not life more than food, and the body more than clothing? Look at the birds of the air: they neither sow nor reap nor gather into barns, and yet your heavenly Father feeds them. Are you not of more value than they? And which of you by being anxious can add a single hour to his span of life? And why are you anxious about clothing? Consider the lilies of the field,

how they grow: they neither toil nor spin, yet I tell you, even Solomon in all his glory was not arrayed like one of these. But if God so clothes the grass of the field, which today is alive and tomorrow is thrown into the oven, will he not much more clothe you, O you of little faith? Therefore do not be anxious, saying, 'What shall we eat?' or 'What shall we drink?' or 'What shall we wear?' For the Gentiles seek after all these things, and your heavenly Father knows that you need them all. But seek first the kingdom of God and his righteousness, and all these things will be added to you. 'Therefore do not be anxious about tomorrow, for tomorrow will be anxious for itself. Sufficient for the day is its own trouble. (Matt. 6:25-34)

Our anxieties reveal what our hearts are ultimately seeking. Just like adults, our teens may act more like unbelievers, anxiously focused on what we are eating, drinking, and wearing. This will keep us in general anxiety all of our lives—a place where believers should not be.

So, because God perfectly provides for all our needs, Christians are able to seek after something much bigger and better—the Kingdom of God. This keeps us focused on today, rather than tomorrow. It fixes our eyes on the growth and expansion of the Kingdom in this world, rather than the maintenance of our own personal kingdoms. It doesn't take an expert to understand that teenagers have the tendency to exist in a very small world, which often orbits around self. They need to have a Kingdom-view, a gospel-focus, and a Christ-centric view of everything in their world. This also means that we should regularly admonish our anxious teens to give themselves over to the sacrificial ministry of others, especially those who are 'least' or outside of the Kingdom of God. When we are tempted to worry about so many things, the only comfort is found within the powerful walls of the Kingdom of God.

Confront anxious thoughts

The entire spectrum of anxiety, worry, and fear problems require the teenager to deal with his or her thought life. While we often think about worry or anxiety as a feeling, it is better understood as a thought disorder that produces negative feelings and actions. Consider what the Psalmist says in Psalm 139: 'Search me, O God, and know my heart; Try me, and know my anxious thoughts; And see if there is any wicked way in me, And lead me in the way everlasting' (Ps. 139:23-24). The teen struggling with anxious thoughts needs the Lord to shine His light of truth on them, showing him or her how irrational and unbiblical they are. Teens can become stuck in fearful thoughts of failure, fearing what others think, worrying about getting hurt or rejected, or a myriad of other destructive thought patterns. In order to stop believing lies, the Biblical counselor must confront teens with the truth.

Consider Gary, our 16-year old who says he has OCD. At one level, he is very proud of his organizational skills and his perfectionism. But he confesses to you that his OCD really manifests itself with bad weather, controlling him to such a level that he often won't leave the house on a stormy day. To be clear, obsessive-compulsive disorder is one of the most difficult anxiety problems to overcome, since it is often deeply rooted to a person's identity. It may even require medical treatment at some point. Yet, Gary does need help confronting his anxious thoughts about storms and severe weather. He believes he is best dealing with his obsessive thoughts by giving into his compulsive checking of the news and his avoidance of being ever caught in a storm. Unfortunately, his compulsive behaviors only confirm and promote his obsessive, anxious thoughts. Gary needs self-control—the fruit of the Spirit—in order to fight against the obsessions and compulsions.

To combat anxious thoughts Biblically, our teens must learn to hold on to the words of the apostle Paul to Timothy: 'For God has not given us a spirit of fear, but of power and of love and of a sound mind' (2 Tim. 1:7). If Gary is a Christian, he no longer has an overall disposition (spirit) of fear, but the power and love of God which produces a sound mind. Anxious thoughts produce only unsound thinking. Anxiety convinces us that we are believing the truth, when we are really believing lies. Checking the weather fifty times a day will not ever put Gary in control of the weather. Making sure that all his windows and doors are perfectly weatherproof all the time will not ultimately keep him from harm. As challenging as OCD is, your teen will need to gradually get better at confronting his or her thought life, and resisting giving in to the persistent compulsions. With the power of the Spirit and a commitment to thinking truthfully, your teen will be able to begin to see those anxious thoughts calm down.

Control what you can control

One of the best definitions of anxiety is: Anxiety is the heart's attempt to control what a person can't control. The worrier—the anxious teen—is really a controlling person, whether or not he or she wants to believe it or admit it. Daniel wants to be in control over his school grades and his future success. Fran wants to control which people are in her life and which people aren't, ensuring that she will never be hurt, embarrassed, or rejected. Gary longs to be in control of most things in his life, but the weather for sure. A teen's control often manifests in how he or she treats other people. Or, it may show up in simple avoidance of all things that are risky or hard. Anxiety only increases as situations occur that are well beyond our control. Whenever we can live in the illusion of control, our fears and anxieties subside. Too bad you can't offer your teen a path to the complete control of his or her life!

Here's a helpful exercise for your teen struggling with anxiety: Make two columns on a piece of paper. On the top of one column, write 'My list,' and on the other, 'God's list.' Tell your teenager to first list all of the things that he or she can control. Daniel would write things down such as: Take good notes in class, study hard, and do all the homework. Gary would note things like: Close doors and windows, follow reasonable advice of the weather man, etc. Then, they need to think about what God sovereignly controls—what's solely in His column. God is ultimately in charge of Daniel's grades and future success. He is also totally in control of the weather and our physical safety. Using this exercise, you want your teen to see that he is spending most of his time on God's side of the ledger, instead of taking responsibility for his own. The more he focuses on what only God can do, he will be anxious and worried. If he can actively remain focused on taking care of his own list, he must then trust God to take care of His list.

The truth is: anxiety of the heart that is deep and persistent is fueled by a desperate longing to BE God rather than letting God be God. It's difficult for Christians to admit that, isn't it? But when poked and prodded enough, your teenager may discover he actually thinks he would do a better job of being the one true God of the universe. As was said previously, anxiety and worry puts on full display that we don't really trust God to care for us. So it should make sense that when we are trying to be in control of what we can't control, we are simply attempting to take the throne away from King Jesus, if that were even possible. Another way to describe this heart process to your teen is that it is a basic idolizing of self—thinking way too highly of self. The only way I can be at peace is if I believe I control my life, or until the outcome I desire comes to fruition. The reality is that if any of us had full reign over our lives, we would make a terrible mess of things! Point all your teens to the truth of how grateful they should be that God is sovereign and in control of their lives.

Recognize real peace

Anxiety problems expose an absence of Biblical peace—peace as a fruit of the work of the Holy Spirit in our lives (Gal. 5:22). 'Stressed out' Daniel would love to have peace at school and throughout his daily life. When Fran avoids youth group or interaction with her peers, it may feel peaceful, but it really isn't. Gary only experiences peace when his compulsions make him feel like he is in control. Unfortunately, these teenagers are seeking after the world's peace rather than after God's peace. The world's definition of peace is the calm that comes when everything in my life is running smoothly—at least the way I conceive of 'smoothly.' So that peace quickly dissipates when I am faced with stressors or people or situations that provoke unrest and fear. Even worse, a teen may never feel any semblance of peace because he or she is just looking for the next problem that is coming his or her way.

God's peace is that peace that 'passes all understanding' (Phil. 4:7, RSV). This real peace comes from a growing relationship with the Lord and the operation of the Spirit in our lives. Rather than finding our security and confidence in other people, or our circumstances, we find our peace in Christ. This peace is deeply connected to a heart submission to God's sovereign will for our lives. In a world which is constantly inviting us to be anxious, God's peace is the only real peace available. So, resist the temptation to simply allow your teenager to avoid the problem or the fear-provoking situation. Rather than seeking to help our young people 'relax' and 'chill out,' we point them to the work of the Prince of Peace in their lives. We don't just want them to feel better or even just to think wisely, but to have hearts that are at true rest in all situations. When that level of peace is experienced in their hearts, it will demonstrate a mature trust in God as well as a growing love for other people.

Panic attacks?

Before we leave this group of teenage problems, let's not forget about 17-year old Emily and her struggle with panic attacks. Like so many others who have experienced her symptoms, Emily was originally convinced she was having a heart attack—and thought she was going to die! Shortness of breath, heart palpitation, sweaty palms, dizziness—all very scary experiences that appear to come out of nowhere. Emily certainly needs a medical examination to rule out heart issues or any other physical problems. But if the 'body side' of things checks out, these panic attacks are a type of anxiety disorder that can be greatly helped by many of the Biblical counseling principles already discussed. Because of the physical symptoms, it is often assumed that panic attacks are solely physiological in nature, demanding a physiological/medical solution. Yet, even if there are physical issues that need to be addressed, panic attacks are a problem of the heart, mind, and soul as well.

Often, teens like Emily who experience panic attacks initially claim that these attacks come out of nowhere, and that they are not typically anxious people. But the more conversations you have with your teen, you will most likely find a significant history of worry and anxiety, as well as a possible traumatic triggering event. Sometimes, the teenager has a heart that is so used to controlling things (and people), that when things start to unravel, panic attacks ensue as he or she attempts to regain control. If you think about it, panic attacks are the body's way of telling a person that he or she is in anxiety overload. Whenever our fear, worry, or anxiety produces physical symptoms, it is God's way to get us to truly pay attention to our hearts and minds. Some of the typical anxiety problems can be avoided or covered over; but panic attacks are impossible to ignore. Like all of the more difficult anxiety problems, panic attacks can become such a part of a teen's life that they become tied to her entire identity. Again, the starting place for this type of anxiety problem is to have Emily deal with her heart of control!

Wisdom POINTERS

To enable teenagers to pursue hearts of wisdom, we must give them wise counsel. It's one thing to operate from Biblical presuppositions, understand a Biblical counseling process, and to know Biblical principles concerning a problem; it's quite another to apply it all wisely. A Biblical analysis of each teenage problem will end with some 'wisdom pointers'—some summary 'do's and don'ts'—to help counsel your teen wisely. So, when dealing with the problems of anxiety, fear, and worry:

- Do communicate the love of Christ for sinners.
- Don't allow your teen's anxiety to make you anxious.
- Do show true compassion for the pain the teen is experiencing.
- Don't excuse sinful anxiety as just a normal emotion.
- Do recognize the difference between worry and concern.

- Don't communicate that your teen just needs to relax and stop worrying so much.
- Do encourage a fearful heart with the comfort of God.
- Don't offer ways to simply avoid the fear-provoking situation or relationships.
- Do teach a love for God and a sacrificial love for others, even for our enemies.
- Don't allow your teen to keep trying to control things he or she can't control.
- Do point to the power of the Spirit to produce real peace in the heart.
- Don't encourage the teen to rely simply on anti-anxiety medication.
- Do prod them to truly deal with their own hearts and confront their anxious thoughts.

6.
Depression

'I can't believe it's Monday again and I have to go to school ... how depressing is that!' 'I'm so depressed that my favorite sports team lost again. They just stink.' Just like adults, our teenagers often misuse and overuse expressions of depressed feelings, sometimes making it a challenge to recognize true depression. Then, there are teens who may never describe themselves as depressed—and even deny that there is a problem—who display clear symptoms of this common problem. And, how do we rightly address the belief that it's just normal for teens to feel 'moody' or to be routinely driven by their feelings? Clearly, there are a wide range of depressive experiences on the spectrum from normal sadness and grief, all the way to major disabling depressive episodes. Depression is literally 'pressing down' on many of our teens, sucking the joy out of life. The isolating darkness of depression must be understood and handled Biblically so that it will not become a long-term issue in their lives.

Opening PORTRAITS

- Haley, a 17-year old, has always been a moody person. She seems to either be really up or really down—living life like it is a constant roller-coaster ride. Lately, Haley has been depressed for longer periods of time, followed by engaging in very risky behavior when she becomes her 'happy self' again.

- Iris, a 16-year old, has been sleeping a lot lately. She rarely leaves her bedroom, except for mealtimes, and has become more withdrawn from her siblings. Iris claims nothing is wrong; she is just a loner. She would rather binge-watch her favorite shows than go out with her friends.

- 14-year old Jake has been through some major tragedies this past year. His father died in a car accident, which also left his older brother a quadriplegic. His mother has been emotionally withdrawn ever since then, primarily focusing her energy on his brother. The family was already in financial difficulty, but now it has reached crisis levels.

Typical PROBLEMS

Depressive problems are best understood on a spectrum—with the differences being related to intensity and duration of symptoms. The overall experience of depression is relatively universal: it is painful, feels isolating, sucks the joy out of life, and is an overwhelming, stubborn darkness. The symptoms of depression include: a loss of interest in pleasure, sleep disruptions, feelings of worthlessness and hopelessness, eating problems, and suicidal thoughts. With that in mind, here are some of the typical teenage depressive problems:

1. Major depression

In the past, major depression was described by the psychiatric world as 'clinical' depression. Referring to this problem as major or clinical infers that this is the most serious and intense of all depressive disorders. When your teen is experiencing symptoms of depression more days than not, it is probably a major depression episode. The typical symptoms will also be the most disabling in a major depression. While this form of extreme depression is often reserved for adults (due to its duration), teenagers who are truly depressed since childhood could be experiencing major depression as well. Major depression becomes very identity transforming, as the teen will appear to 'always' be depressed.

2. Situational depression

The teen years are filled with challenging problems, from relational issues, career choices, hormonal changes, struggle with parents, etc. Any of these situations can bring about a short-term depressive episode, best described as a situational depression. Even though this form of depression is connected to a specific event, relationship, or problem, that doesn't always make it less intense.

3. 'Abnormal' grief

Similar to a situational depression, your teenager may not be responding well to a loss of relationship, a death of a loved one, or a devastating change in life. While we should expect our teens to grieve over losses and hardships, it can become abnormal in its duration and even its intensity. Unfortunately, as will be discussed further, it is tempting to see all grief as a depressive problem, thereby not allowing teens to actually grieve. Yet, there will be times when grief becomes extended and ends up becoming a true depression.

4. The 'blues'/general moodiness

On the other end of the depressive disorder spectrum, many teens simply struggle with the 'blues,' or recurring bad moods. These depressive moods may be connected to hormonal changes or simply the overall transition of adolescence. The symptoms can be intense at times, but typically they are more low-grade, and come and go over time.

5. Bipolar disorder

The most unique of all the types of depression, bipolar disorder, is also known as manic-depression due to the pairing of manic episodes and depressive episodes. This disorder should not be considered the same as having alternating 'good moods' and 'bad moods.' Manic episodes are hyper-energy times, where a teenager may not sleep for days, lose contact with reality, and engage in excessive risky behavior (sex, crazy spending, substance abuse, etc.). After literally burning out on this 'high,' an extended depression will occur.

Evaluation PERSONALIZATION

If your teenager is displaying some of the symptoms of depression, these are the essential personal issues to listen for and wisely evaluate:

Overall depressive patterns

1. When did the feelings of depression begin?
2. Was there a significant precipitating event?
3. How many days a week are feelings of depression experienced?
4. Have there been any manic episodes?

Physical factors

1. Is the teen experiencing any physical health issues?
2. Are there any intellectual or physical disabilities of note?
3. Would a medical evaluation be helpful?
4. What is the status of the teen's eating, exercise, and sleeping habits?
5. Have there been any dramatic hormonal changes?

Relational issues

1. Is the teenager isolating self, withdrawn from others?
2. Are there significant problems with friends, or the opposite sex?
3. Is there any apparent bullying?
4. What are the teen's social media habits?
5. Has the depression created other relational issues?

Marriage and family

1. Are there significant family problems that are contributing to the depression?
2. Is the home life peaceful, or full of conflict?
3. How is the teen relating to parents and siblings?
4. Is there a history of depression in the family?

Relationship with God

1. What is the teen's basic understanding of God?
2. What about his or her devotional life? Prayer and Bible study?
3. How does the teen describe his or her relationship to Jesus Christ?
4. What about the role of the Holy Spirit in spiritual maturity?
5. Is the teen angry with God?

Suicidal ideations

1. Is the teen talking about suicide?
2. Does the teen have a plan to commit suicide?
3. Does the teen need to be put on an intensive suicide watch?

Other related problems

1. Is there any drug or alcohol use involved?
2. Is the teenager angry or anxious?
3. Are there any other problems that could be connected?

Biblical PRINCIPLES

Depression is one of those teenage problems that parents and youth workers can either overreact to, or severely underreact to. Fearing a potential suicide attempt, helpers or family members can overreact and end up potentially creating more of a problem instead of addressing it in a balanced way. On the other hand, viewing teenagers as too emotional, hormonal, and immature may lead us to dismiss any symptoms of depression, risking complications in the future.

Hopefully, the depressive problem will be addressed wisely, giving the teenager a great opportunity to grow and mature in Christ. Believing that God's Word gives hope and answers to those who are struggling with various types of depression, we can lead our teens through the potential minefields. The following Biblical principles can act as your guide to giving wise counsel that goes to the heart of the matter.

Get the big picture

When your teenager speaks about being depressed—or is displaying some of the common symptoms—it is essential to step back and get a bigger picture, a better view, of the problem. Why do we need to get the big picture of depression? *Because it keeps us from oversimplifying the problem and assuming a singular, universal cause to all types of depression.* A first common error is the belief that depression is always the result of a physiological, chemical, or hormonal problem. In this view, depression is a SICKNESS, an illness that needs medical attention. Another typical error occurs when we believe that depression is always a moral problem—a SIN that requires confession and repentance. If this view is held, then the teen simply needs to have a change of heart and mind. Starting further back, the 'bigger picture' way to begin to understand teenage depression is to see it first as a form of SUFFERING. Whatever the causes or contributing factors that lie behind the unique depressive problem, it is primarily experienced as deep suffering. So, this also means that we begin with compassion for the sufferer.

Understanding depression as a form of suffering forces us to recognize and consider the various causes of human suffering:

- We can suffer at the hands of other people who sin against us, betray us, abuse us, etc.
- Our bodies can cause our suffering, with disease and dysfunction, hormonal and chemical issues, etc.
- We can cause our own suffering, with our own sinful hearts, minds, and actions.

- Our great adversary, Satan, can bring great suffering into our lives.
- Ultimately, we know that God is control of all things, including our suffering. God brings suffering into our lives for His purposes.

When we first view teenage depression as suffering, we acknowledge that it can enter our lives for one or several of those reasons: the sins of others, a breakdown in our bodies, our own sin, the oppression of Satan, and God's sovereign plan. This viewpoint makes us remember that depression may be a universal experience, but it does not necessarily have a singular cause or solution. So, as also goes for many other problems, see the teenager as a sufferer first in order to deal with depression Biblically.

Look past the surface

Let's think about Iris, our 16-year old, who is displaying symptoms of some type of depressive disorder. What do we know so far? She is sleeping a lot lately. She rarely leaves her bedroom, and has become withdrawn from friends and family. Iris would rather spend her time watching television alone than doing just about any other activity. With this information in mind, it may be tempting to quickly jump to a solution to the problem. After all, if Iris is freed from her depression, then she will rejoin her family and friends, become active again, return to normal sleep patterns, and be happy again, right? This is a suitable theory if we understand teenage depression to be a root problem that needs to be cured or changed. But a better approach— more in line with a right view of human suffering—is to see depression as a *surface symptom* rather than a root problem. Depression is an emotional indicator that points to a vast array of teenage problems. In this view, depression will only be truly relieved when underlying root problems are handled Biblically.

Going below the surface forces us to ask 'why' Iris is depressed rather than simply trying to get rid of her emotional symptoms. We have a lot of questions to ask Iris, since much more information is required. But, before we ask those questions, consider two Biblical examples. Think about Cain in Genesis 4. He is described by God as being angry and having a 'downcast face' (Gen. 4:5-6), which conjures up a picture of depression. So why was Cain depressed? He was angry over having his sacrifice rejected, and he was clearly envious of his brother, Abel. What about David's depression? In Psalm 38, he describes his experience as 'a heavy burden ... too much for me. I am bent over and greatly bowed down; I go mourning all day long.... I am benumbed and badly crushed; I groan because of the agitation of my heart' (Ps. 38:4, 6, 8). So, what does David see as the problem? In verse 4, he states: 'For my iniquities have gone over my head.' David's depression was rooted deeply in his own sinful actions. These sins literally pressed him down into the depths of despair.

From these two examples, can we say with certainty that all depression is caused by envy and unrighteous anger (like Cain), or by our own sinful actions (like David)? Unfortunately, it's not that simple. Stories like these, as well as many others, demonstrate that the symptoms that we normally describe as depression require us to go below the surface by asking WHY. As was discussed earlier, we must always move from the feeling level, through the doing level, to the heart level in order to solve problems Biblically. Simply seeking to get rid of the troubling symptoms of the various depressive disorders will keep us from solving the real root problems. While depression in our teenager certainly requires action, don't neglect to seek answers to what is truly causing, as well as contributing to, the surface symptoms.

Recognize the downward spiral

Most likely, Iris didn't wake up one day in a fully depressed state, unless there was a major precipitating event involved. As we begin to listen to her story, we discover that she has struggled to 'fit in' ever since her freshman year of high school. In order to make friends, Iris developed a pattern of exaggerating about her abilities, family life, and aspirations—just about everything in her life. This seemed to work for her for a period of time, as she moved from the social fringe to the inner, popular teen circles. Once there, her grades suffered as she focused more on attending parties and social activities most days of the week. Iris' parents were actually happy that their daughter had started 'having a life.' But, then, Iris began to be exposed in some of her lies, and the gossip began traveling quickly. Eventually, she was treated like a pariah, and was also failing some of her classes. Iris did a good job of hiding all this from her parents and siblings. In the end, it was just easier to avoid people as much as possible, and develop a comfortable, withdrawn, solitary life.

Iris is an example of a teenager living on a downward spiral that eventually ends up in depression. A normal longing for friendship coupled with the pain of being on the 'outside' led to a sinful response. Rather than solving the problem, a growing popularity led Iris to a lifestyle of partying and over-socializing. Add to those situations a neglect of studying and classwork, and Iris continued on a downward path. It may be that Iris would have never ended up in a depressed state if she would not have been exposed as a liar by her friends. But she was, and that just created another opportunity to make a decision to get off the downward spiral. She could have talked to her parents, repented of her sins, and sought solution and reconciliation. Instead, Iris avoided all of those difficult actions, settling in the bottom of the pit. Do you see the downward spiral at work? A problem becomes a complicating problem; a poor response leads to another complication; and on and on it goes. Recognizing the route she took to arrive at her symptoms of depression is a necessary start to dealing with the essential issues. With this sort of causation, the challenge is to help Iris make new choices even when the depressed feelings make it feel nearly impossible to do so.

Crossing the line

Another fundamental way to understand certain types of teenage depression has to do with depression's relationship to normal sadness and grief. Think about 14-year old Jake and all of the tragic occurrences in his life. His father died in a car accident, his older brother has quadriplegia, his mother is an emotional wreck, and the family has significant financial difficulties. Jake has all sorts of legitimate reasons to be extremely sad! He is grieving so many losses—all with extensive impact on his life. If you were counseling Jake, and he claimed not to be sad, you would be much more concerned about him, wouldn't you? Tragic and painful situations will clearly produce sadness in our lives. Made in His image, God has given us the capacity to grieve. To believe we should always be happy as Christians denies the fact that sadness is a part of living in this fallen world.

So, when does normal sadness and grief turn into depression? Some would say that it has to do with duration—if the grief is prolonged for a certain amount of time, then it is 'officially' a depressive disorder. But how long is too long? When will Jake have grieved too much? Another common theory is that grief becomes depression as the symptoms become more and more intense. That understanding has some merit to it. But, exactly how intense is 'depression-level' intensity? Normal grief and sadness can produce some extreme thoughts and emotions as well. When helping teenagers, we must take great care not to confuse grief with depression. Yet, there are clearly times when sadness and grief 'cross the line' and become a depressive disorder. The fundamental question is: What is that line?

The Psalmist actually helps answer this question by asking: 'Why are you cast down, O my soul, and why are you in turmoil within me? Hope in God; for I shall again praise him, my salvation and my God' (Ps. 42:11). Normal, healthy grief and sadness still hopes in God. It says: 'God is sovereign. He loves me. He alone is my God and my salvation. I will put my hope in Him!' Depression, on the other hand, crosses the 'hope line' and says: 'I don't trust God. He doesn't love me.

I want to be in control. He has failed me. I can't put my hope in God.' Do you see this important distinction? Righteous grief and sadness hopes in God, while depression hopes in self or something/someone else. Crossing the hope line is what prolongs the grief and intensifies it. As described in Jeremiah 17:5-6, it ends up shriveling up our hearts and putting us into parched places in the wilderness. When a grieving teen, like Jake, moves from hoping in God to trusting in self—then he will certainly become depressed. Our task, then, is to help our teens to travel back over the hope line into God-glorifying, normal sadness!

Pursuing rather than avoiding

Let's imagine that Jake has clearly crossed the line and has fallen into depression. As he talks to you about his thoughts, emotions, and beliefs, he communicates how he will not survive if more tragedy ever comes into his life. That sentiment is certainly understandable! Like Job, the Old Testament embodiment of righteous suffering, Jake has had more than his 'fair share' of tragedy. Thus, we should sympathize with him, and mourn with him as well. Yet we must also address his heart attitude that is expressed in his anxiety-filled thoughts and words. Depression has a way of putting a teenager into 'avoidance mode,' where he or she longs to never face a painful situation ever again. Unfortunately, this pain avoidance only fuels depression, keeping a person captive to fear and self-protection. Again, this connects to a false trust in self at the expense of hoping and trusting in a sovereign, loving God.

As difficult as it is, your depressed teenager needs to reject a life of habitually avoiding pain. He needs to learn that pain avoidance will end up making him more focused and even consumed by the pain. Instead, the path out of depression comes from a Spirit-led pursuit of the joy of the Lord. God's Word repeatedly tells us that the joy of the Lord is our strength (Neh. 8:10). Spiritual joy must be actively pursued to counteract the passive lifestyle of pain avoidance. To be clear, we are not just telling teenagers: 'Don't worry, be happy!' That might make for a good moralistic mantra, but it fails to capture the necessary Biblical truth. When pain avoidance—or even conflict avoidance—is the root of depression, then becoming active in seeking joy is a significant part of the solution. Instead of internalizing all that anxiety and anger, Jake must find his joy in the Lord.

Persevering instead of quitting

A corresponding Biblical principle that is vital to bring change to depressed feelings takes us back to our teen, Iris. Basically, she has quit on life. Relationships are just too risky. She has dug a hole that doesn't seem possible to climb out of. So, Iris has taken to the solitary life, hiding behind closed doors and personal technology screens. Depression has a way of tempting a person to give up, doesn't it? It says, 'Surrender! Quit! Everything is too hard!' This heart attitude makes it a small step to end up with suicidal thoughts, and even to the committing of suicide. Even though Iris has brought much of her pain on herself, we can sympathize with her struggles. Relationships are just plain hard, especially for many of our teenagers. It does seem that we can't get out of corners into which we have painted ourselves. Life is difficult, and Satan uses this truth to lie to us that it is actually impossible. We must take great care to help teens like Iris to not give up on life—emotionally, mentally, relationally—and definitely not ultimately.

As much as we understand and sympathize with Iris, if she is a follower of Christ, she is called to persevere. As James writes: 'Blessed is the man who remains steadfast (perseveres) under trial, for when he has stood the test he will receive the crown of life, which God has promised to those who love him' (James 1:12). Whatever the trial or tribulation, Christians are able to persevere because God perseveres with us! In some cases, depression can simply be battle fatigue in the war of everyday life, the war against sin, and the spiritual war against demonic forces. Now, calling on a person to persevere isn't equivalent to telling someone to 'hang in there.' Perseverance is a work of God's grace through His Spirit for all who are His. This is the power and hope of the gospel of which Iris needs to be reminded. As our salvation is preserved by God, we are then empowered to persevere and not give up.

Stop listening to self

Whether you are a parent of a teen or a youth ministry worker, you probably know the challenge of getting teenagers to listen. Sometimes it seems as though they rarely listen to anything of importance you have to say! But the reality is that our teens are listening—and often very intensely—to many different voices. So when seeking to help teenagers who are struggling with depressed feelings, it is important to assist them to recognize the various voices to which they are listening. Sometimes, they are listening to other people's oppressive voices—from both their past and their present situations. Or, they are listening to their own inner voice of hopelessness, anger, and despair. Satan is certainly 'speaking' to them as well, lying to them about a myriad of things. And, finally, there is the world's voice of pessimism and negativity that is often listened to by teenagers. All of this sort of listening is entirely passive, as the teenager just agrees with whatever the voice of depression is saying. No, we're not talking about some sort of delusional psychotic break! We are all tempted to listen to lies, myths, and all sorts of deceiving words that bounce around in our heads.

What's the remedy to listening to all the wrong voices? Certainly, we can encourage our teens to listen to sermons and read gospel-laden books and resources in order to deal with their depression. But in order to stop listening to those harmful voices, teenagers need to learn to talk to themselves more. This moves someone who is depressed from passivity to activity, from listening to lies to telling themselves the truth. How should our depressed teens like Iris and Jake talk to themselves? They must learn to speak God's Word to themselves, preaching the gospel to themselves every day. They need to address the difficult situations and relationships in their lives with the truth, using wisdom and discernment to think things through. This is where a parent or youth ministry worker is essential—to speak the truth which can become the life-giving, active voices in their minds. When struggling with depressed feelings, we need the Spirit to apply the truths of the Word of God to our lives in order to combat lies from the devil, our own hearts, other people, and from the world.

Self-righteousness and self-pity

Among the plethora of heart problems that fuel depressed feelings, two connected 'self' issues are often predominant, especially among teens who are Christians: self-righteousness and self-pity. Self-righteousness is the belief that I can earn or retain my salvation as well as God's love by all of my law-keeping and good works. Whether it's going to church every time the door is open, reading the Bible and praying, remaining pure and abstaining from sinful activities—whatever is considered 'being a good Christian'—can be relied upon for eternal security and happiness. But what happens if a teenager is 'doing all the right things' but life isn't working out very well? He or she could come to believe that life isn't fair anymore—and God isn't perfectly just—potentially producing feelings of hopelessness and despair. After all, what's the point of living right, being different than all of those pagan teens out there, if there aren't some temporal rewards? Do you see how easily self-righteousness in the heart can produce some type of depression? Unfortunately, for the 'good' teen, the depressed feelings can then be experienced as sinful, shattering their dreams of self-righteousness further, producing more depression.

So your teen who is inclined to think in self-righteous ways can easily end up in self-pity—the companion self-problem. No, we are not simply criticizing teens as being whiners or complainers. Self-pity is a much more stubborn issue of the heart. To pity self is to be excessively preoccupied with one's own sorrows and afflictions. It is akin to being a perpetual victim of any number of people and situations. Do you see the connection to self-righteousness? Self-pity says: 'I am not getting what I deserve' or, 'things never go the way they ought for me.' Because self-righteousness is rooted in false hopes, it easily degenerates into the hopelessness of self-pity. Believing that I deserve a happy life because I am such a good person weighs on the heart and mind when things repeatedly go wrong. So, if these twin heart attitudes of self-righteousness and self-pity are present, depression will often result. The good news is: Your teenager needs to have these heart issues exposed! Depression often points to a self-focus that the Spirit and the truth can and will change.

Two simplistic (but helpful) equations

Always remember that it is better to look at most depressive disorders as a surface symptom experience that is revealing a deeper heart problem—especially when physiological causation is ruled out. With that in mind, here's the first of two overly simplistic equations that may, nevertheless, be very helpful:

Anger + Overwhelming Sorrow = Depression

Many people who are depressed are really just very angry. Iris could be an example of this first equation. If you think about it, she has a lot about which to be angry! She has lost all her friends, been exposed as a liar, and has incurred failing grades. While Iris may not seem angry, her anger is likely deeply submerged below overwhelming sadness and grief. Many teens who present symptoms of depression are angry at God, angry at others, and angry at self. Rather than deal constructively with all the anger (see Chapter 4), they give up and become resolved to perpetual anger and frustration. So, rule out anger when talking with your depressed teen.

While anger is a regular culprit in teenage depression, there is one more equation that helps us here as well:

Anxiety + Overwhelming Sorrow = Depression

Remember that Jake was rightly grieving over all of the losses in his life. His normal sadness ended up turning into a prolonged depression as his hope was more in self rather than it was in God. But another heart problem that has contributed to his depression is his growing anxiety. He began to worry about and fear when the next 'shoe would drop.' Jake became convinced that he could not go through another tragedy. So anxiety combined with excessive grief and sadness became the fuel for more depressive symptoms. Thus, when dealing with your teenager, listen for anxious thoughts and a fearful heart. Seeking to solve the anxiety first will end up relieving the depressed symptoms as well. Again, the problems of anger and anxiety are not the only sources of depression, but they are certainly high on the list of factors that end up being the root problem.

Bipolar Depression?

Finally, we need to touch briefly on one of the most challenging of the teenage depressive disorder, typically known as bipolar disorder. Haley, our 17-year old 'moody' girl, may be diagnosed with one of the variations of this disorder. Originally labeled manic-depression, bipolar is characterized by lengthy depression punctuated with brief periods of hyper-energy, and often risky behavior (mania). True bipolar disorder is much more extreme and prolonged than simple emotional 'ups and downs.' It is often thought of as more of a psychiatric problem requiring medication and medical intervention. There may also be a greater risk of suicide than occurs with other depressive disorders, as well as severe consequences due to the risky, manic behavior. Bipolar disorder may require the help of more experienced Biblical counselors as well as proper medical help in order to see real change, rather than just symptom relief.

With that in mind, there is one specific illustration that may help a teenager, especially if he or she is just beginning to experience symptoms of bipolar disorder. Imagine you are driving down the highway, very late at night. You are having such a problem keeping your eyes open that you are starting to swerve onto the shoulder. Finally, your eyes close, and you begin heading for the ditch when your tires suddenly hit the rumble strip. Startled, you swing the steering wheel with such force (to avoid crashing into the ditch) that you end up over-correcting and end up in the ditch on the other side of the highway! This is a dramatic picture of what may be happening with bipolar disorder. When a person is stuck down deep in a depression, the natural tendency is to do something 'extreme' to pull self out of it. That over-correction becomes the manic stage of bipolar, creating even more problems. So, it may help a teen like Haley to recognize the temptation to over-correct her depression by engaging in manic behavior. Over time, this can easily become an emotional habit, where it seems like the only way to stop being depressed is to become a different 'happy' person. Ultimately, solving the actual source of the depression should take the fuel out of the bipolar disorder. Yet, the habit of becoming more addicted to a lifestyle of extreme 'ups and downs' must be addressed as well.

Wisdom POINTERS

Helping your teen get to the heart of his or her particular type of depression will take great wisdom and care. The following are some 'do's and don'ts' to keep you grounded in God's Word and focused on true, gospel-driven change:

- Do see your teen as a sufferer, not just as sick, or as a sinner.
- Don't settle for just symptom relief, but for true heart change.
- Do show compassion for the pain the teen is experiencing.
- Don't ignore symptoms of depression as simple moodiness.
- Do look for a heart of anger, or a heart of anxiety.
- Don't think of all types of depression as having the same cause.
- Do recognize all of the life factors that contribute to depressed feelings.
- Don't forget to challenge the teen to pursue true joy.
- Do teach sacrificial service for others, even though he or she won't feel like it.

- Don't ignore any suicidal ideations.
- Do point to the power of the Spirit to produce the joy of the Lord.
- Don't encourage the teen to rely only on medication.
- Do become one who helps to bear your teen's burdens.
- Don't forget to watch for the downward spiral.

7.
Drugs and Alcohol

Experimentation with drugs and alcohol has long been considered by many as simply part and parcel of the teenage years. Fueled by typical teenage experiences such as peer pressure, boredom, depression, stress, and outright rebellion, the use of mood-altering substances is commonplace. Today, it continues to become easier and easier to access drugs and alcohol, and there are more and more substances that can be abused. While this may be a problem that seems to present a simple solution ('just say no' to drugs), true change will be more challenging. Drug and alcohol use and abuse should not just be dismissed as a normal part of teenage development, nor should it necessarily be approached as an addiction that will haunt your teen forever. As with other problems that occur on the 'doing level,' substance abuse should lead us to help our teens pursue a heart of wisdom rather than a heart of folly.

Opening PORTRAITS

- Kevin, a 16-year old, is one of the core members of the church youth group. He leads the praise team, a small group Bible study, and is a top student in the Christian high school. Two other members of the youth group tell you that they saw Kevin with a beer in his hand at a school party.

- Laurie, a 17-year old, confesses that she had a couple of beers and a few other alcoholic beverages at her best friend's house—after Laurie's parents smelled alcohol on her breath. During further conversations, she admits to having a pretty bad drinking problem a few years ago, but she has it under control now.
- 15-year old Mack has been smoking marijuana for a year or so, as well as experimenting with a few other 'random' drugs. When confronted, Mack is defensive, asserting that 'weed' isn't addictive, and he is just having a little fun.

Typical PROBLEMS

Some of our teens are simply experimenting with drugs and/or alcohol. Others are chronically abusing one or various substances to the point that it is becoming an addiction. In a very real sense, any use of drugs or alcohol is a problem that must be understood and confronted, not simply when abuse or addiction is present. While we certainly must address the problem of drug and alcohol use when it reaches the level of dependence, it is much better to prevent it from ever getting there. So, before considering the Biblical principles that will lead to solution, here are the typical substances that teenagers abuse:

1. Alcohol

From beer, to wine, to hard liquor of all kinds, alcohol operates as a depressant that is extremely popular with teens. While it may give an initial surge of energy, the teen's vital functions will slow down, bringing impairment and lack of judgment.

2. Nicotine

Whether in cigarettes, e-cigarettes, cigars, or chewing tobacco, nicotine is an extremely addictive substance. While it may not appear to be as harmful as other drugs, nicotine has some of the worst side effects that appear over time.

3. Marijuana

The legalization of marijuana in many states has made this drug more socially acceptable, and more of interest to teenagers. Marijuana acts like a hallucinogen, but also has depressant qualities. It also has medicinal value, which also leads to possible addiction.

4. Opioids/Painkillers

Opioids are substances that act on opioid receptors to produce painkilling, morphine-like effects. Some familiar prescription opioids are: Hydrocodone, Vicodin, Oxycontin, and Percocet. Heroin and opium fall into this category as well. Opioids can be smoked, eaten, drunk—but are most often taken in pill form.

5. Stimulants

Substances that impact the central nervous system in a way that is experienced as a 'speeding up' are known as stimulants. These drugs increase alertness, raise blood pressure and heart rate, and increase breathing levels. Many teens have already been used to taking a stimulant like, Ritalin for their ADHD, or caffeine in coffee and 'energy drinks.' On the severe end of the simulant spectrum are cocaine, methamphetamine, and ecstasy.

6. Depressants

By their very label, depressants have the opposite impact on the central nervous system than stimulants. These drugs slow everything down, producing a sedative-like experience which is often used as an escape from everyday stressors. The most popular depressants (other than alcohol and marijuana) are Valium, barbituates, Xanax, and benziodiazepines.

7. Hallucinogens

These sorts of substances create an experience for the user of rapidly changing emotions and perceptions. Hallucinogens allow a person to see and hear things that aren't really there, resulting in either terrifying or pleasurable illusions. The most popular hallucinogens are LSD and peyote.

8. Inhalants

The use and abuse of inhalants are particularly dangerous because they are usually toxic substances. Teenagers have been known to inhale paint, gasoline, glue, paint thinner, aerosol sprays and even room deodorizers. Each different substance produces a different sort of 'high,' as well as damaging effects on the body.

Evaluation *PERSONALIZATION*

If your teen has confessed to drug and alcohol use, or you see some possible signs of it, then you will need to have many more questions answered:

Overall patterns
1. When did the use of drugs or alcohol begin?
2. Was there a significant precipitating event?
3. How frequent is the drug or alcohol use?
4. Is this experimentation or addiction?

Drug use
1. What drug(s) have been used?
2. What effects has the teen experienced from the drug(s)?
3. How did the teen acquire the drug(s)?

Alcohol use
1. What type(s) of alcohol is the teen using?
2. How extensive is the drinking habit?
3. How is the teen acquiring the alcohol?

Physical factors

1. Is the teen experiencing any physical health issues?
2. Are there any intellectual or physical disabilities of note?
3. Would a medical evaluation be helpful?
4. What is the status of the teen's eating, exercise, and sleeping habits?
5. What impact have the drugs or alcohol had on the body?
6. Is the substance abuse connected to self-medication for pain?

Relational issues

1. Is the teenager isolating self or withdrawn from others?
2. Are there significant problems with friends, or the opposite sex?
3. Is there any apparent peer pressure involved?
4. Has the teen been tempting others into drug or alcohol use?

Marriage and family

1. Are there significant family problems that are contributing to the issues?
2. Is there a history of substance abuse in the family?
3. How is the teen relating to parents and siblings?
4. How honest is the teen being about his or her activities?

Relationship with God

1. What is the teen's basic understanding of God?
2. What about his or her devotional life? Prayer and Bible study?
3. How does the teen describe his or her relationship to Jesus Christ?
4. What about the role of the Holy Spirit in spiritual maturity?
5. Is the teen involved in rebellion against God?

Other related problems

1. Is the teenager depressed or suicidal?
2. Is the teenager angry or anxious?

3. Are there any other problems that could be connected?

Biblical PRINCIPLES

Why is teenage alcohol use a problem? There are those who believe a little underage drinking is a rite of passage, or just a normal aspect of teenage rebellion. Drug use is much more serious—at least the harder drugs like crack, meth, and LSD. Smoking cigarettes or marijuana, on the other hand, is not that big of a deal to many. Do you see the problem? There can easily be disagreements on what substances are the most destructive, or whether experimental use is as bad as serious abuse. Wherever you stand as a parent or youth ministry worker, this chapter will treat all substance use as a teenage problem—alcohol as well as all types of mood-enhancing drugs. This doesn't mean that every substance does the same amount of damage to a person's mind and body, or that they all carry the same addictive power. Choosing to treat all teenage drug *and* alcohol use *and* abuse as a problem to be addressed will help to make the underlying Biblical principles clearer. In other words, consider all these Scriptural truths in order to apply them to the particular drug or alcohol problem in your teen's life.

A symptom of folly

Why has Kevin, your 16-year old, been drinking at high school parties? If asked, he may give you any of these reasons: 'I succumbed to peer pressure.' 'I was trying to be cool.' 'I wanted to see what it was like.' 'I was bored.' 'I was just being stupid.' Any of these answers should lead you to a conversation about wisdom and folly. Proverbs 20:1 states it this way: 'Wine is a mocker, strong drink a brawler, and whoever is led astray by it is not wise.' Alcohol and drugs have a way of taking advantage of foolish hearts. To put it more precisely: Teenage alcohol and drug use reveal a heart that is filled with folly. Consider how foolish all of Kevin's possible reasons for drinking are; not one of them emanate from wise thinking. While we may understand how easy it is to give in to peer pressure, how boredom tempts us to do stupid things, or how teens want to be popular—there is still a heart problem present. Foolishness in the heart enables the teen to be easily tempted to use drugs and alcohol.

If we believe the truth that teens who are experimenting with drugs and alcohol are fundamentally foolish, it's essential for them to understand why they are foolish in the first place. Folly is not just found in the heart of children, which they grow out of through the years. In Matthew 7, Jesus gives us the reason why human beings are foolish: 'Everyone who hears these words of mine and does not do them will be like a foolish man who built his house on the sand' (Matt. 7:26). Foolishness is fueled by our rebellion against Christ's commands. What may begin as childishness and immaturity only remains that way during the teenage years when there is a rejection of God's ways, and disobedience to His Word. So it is not good enough to just hope our teenagers will grow up and out of their foolish ways. They must be taught to see their alcohol or drug use as a symptom of foolishness that is rooted in a sinful and rebellious heart. Only when teenagers begin to fear the Lord will they seek wisdom rather than folly (Prov 1:7).

A body problem

What begins as a sinful and foolish desire can quickly become a body-based problem. Now, there are many experts who understand drug and alcohol abuse as *only* a body, or a physiological problem. They believe a uniquely diseased brain is to blame, rejecting the view that alcoholism or drug addiction is a moral problem of any kind. It is beyond the scope of this current chapter to debate whether substance abuse is a disease of the body or a disorder of the heart and soul. We will stick with what appears to be clear about drug and alcohol use: it does have a clear impact on our body chemistry, especially with long-term use and abuse. Therefore, it is most helpful to view addiction to any substance as a spiritual problem AND a body problem. Whatever the cause, or the effect, the body side of things must certainly be taken into account.

To ignore the physiological consequences and contributing factors denies the chemical nature and effects of the substances themselves.

Laurie, our 17-year old, has confessed to a pretty serious drinking problem, even though she claims to have it under control now. What has all that drinking done to Laurie's brain chemistry or hormonal balance? While you are probably not a neurologist or a brain specialist, modern medical research has shown us that alcohol has a way of hijacking normal brain pathways creating some level of physiological dependence. Since that is common wisdom, then we can believe that it is harder and harder to quit drinking or using mood-altering drugs over time and use. In other words, Laurie has made it more difficult on herself to exercise self-control over her drinking because of body changes brought on by her drinking. So, are we to tell Laurie that it is now impossible for her to ever be free from drugs and alcohol? That is taking the medical research a bit too far, seeing the human as body only, without a changeable mind, heart, and soul. Prolonged drinking does not make her an alcoholic for life, but some level of physical dependence does make it tougher to beat.

Counseling from a Biblical worldview recognizes that the human being is both body and soul, internal and external, physical and spiritual. We do not fully understand how our repeated sinful and foolish choices impact our bodies, or how hormonal and chemical changes in our bodies impact our moral decisions. Yet, this is a big reason why we should proactively address even the experimentation with drugs rather than viewing this activity as a passing folly. Common sense says taking early teen drug and alcohol use seriously will prevent harmful physiological changes and dependence. Even at seventeen years old, Laurie could already be considered an alcoholic. Biblical counseling will be extremely helpful at her age to turn the tide of her addiction. She must know how 'hooked' her brain is to alcohol, but also have the mindset that her body chemistry can return to a more normal state. Understanding addiction as a body and soul problem keeps our teens from the more hopeless 'disease model' of substance abuse, while taking seriously the impact on their changing bodies.

A life-dominating problem

Let's return to Kevin, our 16-year old who seems to be living a double life of sorts. He is active in youth groups and is a top student. He even leads Bible studies and the youth praise team. So, why is he drinking at high school parties? Could it be that he was falsely accused, just holding the beer for a friend? Possibly. But we'll assume for the moment that Kevin has been drinking quite often—and not just at parties. What began as just hiding a shameful sin may grow into a life of deception. He may end up with two sets of friends, two types of activities, and even two kinds of personalities. How long can Kevin keep it up? When will the worlds collide? Without changes at the heart level and at the doing level, his drinking will become a life-dominating problem. There will be only one life—one that centers on alcohol and drug use.

When drug and alcohol use approaches addiction levels, it is best understood as a life-dominating problem. Picture a hub of a bicycle tire with spokes extending out to the rim. In alcohol addiction, alcohol is the hub of the tire. The spokes are life factors such as: school, relationships, family life, hobbies, work, church, etc. As alcohol use becomes more intense, it begins to impact Kevin's school grades, his choice of friends, and his relationship with his parents and siblings. Kevin eventually decreases his church attendance, quits the Bible study and praise team because he is 'too busy,' and avoids his youth director. Do you see how alcohol use is dominating his life? It is dictating his choices and dramatically shaping his lifestyle. Increasingly, he denies that his drinking is really that bad, even convincing himself that it is not controlling his life. At some point, he will attempt to shut out the Lord and any other Christian who confronts his choice of activities and lifestyle.

Recognizing the potential for drug and alcohol use to become life-dominating reveals that something much better must become the 'hub' of the wheel. If alcohol use is removed from the center, what will replace it? We'll address this part of the solution later. The point is that abuse of alcohol or drugs demonstrates what really is operating at the hub is *self*. Pleasing self is priority one. Self is on the throne of the heart. So, it's not just about getting Kevin to choose better friends or start going back to youth group again. It's not even really primarily about stopping his drinking. Seeing how easy it is for sin to dominate our lives shows the power of self—the flesh—to ensnare and control us. When anything reaches the level of life domination, our teen is faced with the fact that Jesus is not the dominating and controlling power of and person in his life. Show your teen the hub and spokes of the 'addiction wheel' and how they are connected to one another. External behavioral change will do little in the fight against a life-dominating sin.

Bondage and slavery

The previous principle needs to be more fully grounded in a Biblical understanding of addiction. Rather than seeing that some of our teens are prone to addiction while others are not, God's Word teaches us that bondage is normal to all human beings. Since we are all born sinners, we are all born as slaves to sin. Listen to the words of Jesus: 'Truly, truly, I say to you, everyone who practices sin is a slave to sin. The slave does not remain in the house forever; the son remains forever. So if the Son sets you free, you will be free indeed' (John 8:34-36). Living in bondage to sin is as normal to the fallen human being as eating, drinking, and breathing. From the root of that sinful bondage comes the fruit of a particular addiction. Due to growing up in various families, as well as developing different personalities and experiences, each of our teens is prone to a particular addiction more than another. In the end, because of our sinful hearts, any of us can become addicted to just about anything in this life.

One of the best Biblical analogies of addiction is the history of the Israelites after they were freed from four hundred years of slavery in Egypt. Think about the various responses of God's people to their new-found freedom, as described in the books of Exodus, Leviticus, and Numbers. They often whined and complained, doubting that God would provide for them in the wilderness (Exod. 16:2). Shockingly, many of them actually wanted to go back to Egypt—back into bondage (Num. 14:4)! In a total lack of sanity, they conceived of their hundreds of years in slavery as a time that they sat around pots of meat—being well-fed, secure, and protected (Exod. 16:3). What were they thinking? Quite possibly, they were simply more comfortable in their bondage, and totally terrified of freedom. This is the power of bondage and addiction! As a teen's alcohol or drug use rises to a level of addiction, he or she can feel better about being controlled than about being free. He or she may even be afraid of being fully delivered from these domineering substances.

Sadly, even Christians can return to bondage and be enslaved to addiction, even though we have been set free by the power of Christ. If your teen is a professing Christian, yet is showing signs of being addicted to drugs or alcohol, he or she needs to be reminded that he or she no longer has to be a slave to sin. Relate to your teen Paul's gospel logic in Romans 6:5-7:

> For if we have been united with him in a death like his, we shall certainly be united with him in a resurrection like his. We know that our old self was crucified with him in order that the body of sin might be brought to nothing, so that we would no longer be enslaved to sin. For one who has died has been set free from sin.

Even though we are born in bondage to sin, Christ's death has set us free! Paul finishes his thought in verses 16-18.

> Do you not know that if you present yourselves to anyone as obedient slaves, you are slaves of the one whom you obey, either of sin, which leads to death, or of obedience, which leads to righteousness? But thanks be to God, that you who were once slaves of sin have become obedient from

the heart to the standard of teaching to which you were committed, and, having been set free from sin, have become slaves of righteousness.

Ultimately, Christians have been delivered from the bondage and slavery to sin in order to enjoy the freedom of being slaves to Jesus and righteousness. Obedience of the heart comes from being totally bound and committed to lives of righteousness in Christ.

A worship problem

Another Biblical construct that will be helpful to solve teenage drug and alcohol use and abuse is the truth that we are all born worshipers. Mack, our 15-year old, has been experimenting with 'random' drugs for quite some time. When confronted by his parents, he is defensive, claiming not to be addicted. He's just having a little fun! So rather than challenge him to admit that he is enslaved to drugs, we need to get him to think about the nature of his worship. Mack may think he is just goofing around, but he is more serious about his drug use than he is admitting to himself or others. He has gone from foolishness, to an infatuation with a drug-induced lifestyle. His idol of pleasure is manifesting in the requirement to worship the false high, or false peace, that drugs demand. As Mack's 'love' grows for various types of drugs and the experiences they deliver, his love for Christ fades. So he needs to admit that his natural inclination to worship something has been redirected to false gods.

Yet again, the best solution is not just convincing Mack that he needs to stop experimenting with drugs, but rather *to recover the right worship of God in his life*. He must admit that his drug use is akin to an adulterous affair—cheating on the true love of his life. If he sincerely desires to regain his love for Christ, that longing will give him the strength to fight against his wrong affections. Mack must remember God's love for him, and Christ's perfect sacrifice that gave him life in the first place! He needs to delight in the Lord once again, or for the very first time. Simply put, Jesus and His righteousness has to become worth more than everything else, especially drugs. Teens who are enjoying experimenting with drugs and alcohol may believe that they are also enjoying Christ, but they just can't effectively serve two masters. The more they return to the worship of the one, true God, the less they will worship substances that only produce temporary happiness or peace.

Unbiblical thought patterns

As much as it's vital to deal with heart issues like spiritual slavery and worthless false worship, our teens' sinful thought patterns must be addressed as well. We literally have to answer the question: 'What are they thinking?' Now, getting into the mind of a teen is not an easy task. Many of them have just recently developed rational thinking, and are often more driven by their emotions than by rational thought. And yet, their minds need to be renewed so that they will be transformed by the power of the Spirit rather than conformed to the spirit of this world (Rom. 12:2). While teens like Mack may appear to be simply driven by the pleasure principle, we need to help them examine their thought life. Even if your teen stops drinking or using drugs for a time—if thought patterns don't change, then it's likely they will return to bad habits. Persistent wrong thinking will produce wrong behavior over time.

So, what are some of the typical thought patterns of drug users and abusers that could be found in Mack's mind? He could be thinking himself as a victim—mistreated, bullied by enemies or misunderstood by parents or friends. Angry, bitter, and resentful thoughts are often quite common in teens who turn to drugs. Also, anxious thoughts could be pervasive when substances are used to seek some sort of peace. Has Mack experienced some recent trauma or loss in his life? He may have developed apathetic thoughts due to the unfairness or misery of this life. Many teens have constant thoughts of potential failure, insecurity, or a fear of being alone that drugs can mask. Finally, Mack may just be full of prideful and arrogant thoughts, thinking he is better than others, and in control of his life. As you can see, there are

131

all sorts of possible thoughts and attitudes that need to be challenged and changed. Ultimately, a drug user is stuck in a thought pattern that involves a lot of self-deception—destructive thoughts that keep the teen lying to self rather than believing the truth.

Putting off, putting on

In conjunction with the renewing of the mind, a teen who is using drugs or alcohol will need to put off old behaviors and put on new ones. This process is summarized by the apostle Paul in Ephesians 4:

> But that is not the way you learned Christ!—assuming that you have heard about him and were taught in him, as the truth is in Jesus, to put off your old self, which belongs to your former manner of life and is corrupt through deceitful desires, and to be renewed in the spirit of your minds, and to put on the new self, created after the likeness of God in true righteousness and holiness (Eph. 4:20-24).

Kevin, Laurie, and Mack certainly need to put off (stop) their illicit drinking and drug use. If they are new creations in Christ, they need to put off all the manners of life that belong to the old self. But, as was mentioned earlier, if they truly put off these behaviors, what will they put on (start) in their place? Understandably, the priority here is often on never doing drugs or drinking in excess again. Yet, the change process described in Ephesians includes both mind renewal (our last section) and the need to 'put on' behaviors consistent with the new self. So, again, the question is: What will Kevin, Laurie, and Mack *start* doing if they *stop* doing drugs and drinking alcohol?

In order to 'put on' godly alternatives to drug and alcohol use, there are several other areas of life that need to be addressed. Our teens will need to put off relationships that tempt them to wrong behavior, and put on new friendships that will encourage righteous behavior. Then, any and all activities that are connected to the drinking and drug use must be changed. Going to parties, or sporting events, or other extra-curricular activities may need to be put off, while participation in healthy activities need to be added. Remember how Kevin used to be more involved in youth group, Bible studies, and the praise team? He will need to be encouraged to add those back into his life—not to hide his alcohol use with 'holy behavior,' but to focus his heart and mind on the worship of God instead of the worship of self. Helping your teen to take stock of all his or her 'free' time must include decisions to cut out activities and relationships that are destructives, and add in those that lead to godliness. As their minds are being renewed, behavior must be changed as well.

Heart transformation

The behavior changes that are required to either keep from addiction or to break free from it, require a corresponding heart change. As one who has worked in the addictions industry, it often appears that the goal of drug and alcohol recovery experts is to help a person cope with the addiction rather than actually overcome it. Certainly, a non-believer has no real power to do anything but attempt temporary behavior change and to just survive an addiction. Even a Christian teenager must recognize the power of temptation and the indwelling sin that still exists. Yet, for all believers who are ensnared by drug and alcohol use, the gospel of Jesus Christ gives us the hope of heart and life transformation. This must be the ultimate goal of our counsel and help for teenagers struggling with these unhealthy behaviors. Just saying no to drugs is not enough. We are looking for a total heart change!

Just look closely to what the apostle Paul writes in 1 Corinthians 6, to see if he was satisfied with mere external behavior change:

> Or do you not know that the unrighteous will not inherit the kingdom of God? Do not be deceived: neither the sexually immoral, nor idolaters, nor adulterers, nor men who practice homosexuality, nor thieves, nor the greedy, nor drunkards, nor revilers, nor swindlers will inherit the kingdom of God. And such were some of you. But you were washed, you

were sanctified, you were justified in the name of the Lord Jesus Christ and by the Spirit of our God. (1 Cor. 6:9-11)

These are some of the most hope-filled verses for people struggling with life-dominating problems and sins—like drug and alcohol use. In the list of the unrighteous people who will not inherit the kingdom of God are *drunkards*—people addicted to alcohol and other substances. But then comes the words of grace: 'And such *were* some of you.' Because of the cleansing power of Jesus and the work of the Spirit, heart transformation is possible. Christians no longer have to be conformed to this world, but can be transformed into the likeness of Christ. So make sure your goal for your teenager moves beyond simple recovery (or coping) on to real heart change.

Being led by the Spirit

As much as our teens may think they are in control of their drinking or drug use, we know that, as addiction sets in, they end up being led around by the nose. The use and abuse of mind-altering substances can easily turn teens into passive followers, looking for the next 'buzz' or 'high' in their lives. Instead of running after the things that grow them more into Christ followers, they end up moving in the opposite direction. But where secular counsel may say something like: 'Take charge of your own life rather than letting drugs control you,' Biblical truth teaches something bigger and better. Rather than being led by our own desires, or even taking charge of ourselves, we are to be led by the Spirit of God. While all Christians have been born again in the Spirit, we don't always follow the Spirit as we should—which leaves us vulnerable to be led by the flesh.

The apostle Paul describes the Biblical practice that is essential when dealing with drug and alcohol use: 'But I say, walk by the Spirit, and you will not gratify the desires of the flesh. For the desires of the flesh are against the Spirit, and the desires of the Spirit are against the flesh, for these are opposed to each other, to keep you from doing the things you want to do' (Gal. 5:16-17). Paul follows on this thought in

Ephesians 5: 'And do not get drunk with wine, for that is debauchery, but be filled with the Spirit ...' (Eph. 5:18). Being filled with the Spirit is not just some one-time event, but an ongoing work of the Spirit that corresponds with our 'walking in the Spirit.' So our teens can either imbibe alcoholic 'spirits' or drink deeply of the Holy Spirit. Only when they submit to the leadership of the Spirit will they be able to resist the control of drugs and alcohol. Again, the move is from bondage to freedom, from living by the flesh to walking in the Spirit.

Perseverance and commitment

Finally, it should not be ignored that dealing with teenage drug and alcohol use is a battle that requires spiritual strength and perseverance. If the use of substances is in the very early phases, this last principle may not come into play. Yet, as the drug use becomes prolonged and turns more into abuse and addiction, the teen will be in the fight for his or her life. There is a spiritual battle involved, as Satan would love to keep Kevin in bondage and leading a double life. The devil longs for our youth to have a form of religion without experiencing any spiritual power. It's an emotional and mental battle for Laurie as well, against the lies that have been believed and the possible ups and downs of anxiety, anger, and depression. And, addiction to drugs and alcohol is also a physical fight for a teen like Mack, as the body craves the substances and the body chemistry is disrupted. Dealing with any addiction is literally a war for body and soul.

Because of this war, Biblical obedience in these matters is not easy. As parents and youth ministry workers, we should be compassionate for any teen who is caught in the snare of drugs or alcohol. Yet, at the same time, we call them to perseverance and the commitment to fight. It's just too easy to give up and return to the slave master. No, we are not telling our teens to just try really hard on their own. As in all of the problems of life, they need the grace of God to persevere in the battle. The victory will only come in Christ, because He has already won the war for our souls. The commitment to persevere will become extremely necessary when your teen slips up and falls. He or she will need to confess, repent, and get up and fight again. Satan and the human sinful flesh will speak of giving up and resolving that victory is impossible. The grace of God and the power of the Spirit tell God's people to endure and persevere, for the battle is ultimately the Lord's!

Wisdom POINTERS

The following are some 'do's and don'ts' to keep you gospel-centered and Biblically grounded when handling problems with drugs and alcohol:

- Do see addiction as a spiritual problem AND a body problem.
- Don't settle for just quitting or stopping drugs or alcohol use.
- Do recognize the power of life-dominating sins.
- Don't communicate that experimentation is normal for teens.
- Do see the ability of all people to become slaves to sin.
- Don't ignore the nature of disordered worship.
- Do address unbiblical thought patterns.
- Don't forget to help your teen 'put on' new behaviors.
- Do aim for heart transformation.
- Don't lead your teen to take control of his or her own life.
- Do lead your teen to be led by the Spirit of God.
- Don't believe that this will be an easy process of change.

8.
Eating Disorders

When considering the topic of eating disorders, it's tempting just to think of them as only a 'female problem.' While it's true that young women can often become overly concerned with their weight and overall body image, any of our young people can become ensnared in one of the various types of eating disorders. Human beings are prone to abuse the great gifts that God has given us, and that includes food as well as our physical health. In the end, our eating can either glorify God or destroy our bodies, minds—and even our relationships. Eating disorders have been a common problem in the lives of our young people for some time, and they should never be ignored. Connected to our overall health, an eating disorder that is not properly confronted and solved can have life-threatening consequences.

Opening PORTRAITS

- Nancy, a 16-year old, was acting very strangely on a recent youth retreat. She avoided many of the mealtimes, claiming to not feel well. Even when she would eat with the group, she mostly nibbled and pushed her food around the plate. Her best friend tells you that Nancy has been obsessively trying to lose weight to impress her new boyfriend.

- Opal is a very confident, perfectionistic, intelligent 17-year old. Lately, she has become obsessive in her dieting, not liking the extra weight she has gained. But in secret, Opal eats extra large quantities until she gets so disgusted with herself that she purges. As a strong Christian, she is very embarrassed by her behavior.

- Pedro, a 17-year old varsity football player, is meticulous with his eating and exercise habits. He works out at least three hours a day, before and after school. Pedro refuses to eat anything he perceives is unhealthy. Much of the time, he simply ingests his high protein energy drinks.

Typical PROBLEMS

We have been designed by God with bodies that require food in order to live. Yet, we are not mere machines that simply ingest nutritional substances routinely in order to have life. Eating is a physical experience as well as a mental and emotional experience. Because of that, there are many ways teens can misuse food and the entire activity of eating. For our purposes, there are four main types of eating disorders that are typical for teens:

1. Anorexia

An extreme reduction of calories by eating very little is the central distinction of the most common eating disorder: anorexia. The goal of the person struggling with anorexia is either rapid weight loss or the maintenance of an abnormally low weight. With these intentions, anorexia may easily end up in death. Even at dangerous weights, the anorexic perceives of self as still being fat and is constantly afraid of gaining even a little weight.

2. Bulimia

Instead of eating very little, a teen experiencing bulimia binges on a large amount of food, followed by purging. The purging typically occurs by vomiting—but may also be accomplished by the use of laxatives or the practice of extreme exercise. The cycle of binging and purging is the defining quality of bulimia, to the point of addiction. A bulimic teen is obsessed with body image and weight, yet may end up being overweight.

3. Binge eating

From its very description, binge eating is the compulsive habit of eating well beyond the point of fullness. It is synonymous with gluttony, and typically ends in obesity. Binge eaters may also attempt to diet frequently or fast after binging. The binging can often be totally out of control. Late-night binge eating is a variation of this problem.

4. Excessive exercise and orthorexia

These last two types of eating problems typically occur together. Excessive exercise is not just over-exercising, but exercising to the point of exhaustion in order to maintain a certain weight. Orthorexia is the obsessive focus on only eating the 'right' nutritional foods—again in order to stay at a certain weight or body shape. These co-conspirators work together to form an obsessive dietary and fitness regime, at the expense of relationships and other activities.

Evaluation PERSONALIZATION

If your teen is struggling with an eating disorder, or you see some possible signs of one, then you will need to have many more questions answered:

Overall patterns
1. When did the eating disorder begin?
2. Was there a significant precipitating event?
3. What type of eating disorder is it?
4. How long have there been eating problems?

Physical factors

1. What is the current state of the teen's physical health?
2. Are there any intellectual or physical disabilities of note?
3. Would a medical evaluation be helpful?
4. Will a nutritionist be required to teach and supervise eating habits?
5. What are the teen's other health habits like?
6. Is the teen experiencing any unrelated physical health issues?

Identity Issues

1. What is the teen's view of self?
2. What exactly is the teen's body image?
3. Are there any gender issues involved?

Relational issues

1. Is the teenager isolating self or withdrawn from others?
2. Are there significant problems with friends, or the opposite sex?
3. Has there been any bullying?

Sexuality issues

1. Is the teenager sexually active?
2. Has there been any molestation or other sexual abuse?
3. Is the teen involved in homosexuality or other sinful sexual practices?

Marriage and family

1. Are there significant family problems that are contributing to the issues?
2. What is the teen's relationship with his or her mother? Father?
3. How is the teen relating to siblings?
4. How honest is the teen being about his or her eating problems?
5. What is the general nature of parenting?

Relationship with God

1. What is the teen's basic understanding of God?
2. What about his or her devotional life? Prayer and Bible study?
3. How does the teen describe his or her relationship to Jesus Christ?
4. What about the role of the Holy Spirit in spiritual maturity?
5. Is the teen rebelling against God?

Other related problems

1. Is the teenager depressed or suicidal?
2. Is the teenager angry or anxious?
3. Is there substance abuse involved?
4. Are there any other problems that could be connected?

Biblical PRINCIPLES

One of the earliest training subject matters for children has to do with eating. Parents teach a child how to eat, what to eat, what not to eat, and even how much to eat. Some children learn good eating habits, some learn a mixture of good and bad practices, while others are left pretty much to themselves. Then, there is the deeper level of instruction regarding how parents expect their children to 'see' food—whether it be for good health and fitness, simply for pleasure, or actually with a perspective that glorifies God. So, eating is much more complicated than most people think. A teenager may have learned bad habits, or might just be rejecting the good practices of their parents. Or, again, the teen might have been left alone to decide how, when, and how to eat. Finally, questions concerning 'why' a teen eats must be answered: Eating to escape? Eating out of grief? Eating out of anxiety? Eating as a performance? So, let's apply some essential Biblical principles as we seek to help teens struggling with an eating disorder.

The impact of today's culture

Take a moment and make a mental list of what modern culture is teaching our young people about food, weight, health, fitness, and body image. Here's a start:

- Looking young is the ultimate ideal.
- People are simply bodies, so our bodies define our beauty.
- Thinness is desired most, especially in women.
- A sexy female is one with the most unrealistic 'perfect' proportions.
- The male body must be muscular, with zero body fat.
- Physical health and fitness are the only path to a high quality of life.
- A 'selfie' generation is obsessed with self-image.
- Food is either only for pleasure or a pathway for perfect health.

While there are many other cultural messages that relate to food, health, and fitness, these represent many of the dominant ones. The increasing prevalence of eating disorders among our teenagers can clearly be linked to our culture's obsession with physical bodies. It can be argued that this has been the case for most affluent cultures throughout history; yet, our modern communication technology certainly has sent the messages more often and more intensively.

With these various cultural influences in mind, it is important to first see our teens who are struggling with an eating disorder as sufferers. This doesn't mean we treat them as victims, or as innocent of sinful behavior in the midst of their disorder. They are to be held responsible for an improper adoption of a sinful culture's standards. But our counseling of teens struggling with eating disorders must begin with compassion, care, and empathy. The reality is that we are all impacted by the deviant messages about eating and our bodies—not just our teenagers. We should recognize how difficult it can be to see self accurately and to have a right view of food and health. So, many of our teens will also struggle to not give in to the lies the world is teaching them. As we attempt to offer Biblical counsel, it must always be surrounded by compassion for their suffering.

Nancy, your 16-year old, has been dealing with anorexia for a couple of years. Nancy has always had a very bubbly personality, but has become insecure of her weight over time, mainly because her best friend is so skinny—and beautiful. Now that she has fallen in love with a guy in her youth group, the desire to both lose weight and maintain an ideal weight has become somewhat of an obsession. Does Nancy recognize how she is adopting the world's view of her body rather than a Biblical perspective? Her idolatry of the body as well as a boyfriend is a problem that must be confronted. She first needs parents and youth ministry workers who affirm how tempting it is to buy into what the world is trying to sell. Admitting that the world's false narrative has a hold on her helps to begin the process of dealing with the disorder that has emerged from its grip.

Bondage and addiction

Whether the eating disorder is anorexia, bulimia, binge eating, or some other variation, it is best to understand all of them as forms of addiction. As was discussed in the previous chapter: because of the fall of Adam and Eve, we are all born in bondage to sin. Sin is our master, and self is on the throne. Because of that bondage to sin, addiction is as normal as breathing, eating, and drinking. Human beings, then, can turn just about anything into an addiction, even something as 'healthy' as food. The very nature of addiction is that it is a life-dominating sin, impacting our work, relationships, activities, family, worship, etc. The addict thinks and speaks of being in control of what he or she is doing, when it is the substance or activity that is truly in charge. So rather than simply seeing an eating disorder as a simple problem (just start eating right), we must realize that it is a very difficult addiction. It will not be dealt with simply by the sheer force of one's will.

Think about the reasons why eating disorders can so easily turn into addictions. Obviously, the whole process of eating is habit forming—

we tend to eat every day, three or more times every day! God has created us with natural hunger, so our bodies let us know they need nourishment every few hours a day. So for eating disorders that restrict caloric intake, a teen, like Nancy, has to force herself to resist a natural habit. Then she develops a new habit of resisting hunger, which requires a brand new mindset. On the other hand, teens who binge and purge, like Opal, form a new habit that opposes the natural course of eating in a different way. Eating disorders war against God's beautiful design of enjoying food and reaping benefits from its nutrition when our bodies are operating properly. So, the bottom line is that committing to change a natural habit like regular, normal eating will always end up creating a powerful new eating addiction.

Eating disorders also become addictions because of the pleasure that eating typically brings with it. There are certainly times when we eat simply to satisfy hunger and gain necessary energy. Yet, much of our eating is more than simply a repetitive activity—it is an enjoyable experience! We choose foods that appeal to our senses—that look good to us, smell good, and taste good. We look forward in anticipation to meals where we expect to eat some of our favorite foods or try a new delicacy. During and after a meal, we enjoy thoughts and feelings of satisfaction and happiness when the food is just right. All of that gets distorted and twisted by an eating disorder. Binge eaters overindulge and may even worship their food. Anorexics force themselves to not enjoy the food, or at least very much of it. Bulimics aim to have the best of both worlds, but still have their minds on things other than the pleasure of eating itself. In these ways, eating disorders become a very mind-based addiction as well.

Finally, eating disorders easily turn into bondage and addictions because of the reality that eating is a daily requirement. An alcoholic or drug addict can potential never drink alcohol or use drugs again. Similarly, a teen addicted to pornography could never view substantial porn in the future. But a person with an eating addiction must always deal with food! You can't tell a binge eater to avoid eating ever again.

Likewise, it is impossible to tell anorexics or bulimics that they can remove the temptation of food totally out of their lives. Everyone struggling with an eating disorder of some sort cannot eliminate food from daily existence. Because of that, it is unfruitful to exhort an anorexic just to eat more, or a binge eater to eat less. The ever-present requirement of our lives to deal with food, hunger, nutrition, and our bodies makes an eating disorder potentially the most difficult of all addictions to fully conquer. Yet this reality does not make it hopeless! It only communicates that our teens need the power of Christ to break the chains of bondage and addiction to food and eating.

Distorted body image

While most of our teens imbibe the world's view of health, fitness, and food—why don't all of them have eating disorders? One reason is connected to the way a teenager sees his or own body. Our body image is influenced by many factors, including cultural norms, the opinions of people closest to us, and our own desires and expectations. Nancy is convinced that she doesn't have a body that young men would desire. She compares her body every day to the girls in her youth group, especially those she is most threatened by and with whom she is competing. Now, deep in the struggle with anorexia, Nancy's view of her body has gotten even more distorted. The truth is, she is currently the thinnest girl in her grade at church—by a long shot. There are plenty of boys who are attracted to her. But she believes even more weight loss is required, and will only make her life better.

So, how do you help Nancy change the way she is looking at her body? You could tell her all the objective facts: how she is already super-thin, how her body fat is in the 'normal' range, and how the mirror doesn't lie. But talking to Nancy is like telling someone over and over again that the 'sky is blue,' when she says 'it looks green to me.' To those suffering with an eating disorder, objective truth doesn't matter as much as their own subjective experience. So if Nancy 'feels fat' or doesn't 'feel beautiful,' it will not help to present the truth, even if you have charts and graphs to prove it. The lies that she is believing about her body image cannot be refuted—except by the powerful voice of the Holy Spirit. Does that mean you cannot give an anorexic the objective facts about her weight? No, you certainly can—and must. Nancy needs to be lovingly confronted with the truth, until she begins to believe it. Just recognize that our views of our own bodies may begin somewhat accurate, but can easily become distorted and false.

Self-esteem issues

Because of the distorted body image that fuels many eating disorders, common wisdom points to a self-esteem problem. After all, when a young lady like Opal gets frustrated with the extra weight she has put on, this appears to be equivalent to 'hating' her body. And if she hates her body, that means she hates herself—or is displaying low self-esteem. Unfortunately, the assumption that low self-esteem is at the root of eating disorders—especially among young women—leads to all sorts of unbiblical counsel. Opal may be told to learn to love her body just as it is, and therefore love herself more. Or, she may be told to ignore all the 'body-shamers' out there and embrace how perfect she is at any weight, and in any shape. Do you recognize the problem? While Opal's view of self must be dealt with, the solution is not learning to love herself more. Her inaccurate understanding of her body must be combatted with a right view of self, rather than an unbiblical love of self.

So how do we address Opal's hatred of her body that is potentially fueling her eating disorder? The apostle Paul helps us to think about it Biblically: 'For no one has ever hated his own flesh (body), but nourishes and cherishes it, just as Christ does the church ...' (Eph. 5:29). Opal's desire to lose weight is actually connected to a deep-seated love of self. She desperately wants to look attractive and beautiful, which means she has to stay at a particular weight and size. As Paul says, no one really hates his or her own body, even if there are particular aspects that are undesirable and distasteful. Opal needs to see that her love of self has to be confessed and repented of before she can actually look at her body in the right way. This love of self is also connected to pride in our hearts, as we think we are entitled to be healthy, look good, or be at a certain weight. Only by seeing her tendency to love self and to walk in pride can Opal move forward to an accurate view of self. It is normal to desire to be healthy, and even to be at a certain weight. But when it gets twisted up with a wrong view of self, that heart attitude needs to be changed.

Then there are teenagers like Pedro, our 17-year old varsity football player, whose meticulous eating habits and exercise routine have also led to an eating disorder. As you talk to Pedro, you realize he actually has an extreme love for his body, which may mean he loves himself too much. The same Biblical principle applies: both the apparent love of body, or 'hate' for body, point to an unhealthy preoccupation with self. Pedro apparently has an overly high self-esteem that must be addressed, just as Opal's overly low self-esteem. Both teenagers need an accurate sense of self that moves them beyond a body-centric focus. As with all of the problems of adolescence, we must always dig deeper, below the surface, to the heart level. Esteeming self much too highly, or far too low, spring from the soil of a love for self and a deep-rooted pride. Challenge your teens to recognize what their hearts have made most important, and how it distorts their view of self.

The perfectionism problem

Many teens who fall into the trap of an eating disorder also struggle with the heart issue of perfectionism. This is easy to see in someone like Pedro who has to be at the perfect weight with just the right amount of body fat in order to be the complete athlete. As you spend more time with Pedro, he also is perfectionistic about his grades in school and even his relationship with God. His motto to live by is: 'If you're not first, you're a loser—and God hates losers.' While he may be partially joking, Pedro is revealing his core need to have everything in his life as right as possible. His eating disorder is simply a symptom of his perfectionism, which leads to a deeper desire to be perfect—and Pedro actually thinks he can achieve it! The irrationality of a perfectionist mindset becomes quickly apparent when we all know perfection is impossible. Yet, many who are fighting an eating disorder are deceived that maybe—just maybe—they can be perfect in their eating which will lead to a perfect body.

How do you begin to help your teen tackle the problem of perfectionism? First, the impulse to strive for perfection is laudable, since it is an imperfect attempt to reflect God's image. So we can sympathize with our teen's desire to strive for excellence, which emerges from a longing for the impossibility of perfection. But then, we also need to expose the fact that perfectionism is simply idolatry—especially when it is driven by pride, and the love of self. While God calls us to holiness (1 Pet. 1:16), that is not the same as perfectionism. Perfectionism fails to acknowledge our sinfulness and weakness, as well as our utter dependence on the Lord for any scintilla of righteous behavior. You will need to help Pedro to recognize that his need to be perfect is sinful and self-centered. But the remedy for perfection is not irresponsibility or apathy. God calls us to live by His strength, obey His commands, and strive for holiness in Christ. Reducing the need to be perfect will impact the way Pedro looks at all of his life, including his eating patterns.

Check obsessive thinking

Another common characteristic of teens who are actively involved in an eating disorder is a pattern of obsessive thinking. As was discussed in the chapter on anxiety, fear, and worry, obsessions are thoughts that constantly preoccupy or intrude into a person's mind. Obsessions are then typically followed by compulsions—actions done to satisfy the nagging anxious thoughts. So when there is an obsession to maintain a particular weight, shape, or clothing size, then eating habits become the compulsions to deal with those pervasive thoughts. Or, as in Pedro's case, the obsessiveness has to do with choosing just the right foods, the right caloric intake, and the right sorts of fitness routine. As you help your teen, you'll have to distinguish between normal, healthy concern and anxious obsession. How often is your teen thinking about food, weight, and body size? Has it become a preoccupation that colors most of his or her activities? Obsessive thinking may be apparent in other areas of life, not just eating. It is possible that anxiety is the root problem, with the eating disorder being the fruit of that sinful anxiety.

When you think about the amount of control a teenager with an eating disorder has to maintain, it is pretty astounding. That desire for control, and the ongoing efforts at the manipulation of their world, is what feeds the obsessive thinking. Nancy's anorexia dictates that she must be meticulous about how much she eats. Too many calories or even one extra pound gained will ruin everything. Even though Opal's binging and purging may look like she is out of control, it is actually a habitual manipulation of every meal. Even pure binge eaters are often trying to control their emotional state, literally eating themselves out of anxiety, shame, or other painful experiences. So you may find that your teen is a very controlling person in other areas of life, especially in relationships. Eating disorders become obsessive routines that must not be broken. To help your teenager break free, the anxious thought patterns and controlling attitudes must be relinquished—which means he or she will feel 'out of control' for a while. This is actually a good place to be!

Investigate sexual activity

As was mentioned at the outset, eating disorders have historically been primarily a problem experienced by women—often originating during the high school years, and sometimes even earlier. Since body weight and body image are often connected to a way a young woman views her sexuality, it is essential to investigate the teen's current sexual activity. Often times, you will find a teen who is struggling with an eating disorder to be sexually active, often secretively, because she knows it is wrong. The guilt and shame from engaging in premarital sex could be fueling an eating disorder—just to get some control in her out-of-control life. Alternatively, the eating disorder may be connected with sexual rejection, and a desire for young men to find her sexually attractive. This is certainly the case with Nancy, as her view of her body is connected to her longing to be sexually active with a boyfriend. If she does engage in premarital sex, it may only fuel her impulses to continue in her eating disorder to maintain the experience. So, as you are counseling your teen, you may end up having to address their understanding of their own sexuality, as well as their present sexual sins.

Another sexual issue to look for, especially in young women, is the possibility that they have been sexually abused or molested. It should go without saying that great care must be taken when inquiring and discussing such a sensitive issue. An eating disorder can arise from the grief, shame, and manipulative secrecy of past—or even present—sexual abuse. Being able to control one aspect of my world enables me to suffer through everything else that is out of control. Or, in some cases, the eating disorder arises from a twisted way to punish self for false guilt associated with the sexual abuse. Any confessed sexual abuse or molestation certainly complicates the problem, and must be addressed thoroughly. It is understandable if your teen doesn't want to deal with, or even speak of, any sinful sexual violations. Yet, with love and mercy, hopefully he or she can also be freed from the bondage that sexual abuse brings with it.

Understand family dynamics

If you are a parent of a teen with an eating disorder, this next topic may be difficult to properly evaluate without the help of an outside Biblical counselor. In many cases, an eating disorder has either developed, or is being sustained, mainly due to the relationship of the teen to his or her parents. Sometimes, the fault lies more on the parent's end. One or both parents may have very high expectations of the teenager—in the way she looks, her body weight, and even her grades in school.

In Nancy's case, her parents were 'pushing' her too much, adding to her already 'driven' and perfectionistic personality. Or, a mom or dad may be withholding love and affection, especially since the child has developed into a teenager. It could also be that displays of affection and attention are only forthcoming when parental expectations are met. Understanding the teen's unique family dynamics is not to be sought in an effort to blame parents for the sinful actions of the teenagers, but to help in the process of Biblical change.

On the other hand, it may be that it is the teenager who is actually responding poorly to her parents. Opal's binging and purging is connected to a pattern of rebellion against God, as well as her parents. Ever since elementary school, she has resisted family rules and has pushed back at any parental discipline. So as odd as it may sound, an eating disorder may develop as a purposeful rebellion against the moral standards of mom and dad. This may also include the fact that mom is more of the disciplinarian, and dad is more passive—and perhaps rarely present (emotionally or physically). Whatever the case, Opal's rebellion needs to be addressed, both in her relationship to God as well as to her parents. As will be discussed in a later chapter, teenage rebellion is not just something to be treated as normal, especially when it reaches into their physical health and safety. Whether you are a parent or a youth ministry worker, don't ignore the parent-teen dynamic and the necessary changes that need to take place in order to solve the eating disorder.

To the glory of God

Writing to the church at Corinth, Paul teaches on the subject of eating in relationship to the Old Testament law and the Christian conscience. He sums it all up by saying: 'So, whether you eat or drink, or whatever you do, do all to the glory of God' (1 Cor. 10:31). Unfortunately, our eating can often just serve self, rather than be in praise and gratitude to the Lord who has given us the gift of food. Gluttony is condemned in Scripture, not simply because it is unhealthy—but because it is self-indulgent, rather than God-focused (Prov. 23:20-21, 1 Corinthians 10:7, Phil. 3:19). It submits the teen to the control of food rather than the control of the Spirit (Deut. 21:20, 1 Cor. 6:12). This applies to all eating disorders, as the teenager is more involved with the worship of the body than the worship of God. How can God be glorified when His gifts are being used and abused for self-serving purposes? Refocusing on the Lord rather than bodies, weight, and overall outward appearances is the ultimate corrective for teens who struggle with an eating disorder. Always remember to address the spiritual problem the teen has with King Jesus, as well as the mental, emotional and physical aspects of the disorder.

Wisdom POINTERS

The following are some 'do's and don'ts' to help you remain gospel-centered and Biblically grounded when handling the various types of eating disorders:

- Do recognize the impact on the culture on eating and body weight/shape.
- Don't neglect to see the suffering in the life of your teen.
- Do see the eating disorder as a type of addiction.
- Don't communicate that it is normal to be obsessed with weight and body.
- Do look for the idol of perfectionism.
- Don't embrace the world's definition of self-love and self-hate.
- Do address the obsessive thinking pattern.
- Don't avoid questions pertaining to sexual activity.
- Do ask about past or present sexual abuse.
- Don't neglect looking at parenting dynamics.
- Do understand the disorder can easily become a life-threatening problem.
- Don't think that the teen just has to eat more, or learn to eat right.
- Do all for the glory of God!

9.
Guilt and Shame

Even though teenagers have not lived very long on this earth (relatively speaking), there will be times that they will feel 'stuck in the past.' Some may be harboring secret sins that they think would destroy them if anyone found out. Others have faced physical, emotional, mental, or sexual abuse that they are humiliated about, and just can't get past. Then there are words that have been said to our teenagers by parents, siblings, friends, or enemies that keep bouncing around their heads. Guilt and shame have a way of being such overwhelmingly heavy burdens that can immobilize the teen from enjoying the present, or looking in hope to the future. Some teenagers know exactly what has them stuck in the past. Others will just have a vague sense of being 'held back,' which is interpreted simply as depression, anger, or anxiety. While for some other problems may be present, when you dig a bit deeper you may find the main culprit to be prolonged guilt or shame.

Opening PORTRAITS

- Quentin is a very socially awkward 16-year old. He is left out of just about every youth activity and has never had a real friend. Other teens whisper about Quentin being 'gay,' even though he denies it.

- Randy, a 14-year old, is told regularly by his father that he is a 'disappointment.' His decent grades and skills as a basketball player aren't enough for his dad. Randy tries his hardest to please his dad, but it never seems to be enough.
- Stacy, a 17-year old, was caught shoplifting recently. This isn't the first time she has stolen—just the first time she has been caught. When talking to you about it, Stacy says she doesn't feel guilty because it was an exciting 'thrill ride' while it lasted.

Typical PROBLEMS

Guilt and shame are experienced by all human beings throughout their lives. So, when exactly do these normal emotional and mental responses become a problem? You probably won't have a teen come to you for help with his or her 'guilt issue' or 'shame problem.' Typically, problems with guilt or shame will be revealed when dealing with depression, anger, anxiety, self problems, or addictions. These are three of the usual ways guilt and shame become problems in the lives of our teens:

1. Unconfessed guilt

Guilt is often thought of as only a feeling of responsibility or remorse for some crime or offense. But guilt is first a state established by God, whether or not it is recognized in a person's mind, or produces the result of 'feeling guilty.' When a person is declared guilty of a sin by God and His Word, yet doesn't feel guilty about it, then they will suffer from unrecognized and unconfessed sin. Carrying around real guilt—yet denying it—creates other potential emotional, mental, and relational problems.

2. False guilt

On the other end of the guilt spectrum is the perception of guilt when a sin, crime, or offense has actually not been committed. In this case, a person feels guilty—often excessively guilty—when God's Word has not declared him or her guilty. Connected to this problem is the unwillingness or inability to 'forgive self' or receive God's forgiveness, as well as the heart attitude of perfectionism.

3. Sinful shame

It is right and proper for people to feel shame in the sight of God for their sins. Too often, people sin and feel no shame! Sinful shame is the mental and emotional perception of being unacceptable, unclean, and a disgrace. A teen who experiences sinful shame believes he or she doesn't belong, is an outcast, or deserves to be constantly rejected by everyone, including God.

Evaluation PERSONALIZATION

If your teen is struggling with a problem related to guilt or shame, then you will need to have some of the following questions answered:

Overall patterns

1. Should the teen be feeling guilty? Is he or she guilty?
2. What is producing possible false guilt?
3. What is the teen ashamed of?
4. Is the shame sinful or righteous?
5. What is the teen's understanding of sin, guilt, and shame?

Physical factors

1. What is the current state of the teen's physical health?
2. Are there any intellectual or physical disabilities of note?
3. Would a medical evaluation be helpful?
4. What are the teen's other health habits like?

Relational issues

1. Is the teenager isolating self or withdrawn from others?
2. Are there significant problems with friends, or the opposite sex?
3. Has there been any bullying?

4. What is the impact of social media?

Sexuality issues

1. Is the teenager sexually active?
2. Has there been any molestation or other sexual abuse?
3. Is the teen involved in homosexuality or other sinful sexual practices?

Marriage and family

1. Are there significant family problems that are contributing to the issue?
2. What is the teen's relationship with his or her mother? Father?
3. How is the teen relating to siblings?
4. What is the general nature of parenting?

Relationship with God

1. What is the teen's basic understanding of God? Of sin?
2. What about his or her devotional life? Prayer and Bible study?
3. How does the teen describe his or her relationship to Jesus Christ?
4. What about the role of the Holy Spirit in spiritual maturity?
5. Is the teen rebelling against God?

Other related problems

1. Is the teenager depressed or suicidal?
2. Is the teenager angry or anxious?
3. Is there substance abuse involved?
4. Are there any other problems that could be connected?

Biblical PRINCIPLES

People often speak of guilt and shame as synonymous and interchangeable. Your teen may say: 'I feel guilty for letting my friend cheat off of my test.' Then, her next statement is: 'I am so ashamed and embarrassed for not standing up to her.' Even though guilt and shame often occur together, they are not the same mental and emotional experience. A careful study of God's Word will enable us to learn the difference. For example, in Deuteronomy 23, we read: 'If you make a vow to the LORD your God, you shall not delay fulfilling it, for the LORD your God will surely require it of you, and you will be guilty of sin' (Deut. 23:21). Then, in Psalm 44, the Psalmist writes: 'All day long my disgrace is before me, and shame has covered my face' (Ps. 44:15). So, how are we to help our teens understand guilt and shame Biblically, especially since Christians are not to be ashamed, and are free from guilt in Christ? Let's apply Biblical principles to deal well with the co-conspirators of guilt and shame.

Picturing guilt

Imagine a beautiful, wood-paneled courtroom. In front of the room is a judge in his flowing black robe, sitting behind a large mahogany desk. In his hand is a gavel, raised and ready to make a life-altering declaration. No one else is in the courtroom except your teen and the judge—no jury, no witnesses, no audience. The judge alone declares a person either guilty or not guilty. Do you get the picture? Guilt lives in the courtroom of a person's life. Guilt says: 'You are responsible for wrongdoing. You are legally answerable for what you have done. You are wrong. You have sinned.' Guilt tends to be more focused on a particular sin or situation. When a person is declared 'guilty,' he or she expects punishment for the specific infraction. At the same time, the guilty longs to be forgiven. So when your teen *feels* guilt that matches up with the *fact* of guilt, then the only escape from just condemnation is merciful grace.

Guilt and feelings

Your 17-year old, Stacy, has quite a significant habit of shoplifting. When she finally gets caught, she displays no remorse, claiming to not feel guilty at all. 'I'm just sorry I got caught—it was quite the thrill ride,' Stacy asserts. It is common for teens—and even adults—to equate guilt with simply 'feeling guilty.' In other words, if a person doesn't feel guilty, then he or she isn't guilty. But Stacy needs to learn the proper definition of guilt, doesn't she? While there is certainly a 'feeling level' component to our guilt, guilt is fundamentally a fact, established by God. It is not just a subjective, personal experience. While we want our teens to actually feel guilty over their sins and wrongdoings, their emotions are not the arbiters or determiners of actual guilt. A person IS guilty when he or she breaks the law of God, whether he or she actually has the impact of that guilt touch him or her on an emotional level. Stacy can boast in her thievery—and claim to not feel guilt—but she is actually guilty.

So, how do you approach a teen who doesn't feel guilty about her sinful words, behaviors, or decisions? A good starting place is to move from feelings to thoughts. Instead of trying to challenge a person's emotional state, confront the way that he or she is thinking. Ask Stacy if she thinks it is wrong, according to God's Word, to take what is not hers, that for which she has not paid. If she says, 'Yes, I know stealing is wrong—I just don't think it is a big deal,' then you need to talk through why she is emotionally numb to disobeying God's law. But if Stacy says, 'No, I don't think stealing is wrong—especially something as minor as shoplifting,' then you will have a different sort of conversation. Moving from the feeling level to a person's thought life affords a much better opportunity to get a change of thinking. Hopefully, if Stacy actually knows stealing is wrong, and it is sinning against the God she claims to love, she may again become sensitive to feelings of guilt. Even though feeling guilty is not necessary to actually being guilty, we want our teens to not have their emotions detached from their consciences or their thoughts.

The problem of false guilt

When guilt is only defined as a subjective feeling, we can also end up with the possibility of a person experiencing false guilt. False guilt occurs when a person feels guilty, but in fact has not committed a sin, crime, or wrongdoing. Often times, false guilt is experienced in relationships, where another person claims to be wronged when there is no real sin. For example, a teen may tell you that she feels guilty for avoiding a friend who is pretty difficult to love. As you talk to her more, you think that she has actually gone above and beyond in trying to show kindness and grace in this challenging relationship. So while you counsel the teen on what steps she can take to be honest about the relationship, and lovingly confront, you can also caution her about some of the false guilt she is carrying in her heart. It could possibly be the case that she has an expectation about relationships that is too high, as well as an expectation on herself of what the 'perfect' friend should be. While you should not counsel her to sin against her friend, she needs to think if she is truly guilty in the eyes of God.

Not only does false guilt tend be connected to relationships (where others are making false accusations against us), but it can also be tethered to our own definitions and standards or righteousness (that are not God's). In this way, false guilt is a derivation of the idol of perfectionism. You may have a teen who constantly feels guilty for simply making mistakes, that are redefined as actual sins. Or, another teen may feel guilty for not making straight A's after all the money his father has paid for private school. Then, there are also teenagers who expect such perfection out of themselves that they think God is constantly disappointed with them. The challenge with the problem of false guilt is teasing out the places where the person is actually guilty. Was it really a mistake, or could there have been an element of disobedience as well? Maybe failing to get straight A's is nothing to feel guilty about, but what about being lazy in study habits? Certainly, there can be false guilt involved when seeking to always be perfect, but there will also be actual sins involved that require forgiveness. So, if you perceive feelings of false guilt in the hearts of your teen, make sure to ask the question: 'But are you really guilty in the eyes of God?'

The problem of true guilt

Let's imagine Stacy has realized the gravity of her sin, and how she is guilty of it. She is finally bearing the full weight of her guilt. What is she to do about it? On the most practical level, she must deal with the consequences of her shoplifting, and make all the proper restitution. She should apologize to her parents as well as all those from whom she has stolen. Most importantly, Stacy must seek God's forgiveness for her sin. Since God is the Supreme Judge, we turn to Him first, asking for His forgiveness. Then, Stacy can embrace the truth of 1 John 1:9, 'If we confess our sins, he is faithful and just to forgive us our sins and to cleanse us from all unrighteousness.' In that moment of the confession of sin, the ultimate problem of our true guilt is solved. Stacy no longer bears the guilt of her sin. If she is in Christ, she will not have to pay for that sin by going to hell. Stacy needs to be reminded that breaking God's law in one place means she is guilty of breaking all of it (James 2:10). This reminds us of the necessity of God's forgiveness for all of our sin!

While the core problem of true guilt is solved by God's forgiveness, guilty feelings are also given to us by God for our overall sanctification. What if Stacy confessed her sin of shoplifting, but then went out with some friends the next weekend and stole again? She would be guilty again, requiring her to confess her sins again. Stacy could certainly keep stealing over and over again, and be forgiven over and over again—that's the amazing grace of God for sinners! Yet, if Stacy is a Christian, the guilt of her sin is not 'weighing' on her in a positive way, leading to sustained repentance and heart change. Just because she doesn't bear her guilt anymore doesn't mean she shouldn't remember her guilt (and of course, the forgiveness of God) in a way that will grow her in grace. In other words, confessing our guilt to God is intended, by the work of the Spirit, to lead to turning from that sin and forsaking it in the future. Unfortunately, because of our sinful hearts, we can neglect our forgiveness and wrongly use our freedom in Christ. We want our teenagers to know they are free from their guilt in Christ, but we must also counsel them to practice true repentance and seek Biblical heart change as well.

I keep beating myself up

What good news it would be if Stacy never stole again—especially if this corresponded with genuine growth and gospel-driven sanctification! But imagine that six months have passed since the precipitating event. Stacy comes to you and says she is still 'beating herself up' for her shoplifting rampage. She can't believe how stupid and foolish she was—especially for enjoying it so much. She states: 'I don't need my parents or anyone else to be hard on me because I am my worst critic. I can't stop beating myself up.' What's going on here? First, she may simply be struggling with receiving God's forgiveness. It just seems too easy to confess her sin and to receive forgiveness. Similarly, she may believe God should have punished her more for her sin, so she will just have to do it herself. Or, it may be that Stacy just feels better beating herself up, since she is stuck in deep shame (more about that in a later section). Ultimately, teens who are 'too hard' on themselves after confessing sin misunderstand God, themselves, and grace. Continuing to punish self when God is not condemning them puts them precariously 'above' God, acting as the higher judge, jury, and executioner.

Another version of this problem occurs when your teen tells you: 'I know God has forgiven me, and my parents forgive me, but I just can't forgive myself.' Again, this statement reveals a wrongheaded view of guilt, grace, and forgiveness. At the outset, your teen needs to consider the fact that, whatever the sin was, he did not sin against himself— but against God (and possibly other people). Even when we violate our own standards, we are still not sinning against self, since it is God who makes the rules and sets the perfect standard. There is no reason to 'forgive self' or receive forgiveness from ourselves. God is the one, just Judge—the only One who can offer people forgiveness and release from their guilt. So the answer is not to learn to forgive self, but to rest more deeply in God's forgiveness. Show your teen that wrong thinking makes themselves the more important judge, being a higher 'god' than God Himself. As we will see in a later section, this thinking reveals a potential problem with shame rather than guilt. When your teenager seemingly cannot forgive self, point him or her again and again to who God is, and what God's Word says about grace, mercy, and forgiveness.

Enjoying God's forgiveness

The worldly culture and our own sinful hearts give us all sorts of ineffective and false solutions to the problem of guilt. Teens can deny guilt, claiming that whatever happened wasn't so bad. They can redirect the guilt, pointing fingers at others who sin more or are much worse. They could also simply become angry with God, parents, or society for imposing impossible standards which are intended to make people feel bad. None of these efforts will solve the problem of guilt. Worse than that, they keep our teens from enjoying God's mercy and forgiveness. What we desire to see are teens who fully receive God's forgiveness. We want them to be constantly in awe and amazed at how merciful and gracious God is. Our teens also need to see the power of God's forgiveness to change and cleanse our filthy hearts. Remember that guilt recognizes that we deserve to be punished. We deserve condemnation for our sins. The guilty teen needs to enjoy the forgiveness of God that he or she has in Christ! When our teens truly revel in the love of God for sinners, they will mature in their fear and worship of God.

Picturing shame

Where guilt is experienced in the privacy of the courtroom, shame is felt in a much more public way. Picture a typical suburban neighborhood, with houses standing side by side, children running and biking around the streets, and neighbors visiting over white picket fences. Instead of a quiet room with a solitary judge, there are dozens and even hundreds of a person's peers, friends, and enemies around. But in this picture, where is your teenager? He or she is on the outside of the community—excluded from the neighborhood. All of the neighbors are saying things like: 'You don't belong. You are unacceptable, unclean. You are a total disgrace. You are an outcast.' In a way, this neighborhood feels like a courtroom—the court of public opinion. Where guilt is more defined, connected to a particular sin—the experience of shame is broader and more life-dominating. While the guilty expects deserved punishment, the shamed teen feels worthless and expects rejection. What does the shamed person need? He or she needs cleansing, fellowship, love, and acceptance. The shamed one needs to be welcomed back into the neighborhood!

Shame outside of Christ

In Genesis 2, we read this description of our first parents, Adam and Eve: 'And the man and his wife were both naked and were not ashamed' (Gen. 2:25). Then comes the rest of the story: Adam and Eve sinned, becoming naked AND ashamed. Therefore, outside of Christ, all people are not only guilty before God, but they should feel shame, since sin is shameful. As we stand before a holy God, the right reaction to our sin is shame. The problem for non-Christians is that they are often sinning and are unashamed. Unfortunately, even teenagers who are professing Christians are not as ashamed of their sins as they should be. Today, there are many wicked things going on in this world that people used to be ashamed of, but are now either indifferent to, or even celebrate. Activities that used to bring shame upon a person or a family cause little stir in the community anymore. So, it makes it easier for those who reject Christ to not feel the shame they should.

Even though society today appears to be more openly sinful and wicked; in reality, this has always been the case. Writing to the church at Philippi about non-Christians, Paul states: 'Their end is destruction, their god is their belly, and they glory in their shame, with minds set on earthly things' (Phil. 3:19). And to the church at Ephesus, Paul again says: 'For it is shameful even to speak of the things that they do in secret' (Eph. 5:12). People who are outside of Christ 'glory' in their shame and continue to live in ways in secret that should fill their hearts with shame. So, if your teenager is a non-Christian, it is essential that the shame and 'nakedness' be exposed—bringing what is in the darkness to the light. Why? To embarrass them? To humiliate them? Not at all. Our teens who are non-Christians need to see their shame so they will humble themselves and look for the covering, the atoning, of their sins, that is only found in Jesus. As parents and Biblical counselors, we are not attempting to shame our teens or bring ungodly shame into their lives—but to show them a Savior who covers our shame with His perfect righteousness!

The problem of worth

Shame has deep roots in a heart evaluation of worthiness—what a person believes he is worth to God, to others, and even to self. Fourteen-year old Randy is asking those questions currently, especially of his worth to his father. Many of the messages from dad to son, over several years, have communicated deep disappointment and resentment. Randy not only feels of little worth to his father, but also questions if anyone else in his world sees any worth in him. As you speak to him, Randy even sees himself as worthless in the sight of God. As he speaks of his future, all he contemplates is doom and gloom, since he doesn't deserve anything good in this life. In many ways, Randy wants to quit trying to please anyone, since it seems impossible. In his shame, this teenager sees himself as a disgusting creature.

Because of this worthiness component to shame, it is often confused with modern notions of low self-esteem. While Randy certainly has a wrong view of self, the solution is not simply to raise his self-esteem. This approach would offer counsel like: 'Randy, even though your dad doesn't think highly of you, your need to love you ... believe in yourself ... think highly of yourself. Don't let other people dictate your self-esteem; you are infinitely worthwhile as a human being.' This counsel will only lead to potential pride and love of self which

Scripture condemns as sinful (2 Tim. 3:1-2; 1 Pet. 5:5). Telling Randy how great he is will not counteract the shame he feels, because he has already come to his own conclusions. He believes that his grades and his athletic abilities are unworthy of any real praise. His father's words and beliefs outshout and outweigh anything else, including his own assessment. It is impossible for Randy simply to like himself more and see himself as a worthwhile person.

So, what do we do with the problem of self-worth? In Randy's case, we begin by acknowledging that his dad certainly has a low view of his abilities and accomplishments. Unfortunately, his father is teaching him that a person's performance is what determines a person's worth. This is not a Biblical worldview. A right view of our worth begins with the fact that we are made in the image of God. Yet, as fallen sinners, there is nothing in and of ourselves that makes us worthy of the love of God. But God, in His great mercy, chose to save and redeem a people for Himself—solely because of the infinite worthiness of His Son, Jesus Christ. This is the Biblical way to evaluate our worth as saved children of God. Now the question for Randy is: Which view of worth and worthiness will he embrace—his father's or his Heavenly Father's? Clearly, it is tempting to put his father's thoughts into the mind of God. Thankfully, God is not disappointed in His children because of poor performance in the classroom, or on the athletic field. What we enjoy in our relationship with God in Christ is freedom from shame that is based in unworthiness. This leads us to the next part of the process: confronting the source of our shame.

Confronting sources of shame

Sometimes, the shaping influence of our shame is fairly easy to identify. Randy can point to the words and attitudes of his father as the main source of his shame. Whenever the words or actions of other people are to blame, our teens need to be encouraged to Biblically confront them. Now, there are actually two essential confrontations in these types of situations. First, the person who is speaking and acting in a sinful manner needs to be confronted. When it is a parent, as in Randy's case, it is certainly more challenging. Randy will need to speak to his father in a respectful and honoring manner, yet also firmly about the damage done by his words and attitudes. This person-to-person confrontation may not always be possible, and may not even be constructive—but it should be considered. The second confrontation is of person-to-self. Randy's dad may never have a change of heart or attitude. He may keep telling Randy that he is a disappointment to him. In that case, Randy needs to confront his thoughts, taking them captive to the Lordship of Christ, thereby becoming free from the tyranny of his father (2 Cor. 10:5). In many cases, the source of shame is not just a person, but our own willingness to imbibe their words, making them our own truth.

There are various other sources of shame that must be confronted. In Quentin's case, his shame has developed over years in context of the 'neighborhood.' Through a whisper campaign and routine rejection, Quentin has formed a general attitude of self as an outcast and a defective person. He too must be encouraged to confront his thoughts, but may find it more difficult to challenge the perceptions and activities of his peers. For other teens, the primary source of shame may be a specific, hidden sin pattern. Quentin may actually experience same-sex attraction at times, making him very ashamed. When shame is occurring because of a sinful desire or activity, the person needs to be confronted by the Word of God and the Spirit of conviction. A last typical source of shame can be a long-standing life situation, like a disability, an economic situation, or any of a long list of differences that put people on the 'outside.' Quentin is socially awkward partly because he has a learning disability. What needs to be confronted when there is this sort of exclusionary difference? Thoughts of inferiority and worthlessness must be faced and rejected.

Clean in Christ

Teenagers who are weighed down with shame often have to think more deeply about what it means to be clean. Remember, one of the heart attitudes attached to shame is the belief of being unclean in some way. The best picture we have in the Bible is the sad state of affairs that the person stricken with leprosy faced. Not only did people with leprosy suffer from extreme physical pain and deterioration, they were also declared ceremonially and ritually unclean. On top of that suffering, the leper had to live outside of the camp, avoid human contact, and cry out 'unclean, unclean' to alert others of their pitiful state. As sinners, we are all spiritual lepers. Our sin makes us unclean, separates us from God and His people, and carries with it the ultimate shame. So, again, non-believers are living in shame as unclean lepers, whether they realize it or not. There is only one way to become clean and unashamed—through the grace of God by faith in Christ alone!

So what do we do with a teenager who still feels unclean after coming to Christ by faith for his salvation? Certainly, our ongoing sinful habits make us feel dirty, even though we have already been cleansed in Christ. But that struggle with sin can be confused with somehow returning us to the state of a spiritual leper, excluded from the community of believers. Our teens need to be reminded that being cleansed from sin is a fact, whether we feel it or not. They need to believe important Scriptures like: 'Let us draw near with a true heart in full assurance of faith, with our hearts sprinkled clean from an evil conscience and our bodies washed with pure water' (Heb. 10:22), and 'I will sprinkle clean water on you, and you shall be clean from all your uncleannesses, and from all your idols I will cleanse you' (Ezek. 36:25). Our teens that are stuck in shame must see that, as Christians, they are no longer forced to be on the outside because of their sin. They have been fully cleansed by the blood of Christ and the purifying work of the Spirit.

Shame-based relationships

Some of our teenagers are experiencing shame primarily because they lack true Christian relationships and fellowship. Remember, shame tells us that we have been rejected and excluded because we don't deserve relationships at all. We have been banned from the neighborhood! Yet, that shame-based belief doesn't keep the teenager from longing for relationship. Just because Quentin feels deeply ashamed of himself due to how he is treated by his peers, doesn't mean he wouldn't want those same teens to be his best friends. Now, it wouldn't be helpful to counsel Quentin to ignore all of those 'haters' and find some real friends who will accept him. It is possible he may never have friends! Instead, Quentin begins to solve his shame-based relationships by learning to love his enemies, doing good to those who hate him, and praying for those who are abusing him (Luke 6:27-38). The shame begins to lift—not because the relationships improve—but because of the sanctifying grace of God in our hearts and minds. Hopefully, teens like Quentin will get to enjoy relationships within the body of Christ, as their love and compassion will also be a great antidote to his shame.

Fixing our eyes on Jesus

Speaking of how we run the race of the Christian life, the writer of Hebrews states: '... looking to Jesus, the founder and perfecter of our faith, who for the joy that was set before him endured the cross, despising the shame, and is seated at the right hand of the throne of God' (Heb. 12:2). The ultimate shame for Jesus was the cross, and He endured it because His eyes were fixed on the highest goal—the redemption of His people. Because of this marvelous gospel truth, Christians are to fix their eyes on Jesus, and follow His example when it comes to all of their shame. Whether our teens are filled with shame because of sin, situations, or relationships, the ultimate solution is always moving their eyes from self, or others, to Jesus. Fixing our eyes upon Jesus means enjoying His forgiveness when we are guilty. Fixing our eyes upon Jesus means living in a relationship with God and with

His people without shame. While many of our teens are tempted to wallow in their shame, the only way out is through the founder and perfecter of their faith!

Wisdom POINTERS

The following are some 'do's and don'ts' to help you remain gospel-centered and Biblically grounded when handling problems connected to guilt and shame:

- Do distinguish between guilt and shame in the heart of your teen.
- Don't define guilt as simply a feeling.
- Do recognize the possibility of false guilt.
- Don't confuse shame with low self-esteem.
- Do teach the teen to confess, repent, and die to self.
- Don't forget that non-believing teens should be filled with shame.
- Do recognize the pain and suffering of being excluded and rejected.
- Don't allow the teen to avoid important confrontations.
- Do understand the sources of shame.
- Don't give simplistic answers for difficult relationships.
- Do exhort teens to love their enemies.
- Don't neglect speaking of our cleansing in Christ.
- Do fix your eyes on Jesus as you call your teen to do it as well!

10.
Homosexuality and SSA

Including homosexuality in a list of typical teenage problems to be solved is not only politically incorrect today, but reflects an archaic notion of sexuality in general. With ever-evolving definitions of gender, identity, and sexuality, who's to say what is a problem and what is not? Thankfully, Christians who rest in the foundational authority of God's Word are able to know God's view on these subjects; and, by His grace, can seek to offer wise counsel. We don't have to accept modern views or long-standing myths that seek to normalize homosexuality and other sexual sins. Unfortunately, many of our Christian teens have embraced the notion that homosexuality is genetic or, at least, that the same-sex desires can't be sinful. As we seek to help our teenagers who are either committed to a homosexual identity or are struggling with sinful desires, we will also have to address the larger cultural lies. These issues are complex and convoluted in many ways—yet uncomplicated in others—requiring wisdom and compassion.

Opening PORTRAITS

- Tommy, a 15-year old, has just opened up to his two best friends that he is gay. He has always felt different, and now he knows that he was born this way. Tommy doesn't quite know what to do about church or the youth group, because Christians always judge gay people.

- Vince, a 17-year old, has not had any homosexual encounters in his life; but, he is definitely attracted to other men. He'd like to marry a woman one day, but is afraid he will always have these distorted affections.

- Wanda is a 16-year old who has already had a couple of serious boyfriends. On a recent school trip, a girl in her class kisses and fondles her. Now, Wanda is questioning her sexuality, calling herself 'bi-curious' and maybe even a bisexual.

Typical *PROBLEMS*

When human sexuality goes outside of God's designed boundaries, then all sorts of problems will manifest in a myriad of ways. New terms, especially euphemisms, to describe the aberrations are constantly being created, with distinctions that are becoming more incomprehensible. For our purposes, we will focus on the following issues in this category of problems:

1. Homosexuality

Homosexuality is sexual interest and attraction for members of one's own gender. The term 'gay' is typically synonymous with male homosexuality, while 'lesbian' refers to female homosexuality. As will be discussed further, the sin of homosexuality is more than desire or even activity. It is the embrace of an unbiblical identity.

2. Bisexuality and Bi-curious

Bisexuality is sexual interest and attraction for both men and women. The term 'bi-curious' refers to a heterosexual person who is interested in a sexual experience with a person of the same sex. Additional labels such as 'pansexual,' 'queer,' and 'sexually fluid,' are used to describe the desire for diverse sexual experiences.

3. Same-Sex Attraction (SSA)

Same-sex attraction describes the experience of someone who struggles with homosexual desires and feelings, but does not embrace a homosexual identity. As will be elaborated later, there is an ongoing debate among Christians whether or not SSA is sinful, if those desires are not acted upon. Either way, the person with SSA is not yet committed to a life of homosexuality.

Evaluation *PERSONALIZATION*

If your teen is struggling with the problems of homosexuality, bisexuality, or same-sex attraction, then you will need to have some further questions answered:

Overall patterns

1. Is your teen attracted to the same sex, or has he or she engaged in homosexual activity?
2. Is your teen engaged in sexual activity with both sexes?
3. Does your teen embrace a homosexual identity?
4. Is your teen seeking Biblical change or acceptance?

Sexual history

1. Has your teen experienced sexual abuse?
2. Has your teen been seduced by a homosexual?
3. Is your teenager sexually active?
4. Is your teenager viewing homosexual pornography?

Physical factors

1. What is the current state of the teen's physical health?
2. Are there any intellectual or physical disabilities of note?
3. What are the teen's other health habits like?

Relational issues

1. What is the state of your teen's friendships?

2. Does he or she have homosexual acquaintances or friendships?
3. Is your teen withdrawn and isolated?
4. Has there been any bullying?

Media practices

1. What is the impact of social media in the teen's life?
2. What sort of entertainment media is being engaged in?
3. How has his or her media practices changed over the years?

Marriage and family

1. Are there significant family problems that are contributing to the issues?
2. What is the teen's relationship with his or her mother? Father?
3. How is the teen relating to siblings?
4. What is the general nature of parenting?
5. Are there close family relatives who struggle with homosexuality?

Relationship with God

1. What is the teen's basic understanding of God? Of sin?
2. What about his or her devotional life? Prayer and Bible study?
3. How does the teen describe his or her relationship to Jesus Christ?
4. What about the role of the Holy Spirit in spiritual maturity?
5. Is the teen rebelling against God?

Other related problems

1. Is the teenager depressed or suicidal?
2. Is the teenager angry or anxious?
3. Is there substance abuse involved?
4. Are there any other problems that could be connected?

Biblical PRINCIPLES

The world would have our teenagers believe that Christians are anti-sex and anti-love. After all, the reasoning goes, humans can't help whom they are attracted to, and should be free to love whomever they choose. Who are we to take away someone's freedom of their own sexual experiences? With this worldview, the only real problem occurs when teenagers are denied the ability and opportunity to explore their sexuality in their own way. Yet, God's Word fundamentally opposes a human-centered view of sex and relationships. From the very beginning, God ordained our sexual expression to occur within marriage between one man and one woman (Gen. 2:18-25). He created woman to be a helpmate to man, to complement him as the two become one flesh. Homosexual marriage is not the Biblical pattern for marriage, and homosexual desire and behavior is a sinful disorder that requires Biblical change. So let's think through how the Scriptures guide us to help our teens who are struggling with homosexual-based sins.

Homosexuality vs. SSA

Until fairly recently, anyone who experienced any sort of homosexual feeling or desire used the label 'homosexual' or 'gay' in reference to self. Now, the term 'same-sex attraction' (SSA) has been added to the lexicon. So, what's the difference? Let's begin with Tommy, your 15-year old who describes himself as a homosexual, and even a 'gay Christian.' Fundamentally, the use of the term homosexual communicates a particular identity and lifestyle. If your teen says, 'I am gay,' or 'I am a lesbian,' he or she is saying more than I am simply attracted to people of the same sex. The homosexual is committed to this same-sex sexual orientation as a life-defining identity. It's a clear way to describe their entire being, in opposition to normal heterosexual orientation. Therefore, Tommy is declaring that he has embraced an identity of homosexuality, believing he has been created with this sexuality.

Vince, on the other hand, doesn't think he's a homosexual, but is struggling with same-sex attraction (SSA). The use of the term SSA, then, is more limited—as it is used to describe the experience of having homosexual desires and feelings, but without a commitment to a homosexual identity. In other words, a person who embraces a heterosexual identity and lifestyle, yet has sexual desire for people of his or her own sex, is dealing with the problem of SSA. To be clear, this doesn't necessarily mean that SSA is easier to overcome than homosexuality. A teen who is attracted to members of the same sex, whether or not he or she acts on it, is still dealing with a challenging sin pattern. And, someone with SSA can also give in to those desires with homosexual activities. But the difference is that there is no interest in seeking to identify as gay, lesbian, or homosexual—or to seek a homosexual lifestyle.

To make this distinction abundantly clear, we need to answer the controversial question of whether or not a homosexual can be a Christian. A teenager who is attracted to people of the same sex, yet refuses to embrace a homosexual identity and lifestyle, can be a Christian. As will be discussed in the next section, SSA is one of many sinful desires and attractions that Christians can and do struggle with—even while dedicated to submitting to the Lordship of Christ. Yet, it is not Biblically consistent to believe that a person can be a Christian homosexual or a 'gay Christian'—a person who embraces both Christianity and a homosexual lifestyle. These are two opposing and competing worldviews and identities (Lev. 18:22, 20:13; Rom.1:26-28; 1 Tim. 1:8-11). They cannot fit together, even if the person holds to Biblical definitions of marriage. A homosexual can certainly become a Christian, but then his or her identity and lifestyle must change! As a Christian, Tommy would need to reject a commitment to homosexuality, but recognize that SSA may continue to be a problem. To identify with Christ and still desire to remain in a life-dominating sinful identity goes against the reality of the believer's union with Christ.

Genetics and choosing

The central teaching of most modern homosexual advocates is that homosexuality is genetic, thereby making it a normal sexual expression. To put it in the vernacular, a certain percentage of the population is simply 'born gay.' Some scientists have been searching long and hard for the 'gay gene' which would support this pre-determined conclusion[1]. Recently, more and more researchers are admitting that this gene may never be found, suggesting that homosexuality may be 'epigenetic' instead—the result of mutations while the child is in the womb. Unfortunately, when a scientist operates outside of a Biblical worldview, he or she ends up looking in the wrong place to explain homosexuality. While seeking solely a genetic explanation, they do not embrace the truth that all human beings are born with a sinful nature. Sin is our fundamental problem; it has been passed down from generation to generation ever since Adam and Eve fell into sin. Homosexuality is not in God's design for the human being, nor is it genetic; it is one result of a fallen, sinful nature.

One of the main rationales for a belief in homosexuality as genetic has to do with the question of choice. Tommy and Vince may tell you that they didn't just wake up one day and choose to be attracted to other men. So because there was no conscious choosing on the person's part, the explanation is that homosexuality is as normally obtained as heterosexuality. After all, no heterosexual chooses to be 'straight,' right? While, on the surface, this may be a strong argument in support of the genetic theory, it just as easily confirms the existence of a sinful nature. The fact is that there are some people born in this world with the sinful attraction towards people of the same sex. The 'choosing' comes later on, when a person gives in to those interests and desires, and determines to make it his or her lifestyle and identity. So, as you counsel your teen Biblically, you will most likely have to confront the world's efforts to normalize homosexuality as simply an alternative

---

1   Even if a 'gay gene' is discovered some day, that doesn't prove that the lifestyle is right. It simply means the brokenness goes right down to the genetic level!

genetic sexual expression. Holding on to the belief that homosexuality is determined by my biology and thereby 'normal' will prevent any real desire to change. The truth is that our biology is fallen too.

Addressing contributing factors

An important step in dealing with any problem, including homosexuality, is properly understanding how it has originated and developed. While the ultimate cause of all sexual disorders is sin, there are numerous contributing factors that must be recognized and addressed. Tommy, for example, believes he is a homosexual because he has always 'felt different.' But as you begin to counsel him, he reveals that his father has always been a harsh and unfeeling man towards him. Tommy consistently felt that his dad was disappointed in him, and their personalities often clashed. His mother was much more caring and compassionate, yet he often felt smothered and controlled by her as well. Further conversations also reveal Tommy's struggle with rejection by guys and girls alike. He confessed to only find friendships among the outsiders of his school—several who are also gay. So while it is overly simplistic to blame a distant father, controlling mom, or rejection by peers as 'causing' Tommy's embrace of homosexuality, they are certainly possible contributing factors. Early relationships with parents, siblings, extended family, and peers impact how we think of our own identity and sexuality.

In talking to Vince about his SSA, you hear a different story. He was raised in a Christian home with very solid parents, at least in his estimation. Vince has just never really seen himself fitting into the mold of a typical man. He has never cared for sports, even though his father made him participate in football and basketball. All his friends are outdoorsmen, but he'd rather be at home reading a good book. Vince is quite artistic and enjoys using his creativity in a variety of different arenas—music, interior design, etc. As he has lived in his own world as well as observed the outside world via social and entertainment media, he can't help but identify more with gay guys than straight guys. Yet, he does want a wife and family one day, and feels terribly guilty for his homosexual desires. So, how have these personal gender characteristics and greater cultural definitions of masculinity and femininity shaped his identity and affections? Addressing beliefs about self and media propaganda will be essential in Vince's case.

Wanda, your 16-year old who is calling herself 'bi-curious' has other contributing factors in her life that must be understood. On a recent school trip, a girl in her class kissed and fondled her. As you hear her story, Wanda also confesses to being sexually active with two former boyfriends—and the relationships were pretty intense. In a later conversation, you are also told of possible sexual molestation when she was somewhere between five and six years old. The perpetrator was a cousin, and it happened on several occasions. Wanda's story is similar to many homosexuals who have either been a victim of sexual abuse as a child, or have been seduced by older homosexuals. These events have caused Wanda to not only question her sexuality, but to come to believe that she is attracted to both men and women. After all, she must be sending out some sort of sexual 'signals' in order for this abuse, molestation, and consensual sex to occur. You may find these sorts of defining events have a significant impact on your teen's sexual identity—which Satan uses to convince him or her of homosexual tendencies. Again, the unique experiences, relationships, personality, parenting, and education must be addressed in order to pursue Biblical change.

Salvation and sanctification

If your teenager has embraced a homosexual identity and lifestyle, it is essential to answer the question of whether or not he or she is truly saved. Those who reject Christ and Christianity outright will make your assessment very straightforward. The challenge comes from those who claim to be 'gay Christians,' believing they can live as a Christian and as a homosexual at the same time. Here is where 1 Corinthians 6:9-10 comes into play, where Paul writes: 'Do you not know that the unrighteous will not inherit the kingdom of God? Do not be deceived, neither the sexually immoral, nor idolaters, nor adulterers, nor men who practice homosexuality... will inherit the kingdom of God.' Why are homosexuals in this list of those outside the kingdom of God? As was said earlier, it is because a homosexual identity is in direct opposition to Christ's new creation. So, our teens who are identifying as homosexuals must be called to faith and repentance, enjoying the grace of God unto salvation.

Then, we are able to share the rest of Paul's thoughts with our struggling teens: 'And such were some of you. But you were washed, you were sanctified, you were justified in the name of the Lord Jesus Christ and by the Spirit of God' (1 Cor. 6:11). What great news! The gospel of Jesus Christ proclaims that homosexuality is not a permanent state, but one that can be changed by the power of God. In Jesus Christ, salvation breaks the bonds of slavery to sin. By the work of the Spirit and the Word, our teens can be washed and sanctified. Paul is not teaching that salvation and sanctification removes all sinful desires or actions. Yet, this cleansing in Christ enables the teen to find his identity in Christ rather than his sin. In this way, it is helpful to think of homosexuality as a type of addiction, a life-dominating bondage that influences all relationships, activities, and decisions. This slavery to sin is broken as the homosexual is transformed into the image of Christ, and becomes a slave to righteousness instead.

Changing desires and attractions

Let's return to Vince and the problem of same-sex attraction. We need to help Vince understand that, as sinners, we all have sinful desires. All human beings are attracted to the things of this world, whether it is the sinful desire for worldly wealth for our own satisfaction (greed), the sinful desire to have sexual experiences out of marriage (adultery), a sinful desire for pornography, a sinful desire and idolatry for food (gluttony), and a plethora of other sinful attractions. With that understanding, SSA is simply one of a long list of sinful desires that originate in our sinful hearts. At the same time, not all of our desires have the same addictive and/or destructive qualities. SSA is on the higher end of difficulty and complexity because it attempts to define a person, taps into the power of relationships, and is influenced by a sinful culture. As a desire that goes against nature (Rom. 1:26-27), same-sex attraction cuts against our grain as well. Our sinful hearts, the lust of the flesh, and the temptations of Satan misdirect normal passions and affections.

The reality of SSA seriously raises the question: Can our desires be changed? Often times, we tend to take a passive approach to our desires, infusing them with the characteristic of uncontrollable or undeniable emotion. Or, we can buy into the belief that humans are just machines, victims of their chemical and biological make-ups. But the Scriptures teach that God changes people by the merciful power of the Holy Spirit. Dying to sin also means not conforming to this world, by putting sinful affections to death, as our minds are renewed (Rom. 12:2). Homosexuals who have become Christians have testified to a change of heart and desires, as well as freedom from sin. But other former homosexuals still struggle with ongoing SSA throughout their lives. Complete change is never promised to us in this life—of any sinful desire. We will only be fully cleansed of our sin in glory. Whatever the result, the Christian teen who believes the truth of God's Word doesn't just wait for desires to change, but works, by the Spirit, to combat these thoughts and feelings—and not act on them.

Challenges to change

Since homosexuality develops as an identity-forming, life-dominating sin, there are many challenges to real change for the believer. Using our 'addiction wheel' again, a person's homosexuality often occupies that center hub of the wheel. On the spokes (connected and driven by the hub) are the usual elements of life: relationships, work, hobbies, family, church, etc. So for a teenager to turn from a homosexual lifestyle, all of those aspects would be impacted. He would possibly have to break friendships that are leading him in the wrong direction, especially active homosexual relationships. He would need to make new friendships, which is a challenge in and of itself for a teenager. Then there are activities, events, and favorite hobbies that need to be discarded, with new ones added. Finally, your teen would have to address family issues, including relationships with parents and siblings. The experience of change will often feel like a complete life overhaul, which is significantly traumatic. Clearly, the strength and power of the Spirit will be needed to make these transformations—which may be at great cost.

Another obstacle to changing desires as well as identities is the guilt and shame attached to homosexuality. As discussed in the last chapter, our guilt is declared in the courtroom, and our shame is determined in the neighborhood. When our teenagers are convicted of the guilt of their homosexual sin, they also may experience shame, since it is often viewed by the Christian community as far worse than other sexual sins. What happens when the parents of teens in your youth group hear the news about the struggles of Tommy, Vince, and Wanda? Some will demand the teens be kicked out of the youth group. Others may pull their own teens out, or require them not to have any contact with the offenders. So even if Tommy, Vince, or Wanda desire Biblical change, they may face even more shame-producing exclusion for the foreseeable future. How much easier would it be to keep their sin secret—or even keep a homosexual identity—since, at least there would be other people who would include and accept them. You will need to help your teenager deal with the guilt and shame, as well as the marginalization that may occur in their lives.

A last major challenge is the loneliness of the struggle, especially for those teens who determine that their SSA requires them to be single for life. Remember, Vince wants to be married in the future, but what happens if he is never sexually attracted to a woman? Is his only choice to be celibate? So, loneliness and isolation are not just a present problem for many of our teens, but a future challenge as well.

And, what about having children? Is that taken away from them as well? These will be questions that you will have to talk through wisely in your counseling. Again, God can certainly change our desires and affections. Yet there will be some teens who will end up choosing celibacy, since they know it is sinful to be sexually involved with the same sex. Even if they are committed to singleness, that doesn't have to mean aloneness. They will need covenantal and familial relationships, just as any other single person. Even with all of these challenges—and more—the teenager struggling with SSA or homosexuality needs to believe that it is not an inescapable sin!

Bi-curious and bi-sexual

A related problem among Christian teens is what Wanda is facing—the sin of bisexuality. Since homosexuality and lesbianism have become so widely tolerated and even approved of by many, it has made it much easier for teens to explore all possible experiences. So we now hear of teenage girls having 'girl crushes' that they will use to investigate whether or not they are really bisexual. There are websites dedicated to teaching young people how to behave in a 'bi-curious' way. On top of that, teens are being encouraged to describe themselves as 'homoflexible' or 'heteroflexible,' where one can supposedly move back and forth in sexual relationships. Again, the current cultural leaders in this world have opened the bounds of sexuality so wide that nothing seems off-limits or abnormal. When we understand our own sinful hearts, this should not surprise us—but it does make things more challenging.

So, what are the unique issues for those teens who are active in bi-sexual thinking and relationships? The main problem is the desire for self-serving sexual 'freedom.' It is intoxicating and addicting to pursue relationships with both sexes, or to have the power to switch attractions back and forth. The idea that our sexual attractions are 'fluid' makes a mockery of our sexual identities, as well as the God-given institution of marriage between one man and one woman. Digging down deeper, there is often a greater desire for rebellion against God and other people than there is with homosexual sin. Then, there is also the confusion of relationship that bisexuality brings, especially if your teen continues to experiment. Fundamentally, for change to occur, your teen will need to be brought back to the fundamentals of how God created all humans and the place of our sexuality in that creation. The idolatry of sex needs to be broken in the life of a teen who is dabbling in all sorts of out-of-bounds sexual experiences.

Compassion and wisdom

As has been stated already, Christians are routinely excoriated for attempting to speak of homosexuality as a sin, or even a problem that demands solution. Where once we were told to be more tolerant of homosexuality, today we are instructed to approve and embrace it. So, don't be surprised if the teenager who is engaging in homosexual behavior or struggling with SSA resists any sort of Biblical help. He or she may feel judged, rather than loved. If you are a parent of a teen claiming to be a homosexual, you may even feel like acceptance of the sin is the only way to effectively demonstrate your love. These are certainly difficult places for parents, family members, friends, and youth ministry workers. Yet, compassion is significantly different than simply accepting a person in their sin. It is moved by mercy and grace, desiring to see real change and freedom in the life of a teen, rather than a life of bondage. So, while it's true that Christians can be unkind and unloving towards people who are trapped in the sins of homosexuality, SSA, or bisexuality, we are called to show the love and compassion of Christ to all.

Helping a teenager who desires to be free from homosexual behavior and SSA takes much wisdom and discernment as well. Is your teen a Christian who is struggling, or do the desires, attitudes, and behaviors point to the fact that he or she is a non-believer? Whether you are a parent or a youth ministry worker, navigating a relationship with your teen through this problem will require compassion linked to wisdom.

This is especially true when you are dealing with other parents and other teenage members of your youth group! Homosexuality is such a hot-button issue for so many Christians that it is easy to let fear rule the day—which again, will lead to unloving words and behavior. At the same time, wisdom is required to recognize whether or not the teen is genuine about a desire to change. Sometimes, the sins of homosexuality or SSA are confessed, but you will see the teen still gravitating to members of the same sex. Again, our teens need true Biblical compassion (not acceptance of their sin) as well as Biblical confrontation, with godly wisdom.

Advocating for Biblical marriage

Gay marriage is now legal in every state in the USA, as well as in many countries throughout the world. This victory alone seems to validate that marriage only between one man and one woman is an archaic construct. Most human beings have moved forward from our homophobic, repressive ideas, right? So, if we are to help teens like Tommy, Vince, and Wanda, we need to stand for Biblical marriage. This is always the beginning and end of our understanding of all sexual problems, including homosexuality. Our arguments against homosexuality must always be a defense of marriage between one man and one woman. Training our teens to embrace Biblical marriage is connected to having the right view of God, human beings, sexuality, and identity. Whether or not your teen eventually gets married, he or she needs to accept God's institution of marriage with His definitions. Recognizing that gay marriage is unbiblical assists in the understanding of homosexuality as sin, rather than solely genetic. Submission to God's way is the ultimate solution to our rebellious hearts!

Wisdom POINTERS

The following are some 'do's and don'ts' to help you remain gospel-centered and Biblically grounded when handling the problems of homosexuality, bisexuality, and SSA:

- Do recognize the difference between homosexuality and SSA.
- Don't fail to show love and compassion for your teen.
- Do act in wisdom with all individuals involved.
- Don't confuse acceptance of the teen with acceptance of the sin.
- Do teach the teen about desires, affections, and behavior.
- Don't forget to ask about the teen's view of God and faith in Christ.
- Do recognize the pain and suffering of being excluded and rejected.
- Don't allow the teen to believe the world's view of homosexuality.
- Do investigate the contributing factors to the problem.
- Don't give simplistic answers for a complicated problem!
- Do give the hope of Biblical change in Christ.

11.
Identity, Gender, and Self Problems

If you would ask a random group of adults to name one problem that all teenagers will experience at some point, the issue of 'identity' would be named by many of them. Throughout the ages, the teen years have been connected to the question of 'who am I?' as young people develop and mature in their personhood. Add today's changing definition of gender into the mix, and it has become even more confusing for adolescents. So instead of just struggling with a sense of self-worth or a healthy self-image, there are often questions of sexuality and gender to answer. In the past, many adults were more prone to assume their teens would somehow 'find themselves' sooner or later. Unfortunately, for many, it has become much, much later—with many young adults still seeking to understand self. It should also be recognized that identity, gender, and other self problems are being faced by children who have not yet entered their teen years. Therefore, it is essential that this cluster of problems be faced head on, with the clarity needed to cut through the confusion fostered by the world, Satan, and our sinful flesh.

Opening PORTRAITS

- Angie, a 16-year old, has always struggled with low self-esteem. Even though she claims to be a Christian, Angie is still trying to 'find herself' and figure out who she really is. She is also totally preoccupied with her body, causing her to be depressed.

- Barry, a 17-year old, is visiting your church's youth group with a friend. During a small group Bible discussion, the whole topic of transgenderism comes up. Barry speaks up and asks to be called Mary, because he is about to start hormone treatments in order to transition to a female.

- The parents of 14-year old Cassie brought her to a psychiatrist recently because she was depressed and angry. The psychiatrist diagnosed her with Gender Identity Disorder (GID). Cassie just doesn't identify with any of the girls in her life, but she is also afraid to think of herself as the other gender.

Typical PROBLEMS

When teenagers are seeking to understand 'self,' a variety of problems can develop which touch on gender, body, and even personality issues. There are more complicated identity issues that fall into a more 'psychiatric' category (dissociative disorders, multiple personality disorder, etc.), and thus will fall outside the scope of this discussion. As has been the pattern, we will zero in on those typical problems that impact our teens as they seek to know and live as a person made in the image of God.

1. Gender Identity Disorder (GID)

In a time where gender and sexuality are considered to be no longer synonymous, gender identity disorder occurs when a person does not identify with his or her biological sex. As the problem becomes more persistent, the teen will become increasingly miserable with his or her gender and more desirous to be known by the other gender.

2. Body Image Disorder

Most teenagers don't like some aspect of their bodies—big ears, crooked nose, too overweight, etc. Young people with an actual body image disorder think about their real or perceived body flaws for hours every day. This preoccupation may lead to other problems, including social anxiety, isolation, bitterness, and depression.

3. Low Self-Esteem

The modern notion of self-esteem is the subjective value or worth a person holds for self. A teenager struggling with low self-esteem has a negative or severely deficient view of self. This is also equated with not 'liking self' enough, according to a more psychological view of how a person should perceive self. Low self-esteem can also be referred to as having a deep sense of inferiority.

4. Lack of Self-Confidence

A person who is self-confident trusts in his or her abilities, skills, talents, intellect, or other character qualities. When a teen doubts his or her abilities—whether it be in sports, activities, relationships, academics—he or she is said to lack necessary self-confidence. Another term used here is insecurity.

5. Self-Exaltation

While the focus of many of our teen's self problems is what happens on the 'low' end of the spectrum, God's Word also speaks to the problem of overly high self-esteem. A teen who overly values self or particular attributes of self is prone to the sin of self-exaltation. Everything he or she does is for his or her glory, which is also referred to as 'vainglory.'

Evaluation PERSONALIZATION

If your teen is struggling with identity, gender, and other self problems, then it will be vital to have further questions answered:

Overall patterns

1. Is your teen questioning his or her gender?
2. Is there a desire to actually transition to the other gender?

3. What is your teen's view of self?

4. How does your teen identify his or her personality?

Physical factors

1. What is the current state of your teen's physical health?

2. Are there any intellectual or physical disabilities of note?

3. What are the teen's health habits like?

Relational issues

1. What is the state of your teen's friendships?

2. Is your teen withdrawn and isolated?

3. Has there been any bullying?

Media practices

1. What is the impact of social media in the teen's life?

2. What sort of entertainment media is being engaged in?

3. How has his or her media practices changed over the years?

Sexual history

1. Is your teen sexually active?

2. Is your teen attracted to the same sex?

3. Is your teenager involved in pornography?

Marriage and family

1. Are there significant family problems that are contributing to the issues?

2. What is the teen's relationship with his or her mother? Father?

3. How is the teen relating to siblings?

4. What is the general nature of parenting?

Relationship with God

1. What is the teen's basic understanding of God? Of sin?

2. What about his or her devotional life? Prayer and Bible study?

3. How does the teen describe his or her relationship to Jesus Christ?
4. What about the role of the Holy Spirit in spiritual maturity?
5. Is the teen rebelling against God?

Other related problems

1. Is the teenager depressed or suicidal?
2. Is the teenager angry or anxious?
3. Is there substance abuse involved?
4. Are there any other problems that could be connected?

Biblical PRINCIPLES

Who am I? That's the fundamental question many of our teenagers are seeking to answer. Unfortunately, they don't typically use God's Word as the starting place for their search. Instead, teenagers often find their identity in status, popularity, possessions, beauty, athletic skills, and personality. Thankfully, many of our Christian teenagers mature and grow in Christ, thereby letting go of those identity-forming idols. But then there are those who get stuck in an enslavement to self, a confusion of gender identity, or even a rebellious rejection of God's created order. The reality is that all of our teenagers need to learn what God's Word has to say about the human being. In order to embrace a proper identity as an individual, they need to know what is true about all people. The beauty of our uniqueness comes from the grand design of a Creator, and the love of God for all His people in Jesus Christ! So use the following Biblical principles to address common identity struggles, as well as to teach every one of your teens how they need to view self Biblically.

Image of God

'Then God said, "Let us make man in our image, after our likeness ..."' (Gen. 1:26). While it is a challenge to truly know all that it means to be made in God's image, the primary truth to revel in is that humans ARE made in the image of God! Human beings are not just the same as the animals, or any of the rest of God's creation. We have not evolved from lower life forms, or simply exist as a random mixture of chemicals, proteins, and hormones. Humans alone are image-bearers, designed to understand who we are in relationship to God. We are unique creations in every way. So this is the starting point for the search for identity. Even as sinners, we are still made in the image of God. Even in our weakness and brokenness, we are made in the image of God. When our identities are in anything else but as creatures made in the image of God, we are already confused. When our teens aren't thoroughly God-centered in their understanding of self, they will not view their personhood rightly, which will lead to all sorts of self-related problems.

Sex and Gender

'So God created man in his own image, in the image of God he created him; male and female he created them' (Gen. 1:27). Inextricably linked to being made in the image of God is the truth that all humans are created either male or female. *God's Word establishes that fact of a normative connection between biological sex and gender.* While we are currently being pressed to accept a distinction between sex and gender, this is merely a man-made definition, not a God-made construction. This is not to say that there are people whose behaviors and attitudes don't conform with their biological sex and are thereby confused. What it does mean is that human beings haven't been given the privilege or responsibility by God to choose a different gender than their God-assigned sex. So when one is committed to God's Word, he or she recognizes the sanctity of one's own biological sex. It is only our sin that attempts to create a distinction between our genetic sexuality and the gender we desire.

After visiting a psychiatrist, the parents of 14-year old Cassie are seeking your help. They don't know what to do now that Cassie has been officially diagnosed with Gender Identity Disorder (GID). Their daughter has never identified with typical girls, and she has been doing internet searches on the process of 'transitioning.' So, they are wondering if they should let her explore another gender expression in order to clear up her confusion. Certainly, there would be some experts that would say that the most compassionate parenting would be to just get out of the way and let Cassie choose for herself. Other counselors would even encourage Cassie's parents to proactively seek medical help and treatment to resolve her GID. But a Biblical counselor will work with these parents to stand firm on God's view of sex and gender. They must be the spiritual leaders in Cassie's life, teaching her that she is made in the image of God as a female—and that will never change. As insensitive as it seems to the world's ears, Cassie's parents must not give any ground to a process that would resolve GID by helping her transition to be a man.

Cassie will need Biblical counseling as well, won't she? When a teenager is confused about his or her gender, it's essential to understand where the true problem lies. Why does Cassie not identify with other girls? Does she not enjoy typically feminine activities or conversations? Is she insecure about her body? Or, does it have more to do with relationships with the opposite sex? There are certainly many understandable reasons why a young teenage girl may question her femininity. But she needs to be encouraged to not only embrace her femaleness, but to recognize that not all teenage girls conform to the same expression of femininity. There is a spectrum of what it means to be feminine and masculine, without crossing over to the other biological type. Unfortunately, our teens are often hearing and reading things that tempt them into wondering if they need to change genders. Since that is out of the question Biblically, what they will need is training and exhortation to learn how to properly live out a proper gender identity.

Challenging transgenderism

Barry, on the other hand, is about to begin hormone treatments in order to transition to a female. His announcement that he wants to be called Mary has rocked your church's youth group. Barry has moved beyond the confusion of GID and arrived at the perceived reality that he is a woman trapped in a 17-year old man's body. At this point, parents and youth ministry workers have a responsibility to offer wise counsel to both Barry and all the members of the youth group. There may still be time to talk with a teen like Barry, showing him that there is no God-given freedom given to human beings to dichotomize sex and gender. Even if he feels more like a girl, God has created him male—and expects him to think, behave, and mature as a young man. His desires to transition are sinful and must be confessed, if he seeks to follow Christ as His disciple. To follow through and transition to a woman would be to reject the identity of Christian, as well as the authority of God's Word.

Whether or not Barry becomes Mary, we have a more potentially knotty challenge with the members of the youth group. Our modern cultural virtues of tolerance and acceptance would require them to only be affirming, not judge Barry, not confront or give advice, and only use the desired gender specific labels. But while we certainly want other Christian teens to be loving, gracious, and compassionate, they need to know their responsibility to speak the truth in love. Barry needs to be respected as an image-bearer, but also needs to be confronted in his sin. What good does it do any of our teens to be accepted into a Christian group where no one addresses sin, or even reframes sinful behavior into normal behavior? It may make things uncomfortable for a while, but if Barry continues to come to church and youth group, he needs to hear the truth of God's Word on transgenderism. He doesn't need to be shunned or avoided; he needs loving, Biblical confrontation. The rest of the youth group will need Scriptural clarity from parents and youth workers alike on this sinful identity disorder.

Nature and grace

Logic tells us that our teens can have a fairly accurate self-image, an overly high self-image (where they think too highly of themselves), or a low self-image (where they believe they are worthless). Much of the current focus is how harmful and destructive a low self-esteem is, with the corresponding solution of elevating that self-esteem. While you may believe the teen before you is suffering from low self-esteem, it is essential to first distinguish between the self 'by nature' and the self 'by grace.' When we think highly of ourselves 'by nature,' then we are operating from sinful pride. There is nothing in and of ourselves that should give us a high self-esteem. In other words, teenagers need to understand that, by nature, they are children of wrath (Eph. 2:3), not children of God. The self 'by nature' has nothing to truly esteem, because it is a sinful nature, totally depraved. If your teenager is struggling with low self-esteem, start by affirming to them that there is little in self that we can accept, or even like, because of our fallen natures, other than the fact that we are all made in the image of God.

But you must always follow up that bad news about the natural self with the good news of God's grace for sinners! First, by God's common grace, we have all been made in the image of God. So, as has been already stated, our teen's sense of self and identity must begin with that fact. While the image of God has been marred by sin, we can have a healthy self-esteem because we are image-bearers. Then, if the teenager is a Christian, he or she also enjoys the love of God, mercy of God, and the saving grace of God. A self 'by grace' is something to be rightly esteemed! Our greatest worth, therefore, is not found solely in our human nature, but in the grace of God for sinners. It is vital that teens understand this theological, but practical distinction. We certainly should not want them to esteem self highly based on some human-centered quality or characteristic. And, we don't want them to not esteem self at all, overlooking and even denying God's grace for self. In the end, a positive sense of self-worth, or self-esteem must be rooted in God's gracious creation and providence—or it will produce sinful pride instead.

Self as master and slave

So, Angie, our 16-year old struggling with low self-esteem, needs to be instructed in the truths of the self by nature and the self by grace. But there is another important lesson that will help teens like Angie who are struggling with self problems. The apostle Paul writes that we are to 'put off the old self, which belongs to your former manner of life, and is corrupt through deceitful desires,' (Eph. 4:22). The central problem with the old self is it seeks to deify itself and crown itself as king of its own universe. So the self seeks to first be master of all, making the problem of self-idolatry the most destructive problem of all. Angie's low self-esteem may be driven by the desire to be in control of her life—to be fully loved and accepted by others. What may be really hurting is her pride, as her peers reject her—bringing shame and humiliation. Angie needs to recognize how she is trying to be the master of her universe, unwilling to submit to King Jesus. This is the power of the old self, of which she needs to be set free.

Then, teenagers like Angie need to learn a corresponding truth about the self: the same self that seeks to be master is also a slave. The old self is enslaved to itself and to the sinful nature. This truth is another reason the world's view of low self-esteem is deficient—it leaves out the fact of the sinful nature, only seeing the self as good, or innocent. Our sin has a way of convincing self that we are autonomous, self-determining beings. Angie's self believes it should rule its own universe, but it is fooled by the myth that it is actually free to do so. Any efforts towards being more in control will only bring self-doubt and the related low self-esteem. Even if Angie somehow convinces herself that she is great and wonderful and marvelous, it is only fueling her captivity to her sinful pride. When she understands that the self as master is also the self as slave, she can see that the route to joy and peace does not come by way of a greater self-esteem. The old self must be put off so the new self, 'created after the likeness of God in true righteousness and holiness' can be effectively put on (Eph. 4:24). This doesn't mean that all Christian teens always have a proper self-esteem.

It can be a regular fight to depose the self as king, recognizing that we no longer are enslaved to self, but to the Lord Jesus Christ.

Self-love and self-hate

To some, the solution to each and every identity, gender, and self-related problem is to learn to love self more. This would be especially true for a teen like Angie. At first glance, her body image disorder must be rooted in a hatred for self, and that's why she can't 'find herself.' Yet, the Biblical truth is that we all come out of the womb self-absorbed, with an inordinate love of self. Accordingly, the love of self is not something that has to be learned; it is something all people already do very well. What teens must deal with is their tendency and temptation to love themselves more than they love God or other people. So, while Angie may be extremely self-critical when it comes to certain aspects of her body, this is really out of a deep love and concern for self. The truth is what Paul writes in Ephesians 5: 'For no one ever hated his own flesh [body], but nourishes and cherishes it ...' (Eph. 5:29a). Teaching people to love self more only leads to the problems of the 'last days' where 'people will be lovers of self' that Paul described for his spiritual son Timothy (see 2 Tim. 3:1-2).

One way to help a teen like Angie think more Biblically about her body is to talk about her mirror. What if she woke up every day, gazed into the mirror, and thought things like: 'I am so beautiful! My hair is gorgeous. My eyes, nose, and ears are perfect. My body shape is fantastic. I am a work of art!' Someone may say, 'Boy, Angie, you are one arrogant gal.' But, more realistically, Angie probably wakes up, looks in her mirror and says: 'You are so overweight and dumpy looking. I hate those big ears. Your hair is too frizzy. There's nothing desirable about this body, that's for sure.' So the first approach might be described as 'self-love,' while the latter would be thought of as 'self-hate.' But the reality is that both perspectives share one huge failing: they are totally self-focused. The problem is not what the final assessment of my body is; it is the fact that I'm obsessed with my body in the first place. No, we are not telling teens like Angie to avoid all of her mirrors, or neglect caring for her body. She must be challenged to stop focusing on self—her body most of all—and start focusing on more eternal things. Do you see how teaching Angie to love her body more takes her down an unbiblical path? A self-focus leads to either self-exaltation, or self-pity—which are both sinful.

Denying and dying to self

By their very nature, self problems tend to force us to focus on helping teenagers view themselves in the right way. While that is important, it may overlook the central priority which really aims for the heart. In the search for self, it can become all about 'me,' at the expense of God and others. Listen to the words of King Jesus: 'If anyone would come after me, let him deny himself and take up his cross daily and follow me' (Luke 9:23). What does it mean for our teens to learn to deny self? Clearly, it is much more than denying themselves the luxuries of this life, in some sort of self-deprived monasticism. Yes, to deny self is to say 'no' to the fleshly desires of self. But it is also about making the glory of God our preoccupation rather than our own glory. It is focusing on pleasing God rather than pleasing self. Rather than seeking to feel better about all aspects of self, it is keeping self from being the obstacle to loving God and others. While teens are often caught up in self-indulgence, a life of denying self is what Christ prescribes for them.

Jesus goes on to tell His disciples: 'For whoever would save his life will lose it, but whoever loses his life for my sake will save it' (Luke 9:24). Connected to the obligation of each Christian to 'take up his cross' in order to follow Him, we are to deny self AND die to self. The cross is the instrument of death we take up in order to crucify self and its desires. So rather than simply building teenagers' self-esteem or just helping them to 'find self,' they should be losing themselves in Christ. This is part of what is meant by our union with Christ as believers. The cries of our teens' hearts must be 'less of me, more of Christ' in order to be faithful disciples of Christ. Angie's struggle with her body image will only begin to subside as she seeks to die to her self-idolatry. Your other teenagers who are self-centered must die to self by loving God and other people as well. In your counseling, work on the obstacles your teen has to deny self and die to self. What you will find out is that they are typically resistant to get self out of the way! In other words, it is a painful thing to die to self and its sinful desires. Even the problem of gender confusion is often rooted in a refusal to deny and die to self.

An accurate view of self

The apostle Paul speaks again to the problem of self: 'For by the grace given to me I say to everyone among you not to think of himself more highly than he ought to think, but to think with sober judgment, each according to the measure of faith that God has assigned' (Rom. 12:3). This verse speaks to the great temptation to exalt self, or to think more highly of ourselves than we ought. So, how do we help our teenagers think about themselves with a sober judgment? For one thing, maybe a teen who is 'down' on himself is actually judging self accurately! You will need to find out exactly why the teen has that particular perception. Maybe he sees his sin and is grieving over it. Or, maybe he is fearful of self, knowing how easily he can mess up relationships. Now, this accurate view of sin and weakness can easily turn into self-pity or self-absorption. As Paul says, it takes a God-given faith in order to have an accurate view of self. Our teens need to learn to rely on the Holy Spirit to not think too highly of self, but to know themselves well. A wise Biblical counselor can walk through this assessment with their teens.

Another piece of important wisdom is written to the church at Galatia: 'For if anyone thinks he is something, when he is nothing, he deceives himself' (Gal. 6:3). Many of the identity problems we see in our teens today involve a lot of self-deception. The seduction of a social media culture that is all about 'me,' preoccupied with taking 'selfies,' and constantly looking for 'likes,' takes its toll on the teenage heart. Add to that the deception of thinking that loving self is the highest virtue keeps our teens confused, anxious, and angry. Even Christian teens can come to believe that they are naturally good and righteous people, missing the grace of God in their lives. So again, work with your teen in developing an accurate view of self in this world. To have a right understanding of self, they must accurately know their sinfulness and their need for Christ. Resist the simplistic view of thinking teens only need to be praised and loved when they need to also believe the truth about self!

Trusting God vs. self

Another tricky area of counseling is helping a teenager who lacks self-confidence. Common wisdom leads us to help teens to increase their self-confidence, exhorting them to 'believe in themselves' more. As with all of the typical self-related problems, we must be careful in our choice of words and phrases because they communicate important messages. So while we may understand what we are saying when it comes to becoming more confident in athletics, academics, or relationships, we are hard pressed to find self-confidence as taught in the Bible. Paul tells us that we are to have no confidence in the flesh (Phil. 3:3), but only in Christ Jesus. In Proverbs we read, 'Those who trust in themselves are fools, but those who walk in wisdom are kept safe' (Prov. 28:26, NIV). To simply urge your teenager to be more self-confident misses the mark, and potentially produces sinful pride. If we truly have an accurate view of self, we would have no confidence in self, in our hearts, in our motives, or even in our abilities.

How, then, are we to help teens that seem to be struggling with confidence? First, it is essential to deal with what may be the actual heart problems when you dig down a bit deeper. Most often, low self-confidence is a problem with fear, worry, and anxiety. This is typically the case when it comes to confidence in relationships or abilities. Anxiety will freeze a teen in such a way that he or she doesn't ever want to try again. It is easier to quit activities or just avoid relationships. Along with an anxiety problem, your teen may just be stuck in self-pity. Repeated failures can work over the teenage mind, making a sense of confidence seem elusive. After exposing other heart problems, focus the teen on developing a God-confidence rather than self-confidence. Hopefully, you understand that this is more than a semantic difference. Trusting in God instead of trusting in self is at stake here. As tempting as it is just to praise our teens and tell them how incredible they are, we must seek a higher goal of glorifying God with our praise. Relying on God rather than their own abilities, intellect, or personalities is the true route to a lasting confidence that pleases God.

Esteeming Christ

Here's a final word to teens who are struggling with identity issues: 'For you have died, and your life is hidden with Christ in God' (Col. 3:3). As hard as this union with Christ is to understand, it cuts through the confusion when embraced by faith. Dying to self in the death of Christ means that my identity is in Him, not in myself. So as important as it is for teens to have accurate self-images and a right understanding of sexuality and gender, the better direction is to move them on to esteeming Christ in a greater measure. How much does your teen really esteem Christ? Is he or she seeking to know Christ more, or just to know self more? While it is tempting to focus on who I am in Christ, it is much better to know who Christ is in me. Esteeming Christ should define the Christian life, even in teens who are immature in their view of self. The one way to dissolve any temptation to self-righteousness is to be grateful daily for the righteousness of Christ in our lives. Since we are inclined to love self more than love God and others, the only antidote is a growing love and esteem for Christ!

Wisdom POINTERS

The following are some 'do's and don'ts' to help you remain gospel-centered and Biblically grounded when handling identity, gender, and self issues:

- Do understand the current cultural lies regarding self, sex, and gender.
- Don't fail to show compassion for your teen's confusion.
- Do speak the truth in love, even if it appears intolerant.
- Don't encourage gender transition to solve gender confusion.
- Do teach the teen about the self by nature versus the self by grace.
- Don't neglect to recognize how the teen is enslaved to the old self.
- Do point out the self-focus that produces sinful self-love or self-hate.
- Don't simply encourage self-confidence, but rather God-confidence.
- Do investigate related problems of anxiety and self-pity.
- Don't allow the teen to lack a sober judgment of self.
- Do call the teen to deny self and die to self.
- Don't forget to proclaim a Christ-esteem!

12.
Pornography

It's almost hard to remember that there was a time when teenagers had to work hard to acquire pornographic materials. This is clearly not the case anymore. The evolution of porn mainly found in magazines, then on televisions and computers, and then on our personal smartphones is both astounding and depressing. Accessibility to this sinful drug of the mind, emotions, and heart is only increasing while cultural condemnation is correspondingly decreasing. We have yet to see the full impact of pornography on the last couple of generations as they emerge into adulthood. In many ways, our teenagers are growing up in a pornographic world, with the traditional virtues of chastity and purity quickly falling by the wayside. Christian teens are not immune to the problem, with many exposed to porn even in childhood. For the foreseeable future, pornography use and addiction will be high on the list of teenage problems.

Opening PORTRAITS

- Doug, a 15-year old, has been looking at pornography on his home computer and his smartphone for several years. As a Christian, he is totally ashamed of it, and is fighting against those urges. But Doug is afraid he is addicted and scarred for life.

- 16-year old Evie has been caught up with a bad crowd at her school for quite some time. These friends regularly show each other porn clips on their smartphones. Lately, Evie has even sent a few nude pictures of herself to a boy she wants to date.
- Freddy, a 13-year old, stumbled on to some pornography on the school computer. He is afraid to tell his parents, but he confides in his youth director.

Typical PROBLEMS

In one sense, the use of pornography is a pretty straightforward problem: Teenagers who are viewing pornography need to stop viewing pornography. If only it were that easy and uncomplicated! While there are numerous types of pornography, ranging on a scale from 'soft' to 'hardcore,' they all share the common goal of arousing erotic and sexual thoughts and desires in the viewer. From pictures to videos, and from voyeuristic to interactive, pornography is dispensed in almost all forms of media today. Historically thought of as primarily a male problem, there is more and more pornographic material targeting young women as well. The bottom line is, whatever the type of pornography being viewed, there are a couple of basic problems that require intervention.

1. Porn Use

While it is unrealistic to think that our teens will never be exposed to any sort of pornography, it becomes a problem when they actively seek it out. Whether it's the choice of movies, social media, written materials, or internet videos, any use of pornography is sinful and destructive. Even if the porn use is erratic rather than routine, moderate use is not acceptable. Porn should be thought of as a poisonous drug that is harmful in a singular use as well as because it can easily become a life-dominating addiction.

2. Porn Addiction

Even teenagers can get to a place where their use of porn controls them. Just like all other addictions, bondage to pornography is a spiritual and a brain-based problem, impacting body and soul. A porn addiction will impact relationships and create other mental, emotional, and spiritual problems as well. The teen who is addicted to pornography will often feel that it is a problem that cannot be solved.

Evaluation PERSONALIZATION

If your teen is struggling with the use of pornography, or has become addicted to it, then it is important to have further questions answered:

Overall patterns

1. When did your teen begin viewing pornography?
2. How often is your teen viewing pornography?
3. What type of pornography is your teen viewing?
4. Is it infrequent pornography use, or has it become an addiction?

Physical factors

1. What is the current state of the teen's physical health?
2. Are there any intellectual or physical disabilities of note?
3. What are the teen's health habits like?
4. How often is the teen masturbating?

Relational issues

1. What is the state of your teen's friendships?
2. Is your teen withdrawn and isolated?
3. Has there been any bullying?
4. Is your teen dating, or involved in a serious relationship?

Media practices

1. What is the impact of social media in the teen's life?
2. What sort of entertainment media is being engaged in?

3. On what media platforms is pornography being viewed?
4. What access does the teen have to various sources of pornography?

Sexual history

1. Is your teen sexually active?
2. Is your teen attracted to the same sex?
3. Is your teenager involved in homosexual pornography?
4. Has your teen been sexually abused or molested?

Marriage and family

1. Are there significant family problems that are contributing to the issue?
2. What is the teen's relationship with his or her mother? Father?
3. What is the general nature of parenting in the life of the teenager?
4. Does the teenager have too much freedom?

Relationship with God

1. What is the teen's basic understanding of God? Of sin?
2. What about his or her devotional life? Prayer and Bible study?
3. How does the teen describe his or her relationship to Jesus Christ?
4. What about the role of the Holy Spirit in spiritual maturity?
5. Is the teen rebelling against God?

Other related problems

1. Is the teenager depressed or suicidal?
2. Is the teenager angry or anxious?
3. Is there substance abuse involved?
4. What are the problems that are possibly connected?

Biblical PRINCIPLES

The etymology of the word pornography speaks volumes of its danger. The first part of the term, 'porne' originates from the Greek for prostitute or harlot, and 'graph' is the word for 'writing.' So pornography is literally the 'writing of prostitutes.' With that word origin, we understand why certain 'romance novels' should be considered pornographic, along with all erotic images and videos. Just as the prostitute 'sells' herself for the pleasure of the purchaser, pornography is marketed to our teenagers for their personal sexual pleasure. While current technology may convince us that porn is only a modern problem, these sinful heart issues have been with us from the beginning of time. There have always been prostitutes and their 'writings,' and there have always been sinful human beings who make use of them. Thus, we need to help our teens struggling with this viral problem to remain grounded in God's Word in order to get to the heart of the problem.

Teenage sexuality

The starting point in any effort to help our teenagers ensnared by pornography is recognizing that God created them as sexual beings. They are naturally attracted to members of the other sex, and have an increasing desire for sexual pleasure. These sexual impulses are not to be understood solely as just some sort of animal desire or sinful perversion. So, as parents and youth ministry workers, it should not surprise us when teenagers are tempted to view pornography. Just as they are more interested in relationships with the other sex, there is a corresponding fascination with their bodies as well. While the world tends to chalk it all up to raging hormones, we must not lose sight that this is part of God's created order. Without sexual desire, there would be a lack of interest in marriage or family life. Therefore, a Biblical approach to the battle against pornography includes the affirmation of our God-given sexuality. Without that, teens who are struggling with porn may only feel shame and disgust for sexuality in general, instead of for the sinful distortion of God's design for sex.

As will be discussed further in the next chapter, our teen's sexual desire must be controlled in order to prevent the problem of pre-marital sex. They need to learn to restrain their sexuality, and become committed to a Biblical definition of marriage and sexual expression. So, when our Christian teens seek to be faithful to God's design for their sexuality, that must extend to their rejection of pornography as well. Unfortunately, Satan can tempt our teens to believe that viewing porn is somehow a 'safe' way of taking care of sexual desire in order to avoid 'real' sexual sin with the other sex. This is a patently false lie; but one that is easy to embrace as a rationalization for this secret sin. We must not allow the use of porn in the lives of our teens to ever be seen as a better alternative to pre-marital sex. Not only may it open the door to further sexual sin, it is sinful all on its own. It is an unrighteous way for teens to deal with normal sexual desire, even though it seems safer.

So, as difficult as it may be, you must see your teenager as a sexual being. That includes Freddy, your 13-year old who has inadvertently seen some pornography on the school computer. While he may just be a child in many ways, Freddy can easily be intrigued enough to begin seeking ways to find more porn, especially if he doesn't tell anyone about his temptations. This means that our teenagers need more conversations about Biblical sexuality when they are children, especially now that pornography is so easily accessible. Our instruction needs to be much more robust than simply telling them to stop looking at porn. Yet, a right view of the sexuality of our teens also recognizes their emotional, cognitive, and spiritual immaturity. In many ways, our teenagers are still children, lacking the maturity to rightly control their sexual impulses. They need our protection from themselves as they grow into their own bodies, and into a Biblical understanding of sexuality.

Fantasy versus reality

Pornography is not just perpetuated by a sinful appeal to normal sexual desires, but it also flourishes as an escape from reality. The human body does not look as good in reality as it does air-brushed or photo-shopped for a magazine or video. Sexual intercourse scenes choreographed in pornographic movies or video clips are also totally unrealistic. The reality of pornography is that it makes the body and sexual experience appear better than they are. Certainly, God has created marvelous bodies, and sex between a man and a woman is a beautiful thing as well. But much like the marketing of any product, pornography takes real beauty to the distorted level of the impossible to sell more of it to its consumers. So, our teens need to understand that they are gaining an unrealistic view of people and sex when viewing pornography. This is not what marriage will be like, or any future relationship with anyone—even if they foolishly married a porn star!

Because viewing pornography is a voyeuristic activity, it is nothing but pure fantasy. With that understanding, the question must be asked: Why is the teenager escaping into fantasy in the first place? What is it about reality that is being avoided? Obviously, as has been already said, fantasy appears to be much better than reality. Yet that too is just an illusion. The joy of marital fidelity, as well as the ability to touch and relate to a human being (other than just look from a distance), is beyond compare. So the plunge into pornographic fantasy may simply be a desire to be sexually involved with a person when it is not yet God's providential timing. At the same time, it may also reveal that the teenager is avoiding real relationships, real decisions, and real activities. Pornography offers a place of escape—a way to sinfully engage imaginations—that seems to have no penalty involved. Rescuing our teens from the land of fantasy is a big part of solving the porn problem. We must keep them grounded in the real life that God has created for them, even when that reality is difficult or frustrating.

The distortion of beauty

Just as God has created us to be sexual beings, human beings are also lovers of beauty. Think of Bible personalities like Sarah, Rachel, Esther, Delilah, Bathsheba—all described as being beautiful in the eyes of man. Male and female bodies at their best are glorious to behold, creating a desire to gaze upon them. Unfortunately, that external beauty, and our inclination towards a materialistic worldview, can tempt us to see people only as bodies. That leads us to not only obsess over bodies, but to also focus only on certain desirable body parts as well. If your teen's sense of beauty is only connected to the physical, then pornography will be that much more of interest to him or her. Since men are typically more visually oriented when it comes to beauty, it is easy for them to end up focusing solely on the body rather than on the beauty of the soul. As long as people put their bodies on display for others to watch in a sexual manner, it continues to promote a body-centric view of beauty. This is a distortion of the true beauty of God's creation.

Christian teens need to be challenged to re-orient their view of human beauty. They need to heed the instruction found in 1 Peter 3: 'Do not let your adorning be external—the braiding of hair and the putting on of gold jewelry, or the clothing you wear— but let your adorning be the hidden person of the heart with the imperishable beauty of a gentle and quiet spirit, which in God's sight is very precious' (1 Pet. 3:3-4). In our highly-charged pornographic world, is it even feasible to recapture a proper definition of beauty as it is connected to sexuality? Rather than finding the seductress appealing, our teens should be longing for the person who has a gentle and quiet spirit. Instead of wanting to only gaze at exposed body parts, we want our teens to see beauty in relationship to the whole person. When true body-soul beauty is desired, then the ugliness of vacuous body-only pornography will be rejected. Point your teenagers to engage in what is truly beautiful in God's eyes.

Twisted relationships and intimacy

Relationships between young men and women are hard enough without the addition of a pornography problem. Teenage boys who are regularly viewing pornography cannot help but have a distorted view of teenage girls, and vice versa. Sexual activity will become more desired, as well as pressure to see nakedness that should be covered up. The increase of teenage girls viewing pornography makes this even more complicated. Evie, your 16-year old who regular watched pornographic video clips, has started to send nude pictures of herself to teenage guys she wants to date. How does this new 'sexting' practice impact dating relationships during the teenage years? Our teens who claim to want to follow Christ have to be shown how porn changes the way we handle our male-female relationships. Even if there is no sexual intimacy, a true godly relationship will be elusive where pornography is involved. The focus will be on the physical rather than emotional, mental, and spiritual intimacy.

As much as the use of pornography impacts present girl-guy relationships, how much more is future intimacy adversely affected? A severe porn addiction may keep a person from ever entering into real intimacy that can only be found in marriage. And, for the many teens who will get married one day, the influence of pornography will almost certainly make its way into the marital bed. Sexual intercourse may be disappointing, not living up to the fantasy-based expectations that were developed during the teen years. The sexual desire and practices of a future spouse will never imitate a porn star's sinful appetite that is observed online. So your teen must be challenged to recognize the harm he or she is doing to a potential future marriage. Too many teens expect marriage to quench the desire for pornography, which is typically not the case. Abstaining from the use of porn is a commitment to present purity in relationships, as well as a future purity in marriage.

Bondage and addiction

It is a sad reality that even our teenagers can become addicted to pornography. In days past, the difficulty in accessing porn kept many teens from being in bondage to it. Since teens, and even children, can now view a tremendous amount of even the most hardcore of porn quite easily, it stands to reason that addiction is becoming an ever-worsening problem. Doug, our 15-year old, has already been looking at pornographic images, videos, and websites for years. What was once an every few month's issue is now becoming a daily habit. Even though he is convicted by the Holy Spirit, Doug has seemingly lost the battle at this point. That's the power of sin in a heart that is prone to being controlled by idols. Pornography has a unique power to make itself dominate the heart and mind's desire, as it abuses our pleasures and affections. It is also a progressive sort of addiction, luring its captives into more extreme and extensive forms of pornography. Our teens must not take for granted the Satanic strength of porn that will become harder to resist as the bondage sets in.

Breaking the power of addiction begins with true conversion. If your teen is not a Christian, then bondage to sin—in this case the addiction to pornography—is natural and normal due to our sinful natures. If your teen is a Christian, then he or she is a new creation and has the indwelling of the Spirit in order to break the power of sin. As was discussed in the chapter on drugs and alcohol, there are many more Biblical principles that would be helpful to apply to an addiction to pornography. The teen needs to see that it is a spiritual and a brain-based problem. He or she must also learn about how it is a disordered worship. As with any addiction, porn improperly becomes the center-hub of life—dominating activities, relationships, choices, etc. The good news for teens like Doug is that he doesn't have to live in despair. As a teenager, the addiction is still in its infancy, relatively speaking. More importantly, God is faithful and powerful to smash our idols and give strength to be victorious over sinful desires. For the addicted teen, a big part of the counseling process must be accountability and relationship—and a commitment to fight!

Boredom and loneliness

For our teens like Doug and Evie, how much of their porn addiction is connected to simple boredom? Hopefully, you recognize that boredom is first a spiritual problem. It is truly a discontentedness of soul that rejects all of the good and positive activities that God has given us. So the answer to boredom in our teens is never simply to look for more things to keep them busy. Even those activities will potentially become boring when a heart attitude is apathetic. On the other hand, there is no doubt that too many of our teens have way too much time on their hands. Giving them an overabundance of free time—without productive work and study—is also a recipe for boredom. So it is essential to get a full accounting of how your teen is using his or her time on a regular basis. What activities should be added that would be healthy for your teen? At the same time, how must the teenager recognize the dissatisfaction that is present in his or her heart? Address the problem of boredom and seek Biblical solutions.

A close associate that often fuels both boredom and porn use is loneliness. Yet again, this is first a spiritual problem, not just a relational one. Your teen certainly may be devoid of relationships and existing very much alone in this life. What makes loneliness primarily a spiritual issue is that it is often associated with a passive view of life. 'I'm lonely because no one will befriend me.' 'I'm lonely because no one likes me.' Even though your lonely teen may think he or she is actively seeking friendships and relationships, this is typically not the case. Insecurity and anxiety of the heart is often present in our disconnected teens. So, again, pornography fills that loneliness 'hole,' even if it is pure fantasy and devoid of real relationship. Look for why your teen is lonely, and what can be done to deal with this problem—spiritually and relationally. Solving the problem of loneliness begins with intimacy with Christ, not with another person. As hard as it is for our teens to be alone, they must be encouraged to seek fulfillment in Christ, not in pornography which only produces more isolation.

Self-centered lust

As our sexuality is designed to be activated in marriage, it is also supposed to be expressed within the context of love. In other words, while sexual activity does bring a personal pleasure, it is intended by God to be used to show love to another person. That's why the apostle Paul speaks of our bodies belonging to our spouses in marriage, to seek to bring the other person pleasure, not just ourselves (1 Cor. 7:3-5). Unfortunately, the use of pornography is typically a solitary activity, used to bring self-focused sexual pleasure. And, it is built on the lust of the flesh, not a godly love for another person. Therefore, even if it is obvious, our teens who struggle with pornography need to recognize how self-centered they are being. What you will also find is that your teenager is probably abundantly self-focused in many of the other areas of life as well. In one sense, pornography belongs on the list of 'self problems' since it is such a self-indulgent practice. It also can powerfully shape the teen's view of self, introducing shame that is difficult to overcome.

Another aspect of the problem of pornography that must not be ignored is its connection to masturbation. While a teenager may be struggling with masturbation without also viewing pornography, it is virtually impossible to have a porn problem without a corresponding persistent habit of masturbation. Needless to say, it is the sole intention of the purveyors of pornography to use it to bring a person to sexual climax. So while it may be uncomfortable to talk with your teenager about masturbation, he or she needs to hear from you on the subject. While the world may see it as a normal, and even healthy activity in the life of our teens, it must be recognized as the sinful self-pleasuring that it is. God clearly intends for the coming to orgasm to be a part of our sexual intimacy with our spouse, not for our solitary pleasure. The problems of masturbation and pornography fuel each other, and thus must be defeated together. The heart's desire to satisfy self through masturbation is, by definition, a lust-filled activity. It is part of the sinful nature that must be killed off by the grace of God.

Put off, Put on

The problem of pornography is another good candidate for the 'put off, put on' process of Biblical change that we find in Ephesians 4. The apostle Paul writes that Christians have been taught 'to put off your old self, which belongs to your former manner of life and is corrupt through deceitful desires ...' (Eph. 4:22). The use and abuse of pornography is part of the old manner of life that must be put off and fully stopped. Of course, that is easier said than done. Yet, a good place to start is to examine when and how porn is being accessed. Is your teen only viewing it on his smartphone late at night? Then, he needs to turn in his phone to his parents before going to bed. Is the habit more widespread, including many different choices of media? Then, the teen should seek to discover ways to stop those activities as well. While this is standard behavior modification in some ways, real change cannot happen without a transformation of heart and a work of the Spirit. Teenagers will only persistently put off the old self and its 'deceitful desires' if they have fully learned of Christ (Eph. 4:21).

This process of Biblical change is never complete without the 'put on' component. Here is how Paul puts it: '... and to put on the new self, created after the likeness of God in true righteousness and holiness' (Eph. 4:24). If your teenager is a believer, he or she has been born again and is able to walk in righteousness and holiness. So the focus for your teen is not just on never viewing pornography again, but to seek to 'put on' holy and righteous activities in its place. Again, if your teen is viewing porn on his smartphone late at night, then what will he do instead when he stops that practice? What are some good late-night habits that can be promoted? The challenge is that porn can appear to be much more appealing than any righteous and holy activity that may replace it. Satan is working overtime in the mind of your teen to convince him or her that godly habits are boring habits. Yet, this is the very practical part of solving the problem of pornography. Help your teen discover positive activities, relationships, and disciplines that can replace a lifestyle of self-centered porn viewing.

Spiritual maturity

1 Corinthians 14:20 reads: 'Brothers, do not be children in your thinking. Be infants in evil, but in your thinking be mature.' Wouldn't it great if all of our teenagers were 'infants' when it comes to evil? When our children are not protected from the evils of pornography, they are being introduced to wickedness that is too mature for them. Even the world recognizes this at some level, as porn is described as 'adult content' or 'for mature audiences only.' Of course, the Christian adult has no business viewing pornography either; yet, our teens are certainly not mature in their thinking to be able to even process it correctly. Pornography will only keep them spiritually immature, more focused on feeding their sinful desires than growing in their passion for serving Jesus. Unfortunately, the viewing of pornography deceives a teenager into thinking that he or she is now much more of an adult. In reality, it is an immature and foolish activity that only creates a childish view of our sexuality.

While the world often depicts the teenage years as a time of utter foolishness, Christians challenge their teens to grow towards maturity in Christ. This does not mean that we don't expect and accept that teenagers will make a lot of foolish decisions. They need a lot of grace and mercy in their sinfulness, as well as rebuke and discipline. By the work of the Spirit, our teens can grow in Christ and begin to develop a heart of wisdom. Teens like Doug, Evie, and Freddy don't have to fear that they will be forever scarred or they cannot ever escape from the clutches of porn. Encouraging them to be faithful in the disciplines of grace—listening to the preaching of the Word, studying God's Word on their own, and developing a life of prayer—will grow them up in the Lord Jesus. Spiritual maturity is possible in our teens, but it will take the prayers and ministry of parents and youth ministry workers as well. Sanctification is a life-long process, which is promised to all of God's children, even those stuck in the sin of pornography.

A battle for the mind and heart

The epidemic of pornography in our culture is just one of the many ways Satan has targeted the minds and hearts of our teens. By twisting God's glorious creation of sex, our great enemy is deceiving generations of our youth like never before. So, recognize that this is a spiritual battle for your teen's soul, not just some sort of mental illness or sexual perversion to fix. Our teenagers must view this as spiritual warfare as well, so they will actively put on the armor of God (Eph. 6:10-18). They need the helmet of salvation to protect their minds from the seduction of pornography. They need the breastplate of righteousness to shield their hearts from being captivated by the 'writings of the prostitute.' As with all of the problems experienced by our teens, they present the opportunity for real heart change and the Spirit's renewal of the mind. The problem of pornography may seem insurmountable for many of our teens; yet, we must believe in the power of Christ to change even the stubbornest of heart problems.

Wisdom *POINTERS*

The following are some 'do's and don'ts' to help you remain gospel-centered and Biblically grounded when seeking to help teens struggling with pornography use and addiction:

- Do recognize that your teenager is a sexual being.
- Don't fail to show compassion for your teen's struggle.
- Do speak the truth in love about the destructive nature of pornography.
- Don't simplistically appeal just for behavior change.
- Do seek real heart change and spiritual maturity.
- Don't avoid topics of lust and masturbation.

- Do discuss how the problem of porn affects current and future relationships.
- Don't give your teen freedom that will only be exploited.
- Do talk about the spiritual problems of boredom and loneliness.
- Don't allow the teen to dwell in shame and self-pity.
- Do call the teen to deny self and die to self.
- Don't forget to proclaim the gospel of change in Jesus Christ.

13.
Premarital Sex

If you took a poll of random adults and asked them why teens having premarital sex is a problem, what would be the majority say? For those who actually see it as a problem, it would seem like its consequences would be the main issue—like a sexually transmitted disease or an unwanted pregnancy. If the consequences of premarital sex are the central concern, then the solution to premarital sex is easy: have sex, but use a condom or other birth control methods to avoid diseases and babies. But if there is an even greater and higher reason that premarital sex is a problem (such as, it goes against God's command), then a different solution has to be advanced. When we believe that God created us as sexual beings and gave us the gift of sex, then we are also called to follow His design and commands regarding our sexuality. Biblically counseling teens caught up in the sin of premarital sex moves us beyond just behavioral change, or the prevention of its consequences, to real heart and life change.

Opening PORTRAITS

- Gabby, a 16-year old, has been dating her boyfriend for four years. She claims to have not had sex yet, but the couple has done just about everything else. As a Christian, Gabby is committed to maintaining her virginity.

- Hal and Iris are teens in the church youth group. Several of their friends are concerned that they are too physical in their relationship. Since they are both convinced that they will marry each other one day, Hal and Iris have had intercourse a couple of times.

- Jerry, a 17-year old, is the most popular guy in the church youth group. He only dates a girl for a couple of months before moving on to the next one. To his closest friends, he talks about all of his 'conquests' on a regular basis.

Typical PROBLEMS

Teenagers who are engaging in premarital sex open themselves up to all sorts of consequences: mental, emotional, physical, spiritual, and relational ones. Some of those—such as depression, anxiety, anger, and substance abuse—are covered in other chapters. Others, like the problems of teenage pregnancy or sexually transmitted diseases, are beyond our current scope. Our focus will be on the two broad categories of premarital sex:

1. Premarital intercourse

Teenage premarital sex is any sexual activity between teenagers outside of marriage. Sexual intercourse occurs when there is penetration of the female vagina by the male penis.

2. Premarital outercourse

To avoid the consequences of sexual intercourse, teenagers may engage in various forms of sexual activity that doesn't include vaginal sex. Some examples of this sort of premarital sex include: mutual masturbation, genital massage, 'dry humping,' oral sex, and anal sex.

Evaluation PERSONALIZATION

If your teen is having any form of heterosexual premarital sex, there are several questions that need to be answered:

Overall patterns

1. When did your teen begin having premarital sex?
2. What sort of sexual activity is occurring?
3. How did you find out about the sexual activity?
4. Is the sexual activity occurring in a committed relationship or multiple 'hook ups?'

Physical factors

1. What is the current state of the teen's physical health?
2. Does your teen have a sexually transmitted disease?

Relational issues

1. What is the state of your teen's relationships?
2. What are your teen's dating habits?
3. Has your teenager been sexually abused or molested?

Media practices

1. What is the impact of social media in the teen's life?
2. What sort of entertainment media is being engaged in?
3. Is the teenager viewing pornography?
4. Is your teenager 'sexting?'

Marriage and family

1. Are there significant family problems that are contributing to the issue?
2. What is the teen's relationship with his or her mother? Father?
3. What is the general nature of parenting?
4. Does the teenager have too much freedom?

Relationship with God

1. What is the teen's basic understanding of God? Of sin?
2. What about his or her devotional life? Prayer and Bible study?

3. How does the teen describe his or her relationship to Jesus Christ?
4. What about the role of the Holy Spirit in spiritual maturity?
5. Is the teen rebelling against God?

Other related problems

1. Is the teenager rebelling in other ways?
2. What are the problems that are possibly connected?

Biblical *PRINCIPLES*

It's tempting for Christian parents and youth ministry workers to ignore the signs of teenage premarital sex. Often times, it can feel like a problem that is 'out there,' but not within 'our' Christian community. Even worse, it can be a subject that is rarely talked about in the family or the church, with almost a silent expectation that dating teenagers just need to handle the temptation to this sin all on their own. Yet, when we have a basic understanding of sinful hearts and teenage sexuality, it should lead us to be more suspicious and vigilant. Sometimes, a teenager will come to you admitting the sin of premarital sex, or the temptation to go in that direction. Other times, it is only caught by parents, or revealed by teenage pregnancy or a sexually transmitted disease. How much better it is to get involved early in the process, counseling your teen Biblically to navigate sexual desires and dating relationships. God's Word gives us clear principles to address this problem of the heart, mind, and body.

Teenage sexuality

As was discussed in the last chapter, recognizing our teenagers as sexual beings is often challenging. Parents can see their adolescents as still children, failing to understand their growing sexual desires and interests. Fewer and fewer parents are having the 'birds and the bees' talk' with their children early enough (or at all), allowing teens to learn about their sexuality from various media sources or peers.

Often times, the local church is mute on the subject as well, other than infrequent lessons on pornography or homosexuality. So, preventative conversations are required as part of the discipleship of our children—not just after sexual sin has occurred. Teenagers should not have to figure out their sexuality on their own or, great peril awaits. An approach that either ignores teens' sexual impulses, or just requires them to exert self-control until marriage without ongoing discipleship, will often be ineffective. Parents and youth ministry workers must not be afraid to talk about sex with their teens.

In that same vein, we must be cautious not to adopt the culture's view of teenage sexuality. In the entertainment media, teens are depicted simply as sexual animals with raging hormones that cannot be controlled. The 'beautiful' and 'popular' teenagers think about little else than sexual conquests or physical bodies. Losing one's virginity is celebrated and encouraged as a rite of passage for teens. The ideas of sexual purity and chastity are for bygone eras—totally unreasonable standards for a sexualized culture such as ours. While these messages are certainly reflective of some teens in our culture, they also seek to train other teenagers to think about themselves in these ways. So, we must be realistic in understanding the temptations, but refuse to accept the fatalistic view of teenage sexuality that is resident in the culture. Teenagers do not have to be slaves to their sexual impulses, nor come to believe that premarital sex is a glorious and coveted escapade. They need to learn God's view of sex, as well as Biblical principles to live in purity before marriage.

Honoring marriage

In days past, children were trained to know that certain activities and behaviors were solely reserved for adults. Grown-ups drink coffee, not children (as my grandfather always warned: 'It will stunt your growth'). Adults choose the menu; children eat what they are served. Adults drink alcohol; children cannot. Most of these distinctions have fallen by the wayside through the years, with some changes being more detrimental than others. The point is that children and teens are much more accustomed than ever before to engage in activities once reserved for adulthood. So, that may make it increasingly difficult to tell teenagers that sex is meant only for marriage. Much more often, they hear cultural messages like: 'Only engage in sex if you are truly in love.' Or, 'You need to experiment sexually so you know if you want to be with a certain partner for life.' Communicating that ALL types of sexual experiences (in addition to intercourse) should be relegated to marriage is even more difficult. While teens have always been tempted to act like adults long before chronological adulthood, it appears to be more acceptable than ever and less resisted by adults than in the past.

The writer to the Hebrews commands: 'Let marriage be held in honor among all, and let the marriage bed be undefiled, for God will judge the sexually immoral and adulterous' (Heb. 13:4). While the problem of extra-marital affairs often comes to mind when reading these words, they clearly pertain to premarital sex as well. If the 'marriage bed' represents the complete sexual experience between a husband and wife, then any other form is out of bounds. To keep the marriage bed 'undefiled,' one must first honor marriage! Marriage must be seen as the only intimate human relationship that rightly involves sexual activity. So, Christians wait to have sex with the opposite sex until marriage because God has made marriage honorable and glorious. As Paul writes in 1 Corinthians 7, 'But because of the temptation to sexual immorality, each man should have his own wife and each woman her own husband' (1 Cor. 7:2). Marriage is between one man and one woman, as the two become one flesh sexually—and emotionally, mentally, and relationally as well (Mark 10:8-9). Teenagers who truly revere marriage will also believe that premarital sex is not honorable or desirable.

Dating too early

Gabby, your 16-year old teenager, claims to not have had sexual intercourse with her boyfriend yet—even though they have done just about 'everything else.' She has been with her boyfriend for four years, so she has been allowed to date from at least the age of twelve. There are certainly many Christian parents who see no problem with teens (and even pre-teens) dating very early. The days of teenagers having to wait until their 'sweet sixteenth' birthday have become a thing of the past for many. Yet, common sense says that early dating practices only increase the chances that premarital sexual activity will occur—especially within the context of a singular long-term dating relationship. The very nature of modern dating encourages teenagers to become intensely emotionally intimate which easily spills over into physical intimacy. It seems like a pretty sizeable burden to ask young teens to handle the 'adult' nature of a committed relationship with the opposite sex, yet save any sexual activity for marriage.

While the debate between those who advocate for modern dating versus those who practice courtship or other varieties of dating practices is beyond the scope of this chapter, the subject will need to be addressed when premarital sex becomes involved. Should Gabby and her boyfriend be allowed to continue to date now that it has been exposed they are engaging in certain types of sexual activity? Or, do we encourage the relationship to continue, just instructing them to be more careful and not going any further sexually? Even if they were told to not date anymore because of the nature of the physical relationship, will the couple comply if they believe they are destined to marry? Whatever your stance on teenage dating is, allowing committed relationships too early will most likely open the door to premarital sexual activity. Encouraging teenagers to wisely wait to begin the process towards marriage may be difficult, but it will help prevent the unwanted sexual activity.

So, what can you do if, like in Gabby's case, a teenager has long been allowed to date from an early age? In some ways, it is too late to backtrack on the decision, since there is no such thing as a teenage time machine. Yet, your teen needs to think through what early dating has brought into in his or her life. As will be discussed further, even the 'everything else' outside of sexual intercourse is unacceptable and destructive. Beyond just the physical component, early dating will have taken a toll on your teen emotionally and spiritually. Rarely does it encourage growth in Christ, or the pursuit of maturity emotionally and relationally. So, Gabby may actually desire to take a break from dating to grow in her relationship with Christ. Clearly, it is much better to address this issue at age twelve than at age sixteen, when many other teens are already dating as well. But it is not out of the question for our Christian teens to contemplate waiting several more years to date again, to not only prevent further sexual activity, but to grow up in Christ.

The serious relationship

Hal and Iris are teens in your youth group who are demonstrably too 'physical' in public. When they are challenged, you find out that they have had sexual intercourse a couple of times already. Even though Hal and Iris are professing Christians, they rationalize that this behavior is acceptable because they are committed to being married one day. Their 'serious' relationship has given them the freedom to be fully, physically connected. When asked about their timeline of engagement and marriage, Hal and Iris haven't thought that far ahead yet, wanting to graduate from college at least. So, what do we do with this mindset? Similar to our dating too early problem, there are many teenage couples who have committed to each other too early, giving themselves to one another before marriage. They are acting married while not even being engaged! Sexual intimacy has been regarded as what happens when your heart is committed, whether or not there is an actual covenant of marriage.

This young couple certainly needs to learn to honor marriage above and beyond defining it as simply a serious relationship. They need to be taught about the covenant of marriage and how we become one flesh only when true covenant promises are exchanged before God. As professing believers, they need to know 1 Thessalonians 4:3-5 applies to them: 'For this is the will of God, your sanctification: that you abstain from sexual immorality; that each one of you know how to control his own body in holiness and honor, not in the passion of lust like the Gentiles who do not know God ...' They are being sexually immoral by God's standards, acting in the passion of lust, even if they are rationalizing it as solely based on their commitment to one another. As tough as it may be for the serious teenage couple, continued sexual activity must wait until marriage. Will that mean they need to marry early? Possibly. Or, maybe it will be wiser to end the relationship if they cannot stop the sexual activity. There should be no option given to simply continue having sex because they may get married one day.

The hook-up mentality

Then, there's Jerry, our 17-year old, who is committed to sexual conquests rather than serious relationships. While there have always been teenagers who simply want to have sex with as many people as possible, the 'hook-up mentality' has reached new heights in our culture. Fueled by social media, websites, and apps on smartphones, it is easier than ever to find other people who simply want to engage in sexual experimentation of any kind. Sometimes, like in Jerry's case, this behavior is disguised by weak attempts at dating relationships. Other times, it is a brazen hedonism, sought after by a teenager for simple lustful, personal pleasure. Either way, the consequences of sex with many partners is obvious—physically, emotional, mentally, relationally, and spiritually. This sort of teenage premarital sex is the most like the pagan world, detached from any real desire to please God with our bodies.

How do we counsel a teenager with this mentality and overall pattern of behavior? The first question which needs to be asked: Is he even a Christian? It is extremely difficult to rationalize how sexual conquest with various partners is compatible with a love for Jesus. So, Jerry probably needs to be converted in order for his sexual activity to change. Beyond that, he would need to embrace what God's Word says about sexual immorality. The apostle Paul writes: 'Or do you not know that the unrighteous will not inherit the kingdom of God? Do not be deceived: neither the sexually immoral, nor idolaters, nor adulterers, nor men who practice homosexuality, nor thieves, nor the greedy, nor drunkards, nor revilers, nor swindlers will inherit the kingdom of God' (1 Cor. 6:9-10). Jerry's lifestyle reveals an unrighteous heart that will keep him from the kingdom of God. True repentance, conversion, and sanctification must occur to be cleansed from this sin. Again, it is not right for unrepentant sexual immorality to be a part of the Christian life.

The problem of outercourse

Let's return to 16-year old Gabby and her boyfriend. They are committed to staying 'virgins,' yet are participating in what has become known today as 'outercourse.' As a play on the familiar word 'intercourse,' this cluster of sexual behaviors enables teens to ostensibly abstain from vaginal sex. Gabby and her boyfriend may be engaging in oral or anal sex, mutual masturbation, genital massage, prolonged sexualized kissing, or other sexualized activities. So, while this couple may be considered 'technical virgins,' does that mean their behavior is God-glorifying and acceptable as followers of Christ? Not only are they engaging in sexual sin, Gabby and her boyfriend are deceiving themselves if they think they will not have sexual intercourse at some point in the process. Using these outercourse activities will inevitably increase their sexual desire for each other, not reduce or prevent it. It will only take one small mistake to move from outercourse to intercourse, as passions are enflamed and fanned. These highly sexualized activities are sinful in and of themselves because these teens are abusing each other's bodies for their own sexual pleasure outside of marriage.

The classic question for teenagers has always been: How far is too far? Depending on which Christian you talk to, there are many different opinions on the subject. Some would argue that teens who are dating shouldn't even kiss until engagement or marriage. Others draw the line more on avoiding contact with 'private parts.' While there are no hard and fast rules given to us in Scripture, there are clearly activities that are much too far for teenagers, including oral and anal sex. A teen like Gabby needs solid Biblical counseling to talk through the particular behaviors and their consequences. What's fueling the desire to go as far as possible without sexual intercourse? If they are followers of Christ, what's going on in their consciences? Do they really believe that the choices of outercourse activities is God-glorifying and keeping them pure? This is a place where we want to see our teens pursuing hearts of wisdom, rather than seeking their own personal passions. Rather than simply handing out rules and limits, Christian teens need to mature in their view of sex and dating relationships.

Privacy and privilege

Often times, one of the contributing factors to the problem of premarital sex is the privacy afforded many of our teenagers. Obviously, sexual activity typically occurs in private, so teenage couples who desire to sin in this way will seek to be alone as much as possible. In most Christian circles today, the idea of a chaperone for dating teenagers is archaic, invasive, and nearly impossible. But because of the ease of teens to find places and situations to be alone, are we affording them too much freedom? This is compounded by the unhealthy privacy a personal smartphone gives to our teens. With this technology, they can hide conversations, plans, and online habits more readily than in the past. So along with this era of privacy and solitariness, are we teaching our teens responsible actions and attitudes? Unfortunately, this is not usually the case. Teens are often left to themselves at home too much (with both parents working), or given opportunity to be alone with the opposite sex in other places as well. Again, there may be nothing new here, yet it is a variable to the problem that must be addressed.

Accordingly, teenagers can be given too many privileges too early, including during the pre-teen years. Our changing technology has made a smartphone a required instrument in the hand of teenagers. When teens are of the age to be a licensed driver, many are given the privilege of owning their own car. Teenagers can also be given too much money to spend in whatever ways they desire. These, and many other privileges, are often not tethered to responsibility and maturity—but simply become a right of adolescence. So, a sense of entitlement can fuel a desire to experiment sexually, thereby allowing a teenager to act more like an adult. As will be discussed further, too many privileges granted by parents can mask over the bigger problem: parents who are simply not involved in a teenager's life. How much freedom can be given teens that will only end up enabling them to engage in risky, sexual behavior? When counseling your teen, make sure to challenge his or her desire to be private and privileged, and how that opens the door to wrong behavior.

Heart and mind

It is tempting to make the problem of teenage premarital sex into only a behavioral problem—with the solution being no teenage sex. But, as with all problems, it is essential to dig down deep into the heart of the matter. What is at the root of the particular sexual activity? In Jerry's case, his behavior may simply be coming from a rebellious heart. Fueled by sinful pride, he wants to be the king of his own universe. Yet, for other teens, the behavior may be founded on many other heart issues: anxiety, anger, self-pity, shame, etc. Gabby may have a heart of fear that she won't be loved unless she gives her body away to her boyfriend. Hal and Iris could be idolizing their relationship—worshiping each other rather than God. Many teenagers seek to find their identity in relationships with the opposite sex, falling into the sin of premarital sex as a consequence. As much as we want the behavior to change, it gives an opportunity to expose the teenager's heart. We should always seek heart change as the ultimate goal, rather than to just get rid of the sinful behavior.

Accordingly, sexual sin is connected to a mind that needs to be renewed. In the world's eyes, teenagers barely have a brain, since they are considered to be merely motivated by animal impulses. The reality is that Satan is fighting for our teen's hearts as well as their minds. As the great Deceiver, he is filling their minds with lies about themselves, sex, and relationships. So what is your teen thinking when it comes to his or her sexuality? Does Jerry believe he can't help himself, since he is such a sexual god? Does Gabby believe she is safe and secure in this relationship, creating the need for sexual expression? Do Hal and Iris both think that their sexual activity won't have any real bearing on their future marriage, if they marry one another? It's essential to challenge the belief systems and thought patterns of your teen. You may discover that he or she is not thinking in rational or truthful ways. When the mind doesn't change, behavior won't ultimately change either—at least in a consistent way.

The Temple of the Holy Spirit

Even though it is essential to get to your teen's heart, he or she must recognize that this is still a very serious body problem. To the church at Corinth, Paul writes:

> Flee from sexual immorality. Every other sin a person commits is outside the body, but the sexually immoral person sins against his own body. Or do you not know that your body is a temple of the Holy Spirit within you, whom you have from God? You are not your own, for you were bought with a price. So glorify God in your body (1 Cor. 6:18-20).

There are several applicable truths here for our teens. First, sexual immorality is a sin against a person's own body. God has given us bodies to care for properly and use for His glory, not for our own sinful pleasure. When there is sexual sin between two teenagers, then two created bodies are being violated! Second, the body was created as a home for the Holy Spirit. In our sin, we think our bodies are our own, to do with whatever we please. But as Christians, our teens need to recognize that their bodies are meant to be a place of worship for the Holy Spirit! Even though it is hard to get our heads around this truth, the Holy Spirit resides in us! The third fact is: God is to be glorified by everything the body does. So, to allow our bodies to participate in sexual sin is glorifying self, not God. Your teen needs to embrace the fact that his body is not his own.

Paul makes the solution to the problem of teenage premarital sex abundantly clear: Run from it! Don't just walk away. Flee! Sexual sin has a way of drawing us in, like a huge electro-magnet. If we dabble in it just a little, it becomes more and more addicting, and even 'natural.' Where God's Word says that sexual immorality is a sin against our own bodies, the world and the devil tell our teenagers the exact opposite. How can something that feels so good be labeled as bad? That's just those old Victorian-era Christians who are trying to make you feel guilty! But, again, we bring teenagers back to the fact that, if they belong to Christ, their bodies are not their own. Gabby, Jerry, Iris, and Hal are not allowed to offer their bodies to someone else who is not their spouse. They are not free to use their bodies in any way they choose. If the Holy Spirit is in His temple, they must worship Him alone—not self, or someone else. At the end of the day, you must exhort your teens to worship God with their bodies!

Parental involvement

If you are a parent of a teen who has just been discovered to be sexually active, it is certainly a time to grieve the loss of a certain amount of innocence. You may also feel guilt and shame for not preventing the sin in the first place, or for being naïve and unaware. Use this time to evaluate your level of involvement in the life of your teenager. He or she may be in rebellion against you and the Lord. Or, this may be a way to compensate for the love not felt from mom or dad. Again, it could simply have occurred because of too much freedom and privilege. It should go without saying that a teenager needs parents to be deeply involved in his or her relationships with the opposite sex. Yet, it often appears that too many teenagers are left alone to navigate this essential part of life. Teens need all the spiritual mentors in their lives for a whole host of issues; yet, they can never replace the Christian parent. If lack of involvement has contributed to the problem, then that is one area that a parent does have responsibility to change.

What should parental involvement look like? It will certainly vary from parent to parent. At the core of it, a parent must be emotionally and relationally available to his or her teen. Both mom and dad need to be able to speak to heart struggles and battle the lies that are underlying the sinful behavior. While it can be hard to show the same love and affection that you did when your teen was a toddler or a child, hugs, kisses, and parental warmth should never disappear. It's normal to allow your teenager to be free to make decisions and to begin to 'fly;' it is unacceptable to abandon the teen, leaving him to his own ways and desires. Parents must be parents, continuing to teach, train, discipline, and love. Your teen may act like he has it all figured out and doesn't need you anymore, but you know that's just not true. When teenagers engage in sexual sin, it demonstrates their training is not over, and they are not ready for life as a Christian adult. Teenagers need parents and youth ministry leaders who will speak the truth in love, and shepherd them through every relationship.

The grace of God

While some of your teenagers may have plunged headlong into sexual rebellion, there are many others who have just made a mistake, or series of mistakes. They have mistakenly crossed a boundary they knew they shouldn't, and now feel great guilt and shame. In either case—rebellion or mistake—our teens need to be shown the grace of God for their sin. Unfortunately, some may face the consequences of unwanted pregnancy, sexually transmitted disease, or emotional scarring from the relationship. Yet, all can enjoy the grace, mercy, and forgiveness of God as they confess and turn from their sins. Our teenagers who have committed sexual sin don't have to walk around with a scarlet letter on their chests. Their sin can be washed by the blood of the Lamb. As destructive as premarital sex is, the grace of God is powerful to save and restore. Don't allow your teen to believe lies about their future, as if this sin has ruined their lives. What a great opportunity to communicate grace and mercy, and to point them to their Savior! It may be a hard path moving forward from sexual sin; yet, it is a glorious road when teens are walking it with Jesus, and with other believers who truly love them in Christ.

Wisdom POINTERS

The following are some 'do's and don'ts' to help you remain gospel-centered and Biblically grounded when your teens have fallen into sexual sin:

- Do recognize that your teenager is a sexual being.
- Don't fail to show compassion for your teen's struggle.
- Do speak the truth in love about sexual immorality.
- Don't simplistically appeal just for behavior change.
- Do seek real heart and mind change.
- Don't enable teens to date too early/get involved emotionally too early.
- Do discuss how sexual immorality impacts current and future relationships.
- Don't give your teen freedom that will only be exploited.
- Do talk about the body as the temple of the Holy Spirit.
- Don't allow the teen to dwell in guilt and shame.
- Do call the teen to renounce worldly passions and desires.
- Don't forget to proclaim the gospel of change in Jesus Christ.

14.
Rebellion

The teenage rebel has long been somewhat of a romantic icon in American lore, unless, of course, it is your teenager who is doing the rebelling. Rules, laws, and standards of morality can be so constraining to teens—just begging to be broken, ignored, and gleefully violated. Even in a time where it can be argued that teens enjoy excessive freedom and the widest of boundaries, teenage rebellion still exists and thrives. Those raised in Christian homes may have more to rebel against, even though they too can be indulged more than teens in the past. When we recognize that rebellion is a heart problem that has always existed, it makes more sense why even increased liberty will not do much to eradicate teenage rebellion. Add to that truth the encouragement from the world and the devil, and we have a real problem that must be solved. Teenage rebellion is not something to ignore, hoping youth will just grow out of at some point. The problem will either worsen—or go underground—only to manifest again later in life.

Opening PORTRAITS

- Kyle, a 16-year old, refuses to go to church with his family. The most he will do is wait in the car until church is over. He has been suspended from school several times for different stunts, including bullying freshmen.

- Larry, a 17-year old, stays in his bedroom most of the time, listening to heavy metal music and playing video games. He is barely passing school, even though he is very intelligent. His parents hope that this is just a phase.
- 16-year old Meri wakes up with a bad attitude almost every day. She is either sullen or in a rage—very little in between. She is just biding her time until her eighteenth birthday, so she can get away from her boring small town, and its narrow-minded citizens.

Typical PROBLEMS

Rebellion is any opposition to a person or system in authority. As the rules, laws, and standards multiply, so do the opportunities to rebel. Some teenage rebellion is more overt and obvious, while others are more subtle and hidden. There are three general categories of teenage rebellion that deserve our attention:

1. Rebellion against authority

A refusal to submit to authority is the textbook definition of rebellion. This type of rebellion is most often manifested towards parents; yet, it may occur against any person in authority. Also included is any resistance to and non-compliance of established laws, rules, and standards of morality.

2. Rebellion against society

A second type of teenage rebellion is against the norms or mores of society. Teenagers may dress differently, groom in abnormal ways, or behave in ways that are not considered typical. In a rapidly changing culture, it can be challenging to recognize what is actual rebellion. Most often, the rebellion against society will be accompanied by a rebellious attitude towards much that is considered normal.

3. Rebellious experimentation

A third category of teenage rebellion includes all types of experimentation, including drugs and alcohol, sexual activity, and other risky behavior. These rebellious actions can also be considered rebellion against authority or society. Some experimentation may be considered normal; but most often, it emanates from a rebellious heart.

Evaluation PERSONALIZATION

If your teen is rebelling against authority or social norms, there are several questions that need to be answered:

Overall patterns

1. How is the teen rebelling against authority?
2. How is the teen rebelling against societal norms?
3. Is the teen experimenting with illegal substances?
4. Is the teen engaging in other types of risky behavior?
5. Has the teen broken any laws?

Physical factors

1. What is the current state of the teen's physical health?
2. Does the teen have any physical disabilities?
3. Is a medical examination required?

Relational issues

1. What is the state of your teen's relationships?
2. What are your teen's dating habits?
3. Are the teenager's friends rebelling too?

Media practices

1. What is the impact of social media in the teen's life?
2. What sort of entertainment media is being engaged in?
3. Is the teenager viewing pornography?

4. What 'education' is the teen gaining from news and information media?

Marriage and family

1. Are there significant family problems that are contributing to the issue?
2. What is the teen's relationship with his or her mother? Father?
3. What is the general nature of parenting?
4. Does the teenager have too much freedom?
5. What are the rules that are being broken?

Relationship with God

1. What is the teen's basic understanding of God? Of sin?
2. What about his or her devotional life? Prayer and Bible study?
3. How does the teen describe his or her relationship to Jesus Christ?
4. What about the role of the Holy Spirit in spiritual maturity?
5. How is the teen rebelling against God?

Other related problems

1. Is the teenager anxious, angry, or depressed?
2. Are there any legal problems that need to be resolved?
3. What are the problems that are possibly connected?

Biblical PRINCIPLES

Is teenage rebellion just a normal part of human development? Is it inevitable that all human beings will rebel at some point during the teenage years? There are those who would give a resounding 'yes' to these fundamental questions. When one begins with the belief that the human being is basically good, then what Christians call rebellion is deemed to be good as well. After all, it is reasoned, a child is learning how to be an adult—which means he or she has to begin to think and act independently of authority. Sometimes, that will include some type of overt rebellion, especially if the rules and laws are too binding and constricting. So, does this wisdom originate from Scripture, or from somewhere else? While we may sympathize with the teenage rebel, God's Word brings a radically different perspective on the matter. And if we are determined to offer Biblical counseling on the issue of rebellion, we must be grounded in essential Biblical principles on the matter.

We are all rebels

While it is tempting to view much of humanity as good people who just make mistakes from time to time, God's Word paints a different picture. Adam and Even did not mistakenly eat the forbidden fruit; they purposefully rebelled against God's clear command (Gen. 3:6). God did not treat them as innocent victims of the devil's schemes, but lawbreakers who were fully accountable for their sin (Gen. 3:16-19). After the entrance of sin into this world, all people are now born sinners, with the desire and mindset to rebel against God and His ways. 'As it is written: "None is righteous, no, not one; no one understands; no one seeks for God"' (Rom. 3:10-11). Teenagers rebel because they have rebellious hearts. They are not anomalies among a planet full of good, decent, moral people. This truth may not be comforting, but it is essential when we are addressing the problem of rebellion. Unless God's saving grace intervenes, every child will rebel well into his or her teenage years. As the apostle John writes: 'Whoever makes a practice of sinning is of the devil, for the devil has been sinning from the beginning ...' (1 John 3:8a). Rebellion is truly a historic, universal problem.

So, from the outset, your counseling must be grounded in a right understanding of sin. Teenagers sin because they are born sinners. They rebel because they are rebels. If we are surprised that teenagers rebel it may be because we don't hold a Biblical view of sin. Or, maybe we are willing to accept that teenagers from non-Christian homes or who have 'bad' parents may rebel, but not our own 'good' teenagers.

While it certainly may shock us to discover our teens participating in certain rebellious activities, the reality check is that rebellion is in their spiritual DNA. This does not excuse teenage rebellion or somehow make it acceptable in God's sight. The Biblical truth is that all human beings deserve death at the hands of a holy God since they are a rebel force against God. But the good news is: 'For if while we were enemies we were reconciled to God by the death of his Son, much more, now that we are reconciled, shall we be saved by his life' (Rom. 5:10). The first and only solution to teenage rebellion is to be reconciled to God through Jesus Christ!

Not all teens rebel

If all human beings are born into this world in rebellion against God, does that mean all teenagers will rebel? Not necessarily. All teenagers certainly have the ability to engage in acts of rebellion, given the right (or, wrong) opportunity. Yet, this doesn't mean that all teenagers will rebel against God, parents, or society at some point from age 13 to age 19. To believe that all teenagers naturally rebel is not the same as the belief that we are all born sinners. As was discussed earlier, what is typically proposed is that teenage rebellion is simply a part of healthy human development. The thinking is that to actually move from childhood to adult in a productive manner, one must engage in rebellious activities and have rebellious attitudes. Rebellion as a universal teenage 'rite of passage' actually removes the truth of rebellion as emerging from sin. Holding this view will only make a parent or youth ministry worker applaud and encourage teenage rebellion rather than work to solve it.

The corollary to the belief that all teens naturally rebel is the view that those who don't rebel will develop some sort of mental or emotional problems. Teenagers who are law-keepers or have some level of moral integrity are suspected of not being 'real' or able to express their true identities. While it is certainly true that teenagers who are simply self-righteous or pridefully moralistic also have problems—and are even operating from a rebellious heart—it is a lie that a holy life is somehow defective. People who don't rebel in significant ways during their teenage years may end up rebelling later as adults. And, teenagers who seem outwardly pure and virtuous may be covering up some deep heart rebellion. Yet those truths do not mean it is undesirable or foolish for teenagers to not rebel. Parents should be wildly excited when their young people make it through the teenage years without significant rebellion. But if teenage rebellion does occur, it should be treated as a problem to be solved—an opportunity for Biblical change to happen.

The problem of God's Law

The apostle Paul writes: 'What then shall we say? That the law is sin? By no means! Yet if it had not been for the law, I would not have known sin. For I would not have known what it is to covet if the law had not said, "You shall not covet"' (Rom. 7:7). To the rebellious teen, God's law is the problem. If it weren't for all those rules, life would be free and easy. But the truth is that the law of God is perfect and holy. As Paul states, we human beings would never know we are sinning if it wasn't for God and His law. He continues: 'But sin, seizing an opportunity through the commandment, produced in me all kinds of covetousness. For apart from the law, sin lies dead' (Rom. 7:8). So in one sense, God's law is the problem. It does expose our sinfulness and heart rebellion. But again, our teen must be reminded that the law is not sin; in other words, it is not the real problem that must be eliminated. We need God's law so we will turn to the only one who can save us from our sin.

So, why does Kyle, our 16-year old, refuse to go to church with his family? When you ask him, he first talks about being angry that his parents left their old church (where all his friends worshiped). Then, he shares that the sermons are boring and that they don't do anything for him anymore. Kyle has read the entire Bible already, and has it all figured out. So while there are several important issues to address in Kyle's life, he is clearly rebelling against God's law. He is refusing to worship God and live in community with God's people. He is self-deceived to think he knows the Bible and is living by its truth. Kyle needs to be helped to see how much disdain he really has for God's law. His misbehavior at school and his bullying of other teens just confirm that he is not conforming to God's law. If he is blaming God's law for his rebellion, then he doesn't recognize its purity and holiness.

Ultimately, we want our teen rebels to not just go from hating God's law to simply accepting it as pure and holy. Our goal for them is to actually love God's law. The psalmist gives our teens the right example: 'Oh how I love your law! It is my meditation all the day' (Ps. 119:97). 'Let your mercy come to me, that I may live; for your law is my delight' (Ps. 119:77). 'If your law had not been my delight, I would have perished in my affliction' (Ps. 119:92). Are these just mere sentiments out of the reach of our modern teens, or heart realities that are possible by the work of the Spirit? While it may seem a distant dream when a teenager is in the midst of some deep rebellion, it should still be the ultimate objective. Having this sort of love and delight is not just a matter of trying harder to obey the law, but seeing the glory and goodness of the law-giver Himself. In the end, we want our rebellious teens to imbibe this truth: 'Blessed are those whose way is blameless, who walk in the law of the Lord' (Ps. 119:1).

The problem of parental strictness

If the law of God shows us our sin as well as the holiness of God, what role does the system of rules of particular parents play in teenage rebellion? There have always been those who suggest that parents who are overly strict in their rules and discipline can cause or contribute to rebellious activity. It is common sense to suppose that parents who exert some level of a totalitarian regime upon their children may provoke the production of little rebels. This certainly can be the case when parents have not shifted from the tighter control required in raising younger children, to the training of teens required for healthy decision-making and critical thinking. If one or both parents appear to be treating their teenager as a young child, refusing to give basic freedoms, or being restrictive in a way that is beyond even the law of God, then rebellion may result. In some cases, this may be pretty obvious; in others, it is not as plain. Either way, a good assessment of parental rules and discipline will be important in the process of responding to instances of rebellion.

Yet, any thought that teenagers are not to blame for rebelling against their strict parent's rules must be rejected. While you may understand how hard it is to obey rules that appear far too restrictive or without real justification, disobeying parents is always wrong (Eph. 6:1). Biblical counseling of the teenage rebel always sounds like: 'Yes, I understand that rule or standard doesn't seem fair, but God commands you to obey.' This includes all human authorities—as in the case of Kyle—who continues to be suspended from school because he thinks the rules are stupid. Obedience doesn't begin with an assessment of whether or not a rule is fair or right. In other words, even if the teenager has a clear case of being treated unjustly by his parents, he is still responsible to God to obey with all his heart. No finger can truly be pointed at a parent for causing a rebellious response, even if it is agreed that the rules are too strict. It may be wise for parents to get counsel on how to make changes in their parenting style and their rule structure; but this is not the ultimate solution to teenage rebellion. Teenagers must own the fact that, regardless of the perception of reality of unjust rules, their obedience is required.

The problem of parental passivity

Let's consider the case of Larry, our 17-year old who has turned his bedroom into his own personal condo. He is not only wasting his mind and life on useless pursuits, but he is teetering on the brink of not graduating from high school. As mentioned already, it is tempting for parents to see this as just a natural stage or phase through which all teens must go. Larry's parents seem to be passively hoping that their son will just grow out of this rebellious stage. There is no doubt that many teenagers do learn from their rebellious ways, and mature into law-abiding young adults. But, 'crossing our fingers, hoping for the best' is not the responsible approach to parenting teens. Larry needs a mom and dad who will challenge his choices and behaviors. He needs parents who will call him to a better standard of living. He may not want lectures or criticism, but he certainly doesn't need passivity. In a case like this, parents must do the hard and exhausting work of Biblical confrontation and loving rebuke. Larry, and teens like him, still need discipline—even though he is nearly out of the home. Banking on just outgrowing these behaviors is foolish and irresponsible.

Often times teenagers are rebelling partly because they are longing for the love and attention of their parents. That may sound overly simplistic, but even teenagers can behave in ways simply to get attention—even if it is purely negative attention. Extreme forms of rebellious activities certainly have a way of mobilizing parents to get involved! And, even teens who simply wall-off parents and other loved ones are really wanting someone to take the time and have the courage to break down those barriers. A hands-off, passive parenting approach may seem loving, but it actually screams apathy and rejection. There is no doubt that many parents feel pushed away and rejected by their rebellious teen. Yet, the love of Christ should compel parents to pursue and move towards their teens, not away from them. There are certainly times where it is wise to step back and allow the Holy Spirit to work on the heart of the rebellious teen. Yet, parents as well as youth ministry workers should never communicate a willingness to passively abandon a teenager, and leave him to himself.

Conformity vs. Individuality

Your teen may be rebelling against the real or perceived expectations of society. Often times, this is manifested in style of dress, grooming habits, and entertainment choices. In days past, the classic teenage rebel was the one refusing to conform to everyone else, swimming against the mainstream—standing out as an individual. Your teenager may refuse to be like his or her other siblings, or the family lifestyle in general. He or she may want to stand out in the youth group, pushing against 'prudish' Christian teens. Or, the rebellion may be against society at large, rejecting political, social, or cultural norms. Whatever the case, the desire to be 'different' is fueled by a number of self-issues that have been discussed in a previous chapter. It may be simple pride and the desire to live in a self-exalting way. It may be a deep sense of insecurity, combined with the need to be a people-pleaser, in a distorted way. Whether driven by arrogance or self-pity, anger or anxiety, the non-conforming teen must be challenged to look at motivations of the heart. The question of 'why' must also be followed by an investigation into what the teen is gaining through this quest for individuality.

The central problem of this type of rebellion is that the teenager typically ends up conforming to the world's standards rather than God's standards. How many of our teens see all the sinful behavior around them and decide to 'rebel' by becoming more righteous and pure? How many are growing up in a pagan home and choose to go against the tide by living for Jesus? Thankfully, there are some out there. Yet, if you are leading a youth group or are a Christian parent, you will more likely observe teenagers replacing what is godly with what is ungodly. They need to hear and obey the words of the apostle Paul: 'Do not be conformed to this world, but be transformed by the renewal of your mind, that by testing you may discern what is the will of God, what is good and acceptable and perfect' (Rom. 12:2). The longing for non-conformity should never end up in the refusal to conform to God's standards. Any sense of individuality must be connected to who I am in Christ, not who I am on my own. Re-direct the desire to be different to the activity of not conforming to the ways of this world. Rebelling against the worldly culture and our own sin results in conforming to Christ!

Rebellious experimentation

What if the teenager is rebelling by experimenting with drugs, alcohol, smoking, or other types of dangerous behavior? The problem of drug and alcohol use has been covered in a previous chapter. But the question to answer here is: From where does the desire to try forbidden things come? When the question is put that way, it is natural to think back to our first parents, Adam and Eve. Their decision to eat of the fruit of the tree of the knowledge of good and evil originated with the desire to have open eyes and to be like God (Gen. 3:5). So, ultimately, they were seeking a higher knowledge, apart from conformity to the will of God. Is this the case with our teenagers who are experimenting with unlawful things? Certainly, they are seeking knowledge and experiences that are often 'above their pay-grade.' Rebellious teens often want to be adults when they are not ready for adult responsibilities, nor able to properly process adult experiences. Helping a teenager understand the prideful lust for knowledge and experience in order to be God-like (rather than godly) must be an essential part of your counsel.

Rebellious experimentation of a laundry list of dangerous substances or activities are also fueled by the longing for risk-taking. So, again, what is at the heart of extreme, risky behavior? For one thing, 'safe' can be perceived to be boring. Satan can tempt our teens to participate in sinful, risky activities by convincing them that they are the source of real life. In the extreme, teens can become addicted to the 'rush' of risky behavior, believing that anything normal is life-destroying. While it is thrilling to do something dangerous and live to talk about it, there is no room for risky behavior that goes against God's Word. It's one thing for your teen to attempt skydiving or bull-riding; it is quite another to put illegal substances in their body to experience their effects. Doing sinfully dangerous things in this life will not lead to the abundant life, and could even lead to the teenager's demise. Talking through the heart idol of risk-taking is a must when your teen is stuck in chronic experimentation.

Behavior change

When a teenager is caught up in rebellious activities, it is normal for parents and youth ministry workers to demand a change of behavior. Typically, the focus is on stopping bad behaviors, and avoiding situations and friends that only encourage those wrong behaviors. While Larry's habit of listening to heavy metal music and playing violent video games may not necessarily be sinful behaviors, they are contributing to his rebellion against school and healthy educational endeavors. So, in this instance, do we require Larry to change radio stations and give up his gaming lifestyle? Possibly. But, what behaviors will replace the ones which are associated with an overall rebellious attitude? And, what if Larry just changes behaviors while his parents are watching, going 'underground' with the activities he still desires. Outward conformity without heart change will only last so long.

Yet, when the rebellious behaviors are clearly sinful, unhealthy, and destructive, they must be changed. Kyle must stop bullying younger teens and participating in the other unlawful 'stunts' he is performing at school. Even if there is no heart desire to be righteous, the law demands that we obey—or pay the consequences. Parents and youth ministry workers must not be afraid to counsel the rebellious teen to 'stop it.' This will not be the end of the counseling; but it may be the beginning. Strict accountability may be necessary to ensure that the teen has stopped the rebellious behavior, at least for a time. To be clear, basic behavior change is not the ultimate goal of teenage rebellion, but that does not mean it should not be expected. Future right behaviors must be encouraged, to replace the present rebellious behaviors. Most likely, your teenager will find it very difficult to stop the behaviors, especially if they have become habitual. That eventuality will allow you to teach a reliance on the work or Christ to change stubborn, rebellious behaviors.

The bad attitude

As much as your rebellious teenager needs a change of behavior, an attitude change is also required. Sixteen-year old Meri seems to have a bad attitude almost every day. She vacillates between overt rage and self-pitying sullenness, with very little in between. Clearly, a better attitude would make her parents happy, and probably change the entire atmosphere of the home. So, what exactly is an attitude? An attitude is a settled way of thinking about something or someone. Meri seems to have the attitude that she is better than the citizens of her small town and their narrow, boring lives. This thought pattern of superiority keeps her from being relational—creating destructive, negative emotions. While there are many sources for unbiblical attitudes, they all surround a wrong view of self, God, and other people. Dwelling on thoughts of unfairness and injustice will also produce the attitude of a victim. Then, rebellious behaviors will proceed from those rebellious attitudes.

So, how do we help the teenagers to change that bad and rebellious attitude? By its very definition, an attitude is a settled way of thinking that doesn't just change by a parental command. The bad attitude will certainly provoke anger and frustration from parents and youth ministry workers alike. But turning that anger against the teenager's bad attitude will not be effective. Instead, out of godly compassion, we are to show our teens the futility of their thoughts. The lies they are believing must be challenged with the truth. Attitudes that do not glorify God have to be removed. Not conforming to the patterns of this world includes the renewal of the mind (Rom. 12:2). Only when the Holy Spirit transforms minds, and the teenager begins to believe the truth, will a bad attitude change to a positive one. It's not about just having a positive attitude or a happy disposition, but growing in a Christ-like pattern of thinking.

The heart of a prodigal

At this stage, Kyle, Larry, and Meri are still living at home, with some possibility to change from their rebellious ways. But what happens when a teenager follows the example of the prodigal son (Luke 15:11-32)? If a teenager has either left the family physically, or just emotionally and mentally, parents and youth ministry workers have a much bigger challenge on their hands. It will take great wisdom and discernment to respond to the teenager who is rejecting all parental authority—and ultimately, God's authority. The heart of a prodigal is one that is prepared to walk away from all that is right and true, that which is godly and virtuous. The Parable of the Prodigal Son points us to the truth that we may have to say goodbye to our teens as they walk down the road—grieving as they go. We will have to pray, and pray some more—waiting for them to return one day, after the Holy Spirit changes the heart. It's a tough place to be; but it is the sad reality of long-standing rebellion. The prodigal son essentially told his father to 'drop dead,' wanting only the benefits of independence without the responsibility. Just imagine how the father felt as his son lived out his rebellion!

But then, by God's grace, the rebellious prodigal returns. And how did the father respond? A fattened calf and the party of the century! Clearly, this parable is a picture of all of us rebels returning to a relationship with our heavenly Father. Yet, it also gives us a pattern for how to respond to our rebellious teens after they see their sins and repent. Unfortunately, depending on the situation, parents and youth ministry workers can be less than gracious, and even suspicious, of the penitent rebel. True repentance does require forgiveness and reconciliation, with the opportunity to live according to God's law (and parental rules) again. Yet, it should bring great joy to see real heart change, attitude transformation, and altered behavior. While rebellious behavior may happen again, the giving of grace, mercy, and forgiveness will be used by God to bring about future change, by God's grace alone. While some teens may become perpetual rebels against God, by faith we are to believe that God will soften hearts and restore your teen.

Wisdom POINTERS

The following are some 'do's and don'ts' to help you remain gospel-centered and Biblically grounded as you deal with teenage rebellion:

- Do recognize that your teenager is a rebel at heart.
- Don't believe that all teens naturally rebel.

- Do stand for the beauty and holiness of God's law.
- Don't communicate that strict rules cause rebellion.
- Do consider what rules or discipline need to change.
- Don't look for simple behavior change.
- Do encourage active parenting.
- Don't fail to recognize the desire to experiment.
- Do challenge the teen to conform to God's ways.
- Don't react out of anger towards bad attitudes.
- Do require necessary rejection of sinful behaviors.
- Don't forget to proclaim the gospel of change in Jesus Christ.

15.
Self-Harm and Cutting

One of the more difficult problems for parents and youth ministry workers to understand is when teenagers are purposely cutting themselves. Cutting is one type of problem included in the broader category of self-harm or self-injury. Why would any person deliberately do things to bring harm or pain to their own bodies? It seems to defy common sense, especially if we suppose that teenagers are much more likely to do things that bring pleasure and avoid pain. Acts of self-harm are often confused with suicide attempts, especially the habit of cutting. Teens who self-injure may or may not be suicidal, but an accidental suicide is always possible. Like many addictive sort of teenage problems, self-harm is typically very hidden and secretive. Because these types of behaviors seem so strange, adults can often either ignore the signs or fail to deal with the underlying heart issues. For the Christian, self-harm is more than a body problem—it is a soul-based problem that must be solved Biblically.

Opening PORTRAITS

- Nora, a 15-year old, always wears long sleeve shirts, even on hot summer days. One Sunday, she is caught cutting herself in the church bathroom. Nora claims to not be suicidal, and is embarrassed that her secret is now out in the open.

- Opal, a 16-year old, has been compulsively pulling out chunks of her hair for several years. She now has several bald spots that she covers up with large bows or strategically placed pony tails. Her parents are finally admitting that this is a problem.
- 17-year old Patrick enjoys inflicting pain on himself, especially when stressed out. He punches himself, burns himself with his father's cigarettes, or scratches himself until he bleeds. There are times he even rips or tears small sections of his skin.

Typical PROBLEMS

Unfortunately, there are many ways for teenagers to harm themselves. Some would put drug and alcohol use on this list, which certainly has some merit. Suicide is also certainly a type of self-injury, but will be covered as its own unique issue. Ultimately, the more typical self-harm problems are habitual, repetitive ways to bring controlled, physical pain to the body. The following are the most common problems:

1. Cutting

This habit is typically synonymous with self-harm. It involves making cuts or deep scratches to the body with any sharp object, typically knives or razor blades. The arms, legs, and the front of the torso are most often cut, since they are more easily hidden. Cutting is highly habit forming, and is typically practiced more often by young women.

2. Hair-pulling

Known as trichotillomania, the problem of hair-pulling is often considered as an issue of impulse control. Unable to control self, a person pulls hair from any part of the body, but especially from the scalp. Habitual hair-pulling leads to patchy bald spots, eventually requiring the teen to wear hats, scarves, and even wigs.

3. Skin picking

This behavior includes severely pinching or scratching the skin with fingernails to the point that bleeding occurs, and marks remain on the skin.

4. Impact with others or self

This type of self-harm includes either banging or punching objects or self to the point of severe bruising or bleeding. This group is seen more often in males.

5. Ripping, carving, or burning skin

Self-injury can also be accomplished by ripping the skin, carving words or symbols in the skin (beyond tattooing), or burning the skin with cigarettes or other heated objects.

Evaluation PERSONALIZATION

If your teen is involved in repetitive self-injurious behaviors, there are many questions that need to be answered:

Overall patterns

1. What sort of self-harm is the teen doing?
2. How long has the teen been injuring self?
3. Who knows about the self-injury?
4. Are there suicidal impulses involved?

Physical factors

1. What is the current state of the teen's physical health?
2. Does the teen have any physical disabilities?
3. Is a medical examination required?
4. What damage has the teen done to his or her body?

Relational issues

1. What is the state of your teen's friendships?

2. Is the teen being bullied in any way?
3. Is the teen dating or in a serious relationship?
4. Is the teen isolated or withdrawn?

Media practices

1. What is the impact of social media in the teen's life?
2. What sort of entertainment media is being engaged in?
3. Is the teenager viewing pornography?

Marriage and family

1. Are there significant family problems that are contributing to the issue?
2. What is the teen's relationship with his or her mother? Father?
3. What is the general nature of parenting?
4. Does the teenager have too much freedom?

Relationship with God

1. What is the teen's basic understanding of God? Of sin?
2. What about his or her devotional life? Prayer and Bible study?
3. How does the teen describe his or her relationship to Jesus Christ?
4. What about the role of the Holy Spirit in spiritual maturity?
5. Is the teen rebelling against God?

Other related problems

1. Is the teenager anxious, worried, or fearful?
2. Is there significant stress in the teen's life?
3. Is the teen angry or depressed?
4. Are there any more complex, psychiatric issues involved?
5. What other problems are possibly connected?

Biblical PRINCIPLES

The problem of self-harm illustrates the fact that sinful hearts and minds find all sorts of ways to sin against God, self, and others. Since God is the Creator of our bodies, we have a responsibility to be a good steward of our bodies, to His glory. Where the natural impulse is to nurture and care for self, our sin distorts and suppresses this desire. And, even though it may seem that activities of self-harm only harm self, other people are also harmed in the process. So, how does God's Word speak to our teens who are deliberately injuring themselves? There are no clear examples in the Bible of people cutting themselves. As with all other problems of the heart, mind, and soul, there are basic Biblical principles that apply and illuminate. We need to gain a better understanding of why teenagers want to harm themselves and how they can be freed from such destructive behaviors.

The problem of pain

When all things are working normally, God has equipped our bodies with vital pain receptors that communicate important information to our brains. What would happen if you put your hand on a hot stove and felt absolutely no pain? Your hand would stay in that position way too long, giving you third-degree burns, or much worse. So, we praise God when He gives us the ability to feel pain, as well as the immediate desire to respond in the healthiest of ways. We not only need to respond to pain in normal ways, but seeking to avoid painful things in the first place is normal as well. Therefore, when a teenager actually seeks to inflict pain on self, there is a problem—maybe a number of problems—to solve. Rather than responding to pain with the normal: 'Wow, that hurts. I don't ever want to experience that again,' the teen who is active in self-harm says, 'I want ... I need that pain in my life.' Pain has ceased to accomplish its God-given purpose.

Therefore, a place to begin with a 15-year old Nora is to talk to her about the God-designed purpose of pain. Her cutting of places on her arms and legs is not only painful, but only increases in pain as she re-injures the same area. Nora's body is telling her to stop, to quit the pain-filled activity; yet, her mind is overriding her body. So, at the heart level, any type of self-harm is rebellion against God's created order. It is telling God that I want pain, I need the pain in my life, even though pain is supposed to drive us to find ways to find and solve the source of pain. Subverting God's purpose will not only be physically detrimental, but there are spiritual consequences as well. How can Nora commune with Christ while cutting herself? How can she endure pain that is self-inflicted? Teens who are harming self are creating a life system that is only creating confusion and disorder. Again we ask: Why would our teenager choose pain rather than avoid it? What makes pain the better option?

To feel something

One possibility which should be investigated has to do with the emotional state of the teenager. When an individual is seeking pain—rather than avoiding it—the real disconnect might be on the emotional level. In other words, feeling pain is a way to 'feel something,' even if that something is negative and painful. When you talk to Nora, she is embarrassed about being discovered, but hardened and stoic in her emotions. Asking her how she feels about her cutting gets very little response. Her face is stony as she talks about her habit, even though she admits this is not a healthy behavior. This can be the case for many teens who are cutting, especially teenage girls. For a variety of reasons, they are either detached from their emotions, or are working overtime to suppress any difficult feelings. Again, cutting, or other self-harm activities, don't necessarily make a teen feel more—or even feel better—but, at least feel something.

Therefore, if your teenager is cutting in order to feel, you need to find out why difficult emotions are being avoided. Not all teens express their emotions in the same way; but the purposeful protection or suppression of emotions goes against God's design. Is there sadness and grief that is too hard to face? Or, is there is deep-seated anger that the teen is too scared to let out? Whatever the case, the teen may need to be convinced that it is good and normal to experience emotions. She may need to actually learn what it means to talk about those feelings in a healthy way. Cutting may give the illusion of provoking an emotional response, but it is really subverting normal emotional experience. In other words, if pain is the only way I can feel, then all my feelings will only be connected to pain! And that means pain will actually be the only experience that ends up making me feel happy. So, it is vital to discover what is keeping the teen from being free to experience and express a wide range of essential emotions.

From relief to pleasure

For 16-year old Opal, her compulsive hair-pulling brings her relief from much of the pain in her life. Her parents seem to always be fighting, she is miserable at school, and her friends don't give her much attention. Opal's self-harm allows her to escape from the difficult things she cannot solve. Just the process of choosing which hairs to pull, and the feeling of the tinge of pain followed by release takes her mind to another place. Now that her trichotillomania has become a long-standing habit, it would only bring more tension in her life if she did not pull her hair out. So, parents and youth ministry workers must pay attention to the painful situations that exist in the life of the teenager. Investigate relationships, family life, and everything that is afflicting the teen. While it is unhealthy to find relief in hair-pulling, or any other form of self-harm, it must be recognized how the teen has come to find it effective.

Unfortunately, there are also self-harming teens who move from mere relief to pleasure. In this way, self-harm becomes similar to masochism, but without the sexual element. Again, it is counterintuitive for inflicting pain to become pleasurable; yet our brains can conflate and confuse the experiences over time. In this way, self-harm literally becomes a 'fleshly' experience, with the seeking of pleasure becoming the priority. Our teenagers who are involved in self-harm would do well to dwell on Paul's words to the Galatians: 'For the one who sows to his own flesh will from the flesh reap corruption, but the one who sows to the Spirit will from the Spirit reap eternal life' (Gal. 6:8). We need to lead our teenagers to find relief and pleasure in the Spirit—and in the works of the Spirit, not in the flesh. By harming the flesh, they are acting in the flesh and not the Spirit. Peace and joy are the fruit of the Spirit; where simple relief and self-centered pleasure are works of the flesh.

Failing to cope with life

Whether your teen is cutting, pulling hair, scratching skin, or practicing any other sort of self-harm, he or she could be simply struggling with life itself. The teenage years can be normally stressful, and there may be additional stressors unique to your particular teen. Patrick, our 17-year old, inflicts various types of pain on himself when he is 'stressed out.' When asked, he shares that he feels a lot of pressure to perform in school, in football, and in life in general. He has always been hard on himself, refusing failure as an option. Digging deeper, Patrick admits that living with two very successful parents brings extra pressure into his life. A consistent culprit of many teen problems is the failure to handle the hard things of life. So, there is room for parents and youth ministry workers to empathize and show compassion for struggling teenagers. Living in a fallen world brings hardship from without and within—as well as the temptation to experiment with unhealthy ways to deal with affliction.

A related question is: Why do so many teenagers lack basic coping skills today? Coping is simply the effort and ability to deal with difficult situations in positive ways. This may be painting with a broad brush; yet it certainly appears that each successive generation finds it harder to cope with the typical problems of life. Are parents really doing the necessary training to enable their children to be resilient; or are they actually contributing to some of this fragility? Additionally, there is a higher calling for Christian parents and teenagers. Rather than just being stronger, tougher, and able to effectively cope, we must train our teens to be strong in the Lord. We want them to pursue hearts of wisdom so they can face the trials that will inevitably come their way. In order to put away self-injury behaviors, they will need to learn and embrace strategies that depend on the Lord's strength, not their own. What will often be found is that the teen who is harming self is extremely self-reliant—as well as very unteachable. Hopefully, when the self-harm is exposed, it will move the teen from humiliation to true humility.

Control and power

Another element potentially connected to the problem of self-harm is related to the struggle to cope with reality. When talking to Nora, you discover that she believes she has absolutely no control in her life. Everything is out of control—in her family life, in school, and within her relationships. Cutting has given her a feeling of control that she doesn't feel anywhere else. So, how does self-harm give a sense of control? Part of it is the secrecy, as the teen who is cutting has to be deceptive, covering up with clothing and excuses. Another control aspect is the cutting itself, as the teenager has to learn how much is not too much, where to cut and where not to cut. Similar to the control of a surgeon's hand, cutting has a meticulous and precise nature to it. Releasing just enough blood, or the right amount of pain, takes thought and effort. Finally, the control occurs in context to the risk to life that is involved. The teenager knows, at some level, that she is taking her life into her own hands. Especially over time, Nora will come to believe she has control of her life when she really doesn't.

So, we may need to talk to our teen about his or her need for control. What is so out of control in life that he or she is stooping for the control of self-harm? Relatedly, teens who are cutting often feel a sense of power in almost a God-like way. This is especially true when parents or friends or youth ministry workers are unable to stop a teen from cutting. In almost a threatening way, a teen can resort to self-harm to punish parents or friends. Holding the behavior over their heads ends up making them very powerful indeed. Do you recognize the heart problem here? The desire to be in control, to be all-powerful, has been in the human heart since the Fall of Adam and Eve. You should not be surprised when your teenagers seek ways to take control of their lives, especially if they feel powerless on their own. The solution is not to find healthy ways to obtain power and control, but to rest in the Almighty power and control of their faithful Father. The challenge will be to discover why your teen is not trusting in God's sovereign work in his or her life!

Trauma, neglect, or abuse

Whenever a teenager is engaged in behavior that endangers or abuses self, there is a possibility that he or she has been traumatized in some way. Pain inflicted by another can be transferred to pain inflicted by self. If there was physical or sexual abuse that was covered up or not dealt with well, self-harm can manifest as a sort of self-punishment. All sorts of abuse may bring any of a variety of destructive consequences into the life of a teenager. So, it is essential to check to see if there is any unconfessed trauma, abuse, or even early neglect. Emotional scarring can become symbolized and visualized with the physical scarring of cutting, tearing, or burning the skin. Deep-seated anger and resentment can be manifested in a willingness to harm self in the place of harming another. Trauma from the past can act as a bondage from which the teen is figuratively 'clawing' to become released. For young girls who are sexually abused, cutting continues the punishment they think they deserve.

If trauma, abuse, or neglect is present, it is essential to lovingly confront the victim mentality that is being perpetuated by the habit of self-harm. Compassion and empathy are certainly required when genuine abuse is discovered. But the impulse to continue to harm self after being hurt by another demonstrates a wrong view of self.

The good news of the gospel is that Christians who suffer harm do not have to hold onto an identity of victimhood. While painful and devastating, abuse doesn't have to have the final word in the life of a teenager. Because of the redemptive work of Christ, and the renewing power of the Spirit, old lives can become new again. So, even though the Satanic power of continued victimization is potent in the lives of many teens, it is no match for the perfect power of God. Again, this is in no way minimizing the ongoing effects of abuse or even extreme neglect. There are real consequences in the life of an abused teen that must be addressed. Yet, do not forget to proclaim the rescue of all who are hurting and in pain by our compassionate God!

Cycle of guilt and shame

If the teenager has suffered from past physical or sexual abuse, there is already guilt and shame that must be addressed. In other cases, a teenager may be guilty of a secret sin, or experiencing shame for something hidden as well. As was discussed in a previous chapter, both guilt and shame are co-conspirators in several typical teenage struggles, including self-harm. The problem becomes that cutting, or any other form of self-injury, creates a cycle of guilt and shame. Even if the teen isn't a Christian, self-harm is clearly not within the normal range of human behaviors. For those who are Christians, they will certainly experience true guilt over any self-harm, followed by shame when others discover it. So as much as the activity is in response to guilt and shame, it produces more guilt and shame. This is a cycle that is hard to break when it becomes central to the teen's view of self.

Now that Nora's cutting has been exposed, she is humiliated. Since she was caught at church, 'everyone' in the youth group is talking about her. So, while Nora should be ashamed of her sinful behavior, being rejected or shunned by her peers will bring more shame. When sin becomes a community experience, then it is vital that other Christian teens show Nora the compassion and love of Christ. Always remember that Biblical counseling is concerned with more than just the individual suffering, but the connecting relationships as well. While other teens cannot be forced to accept and love someone who is harming self, they must be trained to act as true followers of Christ. They must heed the call of the apostle Paul: 'If one member suffers, all suffer together; if one member is honored, all rejoice together' (1 Cor. 12:26). The cycle of guilt and shame will be more easily broken when there are supportive parents, family members, and Christian brothers and sisters. When self-harm comes out of the darkness, it should not force a teenager into the shadows, but into the light of the love of the Lord and His people.

Attention seeking

A problem that is intended to be hidden and secretive can also become a form of attention-seeking on the part of a teenager. Opal has desired a relationship with her father for a long time. Due to the busyness of his work and hobbies, Opal's dad has given her little attention throughout the teen years. If he is honest, he just doesn't know how to relate to a teenage girl, and all the emotional 'drama.' Opal's ongoing habit of hair-pulling always gets a response from her dad, when he actually notices it. Now, this doesn't necessarily mean that Opal is consciously harming herself just to get her dad's love and attention. Yet, teens who are not enjoying the time and connection with their parents can end up using negative behaviors to elicit attention. If Opal can recognize that her dad gives her more attention when she is doing 'bad' things, it will help her to resist the temptation. Opal's father also needs to be counseled to get more involved in her life—and not just to solve a problem in her life. This is another example of how all of the problems of our teens are opportunities for the hearts of parents to re-connect with their teenagers.

Teenage attention-seeking behavior isn't just limited to interaction with parents. Some teens who are cutting, scratching, or burning themselves may be looking for attention from their friends or peers. This is especially true if the teen has been doing other rebellious things to make a name for self in the community. Maybe Nora feels on the fringe of her youth group, so she is actually enjoying her newfound attention. Or, as is the case with Patrick, a popular teen may not want to be known for being righteous and good all the time. So, the same community that is needed to be supportive and helpful can be used by the self-harming teen to find a desired self-centric place. What is the wise way to handle a teen who is seeking attention? Not giving attention will probably just give more fuel to the problem, while more attention will possibly build pride and self-centeredness. The only way through this dilemma is to show the teen how his or her behavior is impacting the family and broader community, and challenge him or her to move beyond self. When the teen begins to see the impact on others, it can help the desire to self-harm be transformed into the activity of helping others.

The power of addiction

For all the reasons already discussed, self-harm can become a serious, and even life-threatening addiction. Since it appears to give emotional security and control, cutting ends up controlling the teenager. By their secrecy and hiddenness, self-injurious behaviors can easily entangle the teen into bondage. Even though there is pain involved, hurting self becomes pleasurable and comfortable—which means entrapment. Remember that all human beings are prone to addiction because of our in-born slavery to sin and ongoing fight with sin. Even as Christians, we can turn ourselves back over to our slave masters rather than submitting to the Lord Jesus and His control. Therefore, it is naïve to believe that teenagers can simply quit cutting, or hair pulling, or practicing the various other harmful behaviors. They must learn the power of addiction and how they are not in control of what they think they control. Stopping will require a real break from the stubborn hold of bondage.

So, what part do parents or youth ministry workers play in the handling of this particular addiction? Should razor blades and knives be locked up, fingernails be filed down, and hair be shaved off? While there certainly should be increased accountability between teen and parent or Biblical counselor, there are just too many ways to self-harm for 'blocking' measures to be efficient. The seriousness of addiction must be asserted to the teen, with measures in place when temptation arises. But as with all addictions, there needs to be a change of heart and mind, not just a change of behavior. What will fill the void when a teenager is giving up the habit of cutting, scratching, or hair-pulling? Even though the dynamic is similar to a drug or alcohol addiction, there is not a substance to avoid in the bondage of self-harm. So, the focus must remain on what is going on in the heart, mind, and emotions—in order to deal with the underlying issues. The addiction will lose its power as the teenager enjoys God's grace, and begins to let go of stubborn attitudes of the mind. As with all forms of bondage, it will take time to change a habit and engage in more Biblical behaviors and activities.

The temple of the Holy Spirit

Addressing the sin of sexual immorality, the apostle Paul writes: 'Or do you not know that your body is a temple of the Holy Spirit within you, whom you have from God? You are not your own, for you were bought with a price. So glorify God in your body' (1 Cor. 6:19-20). Even though Paul didn't have self-harm in view here; the fact is that, as believers, the body of the teenager is a temple of the Holy Spirit. Harming self is an abuse of the Spirit's temple. It is ignoring the fact that our bodies are not our own, to do with as we please. If your teen is a professing Christian, he or she needs to know who inhabits the body, thereby owning his or her body. All forms of self-harm to the body are akin to defacing a holy place of worship. This line of gospel-centered thinking is a much better approach than teaching the teen to love his or her body! We are called to honor and respect our bodies out of a sincere love for who owns and reside in our bodies.

In the end, any form of deliberate self-injury does not glorify God, or sanctify us. If your teen wants to pursue a heart of wisdom in this matter, it begins with asking if the behavior glorifies God. This may sound overly simplistic to teenage ears, yet it is gospel truth. The way we treat our bodies either glorifies God or glorifies something or someone else. Who gets glory when skin is cut, carved, or burned? Who is glorified when bald spots are purposefully created on the scalp? Even the teenager who is harming self is not really glorified in the positive sense of the word. Unfortunately, self-harm does magnify the person, showcasing a worship of self rather than the worship of God. So, in a gracious way, we challenge teens like Nora, Opal, and Patrick to focus on glorifying God rather than self. Even though it may be more painful not to inflict pain, the promise of spiritual blessing in Christ should not be ignored. If the body really is the temple of the Spirit, it must only be used in the worship of God, and not self!

Wisdom POINTERS

The following are some 'do's and don'ts' to remind you to remain gospel-centered and Biblically grounded as you deal with the problem of self-harm:

- Do understand a Biblical view of pain and suffering.
- Don't treat self-harm as simply odd or weird behavior.
- Do strive to understand the emotional pain involved.
- Don't just seek to stop the behavior.
- Do consider the addictive nature of self-harm.
- Don't just pile on the guilt and shame.
- Do encourage the community of saints to get involved.
- Don't fail to see the desire for power and control.
- Do look for trauma, neglect, or abuse.
- Don't react out of anger or frustration.
- Do require your teen to see the body as the temple of the Holy Spirit.
- Don't forget to proclaim the gospel of grace in Christ.

16.
Suicide

The tragedy of a teenager taking his or her own life is devastating for family members, friends, and the community. Parents, siblings, and youth ministry workers can be left wondering whether or not they could have done something to prevent the teen from turning to suicide. Sometimes, there are pretty clear signs that may have been overlooked. Yet, for many teens, suicidal thoughts are kept secretive, or only shared with select friends. Depressed feelings, anxiety, bitterness, guilt, and shame can all lead a teenager to think about, or even attempt, suicide. Getting a teenager to open up and talk about his or her thoughts and feelings can be difficult. Then, when a teen actually begins talking to a parent or youth ministry worker about suicide, it can be an entirely different challenge to know what to say and do. The problem of suicide is truly a community problem that demands intervention and response from parents, youth workers, friends, and other family members.

Opening PORTRAITS

- 17-year old Qwan was about to be arrested for drunk driving—[1]which would be his third strike. When the police officers showed up at his house, he asked to get something out of his car.

1

In the blink of an eye, Qwan grabbed his hidden handgun and tried to shoot himself in the head.

- Riley, a 16-year old girl, has battled depression and anxiety for the past year. Lately, she has become more withdrawn and systematically breaking connections with her friends. She refuses to go to youth group anymore.

- Stuart, an awkward 15-year old, shared in a group text message that he doesn't want to live anymore. One of the girls in the group told her parents, who then passed it on to Stuart's parents. Stuart claims he was just kidding, but this isn't the first time he has talked about killing himself.

Typical PROBLEMS

Suicide is the taking of one's own life. Outside of a successful suicide, there are two problems that need to be addressed:

1. Suicidal ideation

Suicidal ideations are thoughts about suicide or the mental activity of planning suicide. Many teenagers have a random thought about suicide from time to time. Suicidal ideation is typically more frequent, and ends up with a plan for committing suicide.

2. Suicide attempt

The next degree of intensity after suicidal ideation is an actual suicide attempt. Teenagers can try to kill themselves by a firearm, drug overdose, asphyxiation, slitting wrists, or various other ways.

Evaluation PERSONALIZATION

If your teen is having suicidal thoughts, planning to commit suicide, or has made a suicide attempt, there are many questions that need to be answered:

Overall patterns

1. How long has the teen been thinking about suicide?
2. How often does your teen think about suicide?
3. Does your teen have a plan to commit suicide?
4. Has your teen made a suicide attempt?

Physical factors

1. What is the current state of the teen's physical health?
2. Does the teen have any physical disabilities?
3. Is a medical examination required?

Relational issues

1. What is the state of your teen's friendships?
2. Is the teen being bullied in any way?
3. Is the teen dating or in a serious relationship?
4. Is the teen isolated or withdrawn?
5. Has the teen talked to friends about his or her suicidal thoughts?

Media practices

1. What is the impact of social media in the teen's life?
2. What sort of entertainment media is being engaged in?
3. Is the teenager viewing pornography?
4. Is the teen viewing sites related to suicide?

Marriage and family

1. Are there significant family problems that are contributing to the issue?
2. What is the teen's relationship with his or her mother? Father?
3. What is the general nature of parenting?
4. Does the teenager have too much freedom?

Relationship with God

1. What is the teen's basic understanding of God? Of sin?

2. What about his or her devotional life? Prayer and Bible study?

3. How does the teen describe his or her relationship to Jesus Christ?

4. What about the role of the Holy Spirit in spiritual maturity?

5. Is the teen angry with God?

Other related problems

1. Is the teenager anxious, worried, or fearful?

2. Is there significant stress in the teen's life?

3. Is the teen angry or depressed?

4. What are the problems that are possibly connected?

Biblical PRINCIPLES

Teenage suicide is always a tragedy—for everyone involved. While Biblical counseling is certainly necessary for family members and friends after the death of a teen, the focus of this chapter will be on the intervention and prevention of teenage suicide. Murder is against God's law, and that includes the killing of self (Exod. 20:13). Being made in the image of God, we are forbidden to shed the blood of others—and by extension, ourselves (Gen. 9:6). Yet, even though Christians should know that suicide is wrong, our teens can struggle with suicidal thoughts, as well as all of the connected problems of the heart and mind that lead to a suicide attempt. It is essential that parents and youth ministry workers recognize the signs of a potential attempt, as well as be prepared to give sound Biblical counsel when a teen confesses suicidal thoughts. While the Bible doesn't give us a step-by-step plan for suicide intervention, there are essential principles that must be applied.

Sign recognition

Unfortunately, teens don't often come out and tell their parents or youth ministry workers that they are about to commit suicide. Consider Riley, a 16-year old young lady who has battled anxiety and depression for the past year. Does that necessarily make her a candidate for suicidal thoughts or a suicide attempt? No. Yet, it certainly increases the possibility, especially as time goes on. Add to these problems the fact that Riley is now becoming more withdrawn, refuses to go to youth group, and is systematically ending friendships—and the red flags are definitely increasing. Recognizing the signs is not easy, and cannot be reduced to some sort of checklist that automatically elicits the right conclusion. In Riley's case, it is certainly worth asking the question and seeking to listen to what is on her heart and mind. Extended depression and anxiety, coupled with social isolation, put the teenager at a much higher suicide risk.

There are several other signs that should be put in the 'immediate action' list, especially if they occur in combination with one another. They include:

- Giving away prized possessions, and getting 'affairs' in order.
- Talking more about death and dying.
- Saying goodbyes to friends and loved ones.
- Collecting items needed for a suicide attempt.
- Social withdrawal and isolation.
- Increasing drug or alcohol use.
- Refusal to do activities that were once pleasurable.
- Increasing participation in risky behaviors.
- Changing eating or sleeping habits.
- Feelings of helplessness and hopelessness.
- Extreme changes in personality.

Clearly, any one of these 'symptoms' demands a parent's attention, even if the teen does not confess to being suicidal. And, unfortunately, there will be many teenagers who commit suicide who don't significantly manifest any of these signs. Recognizing what is going on in a teen's heart and mind solely through outward behavior is extremely difficult. At the same time, parents, friends, and youth ministry workers should be highly vigilant when any sign of suicide becomes apparent.

Direct questions

When there appears to be signs of potential suicidal thoughts—as in Riley's case—it is essential that certain direct questions are asked. This should not be some sort of police-like interrogation, but a compassionate inquiry into what is going on in her heart and mind. If, as a parent or youth ministry worker, you are led by anxiety and fear, these questions will come across in an intimidating fashion rather than driven by love. You must truly be seeking to listen and understand. The teen needs to open up and feel free to be honest rather than feel accused or judged. So, begin with a question like, 'I'm concerned about some of your recent behavior. Are you having any thoughts about hurting yourself?' Depending on the answer to this question, you may have to be even more direct: 'Are you thinking about killing yourself? Do you have a plan to commit suicide?' These are certainly difficult questions to ask a teenager; yet, not asking the questions keeps everything in the dark.

As answers are being given to your questions, it is vital that you listen closely to what is said. You are primarily listening for false beliefs. In Riley's case, you may hear things like: 'I don't have any friends anymore. Everybody has rejected me.' 'I'm tired of being so sad and down all the time. Life is just too hard.' 'I just don't think I have a bright future. It all seems so pointless.' Even if your teen denies having a plan to commit suicide, expressed thoughts like Riley's are clearly on the path towards suicidal thoughts. Therefore, along with asking direct questions and listening to the responses, it is time to gently speak to the lies she is believing. The emphasis here is on the word 'gently.' When a teenager is at such a low place, she is vulnerable to Satan's lies and more easily believes falsehoods rather than the truth. Yet, she needs to hear truth! Instead of lecturing, use good questions to redirect her thoughts. Some examples are: 'How have your friends rejected you?' 'What is most difficult about your life right now?' 'What do you fear the most?' As the conversation continues, remember you are seeking to listen and understand, not just talk her out of a suicide attempt at this point in the process.

Wise evaluation

It should go without saying that helping a teenager who is contemplating suicide takes great wisdom and discernment, as well as compassion. There are consequences for either overreacting or underreacting to what is being said. While it may seem safer to overreact and err on the side of caution, it can sometimes infuse fear and anxiety into the situation. For example, what if Riley says: 'I occasionally have suicidal thoughts, but I would never kill myself.'? How should you respond? If you think that she may not be telling the whole truth—just seeking to downplay the situation—then you may need to take more forceful steps. This may be the wise response! But, on the other hand, if you discern that she is genuinely just struggling with some lies, and isn't really planning to kill herself, then your response would be different. As with all Biblical counseling, it is essential to rely on the Holy Spirit, and not just our own thoughts. Sometimes it is wiser to be more aggressive; other times, the teenager must be trusted to deal with what is going on in his or her heart and mind.

This evaluation must go beyond the words that you are hearing from the teenager. Again, in Riley's case, you already see behaviors that point to suicidal thoughts and desires. But as she talks, what do her non-verbals say? Is she passionate and emotional, or more subdued with little effect? Does she appear walled-off and closed, or receptive and open? Do her emotions match the words coming out of her mouth? Riley may say a lot more to you simply by what she is not saying! To be clear, this doesn't mean that you have to be some sort of expert in reading micro-expressions or emotional output. Spirit-led wisdom is what is needed, trusting that God will give clarity of thought. Whether Riley admits or denies having suicidal thoughts or a plan, her willingness to talk to you about it is very important. When teenagers are closed and withdrawn, there is a much greater reason to be concerned. Talking about the suicidal thoughts doesn't necessarily mean a teenager will not attempt suicide. A wise evaluation will balance what the teen is saying and how it fits with how he or she is acting.

Heaven and hell

In a similar way, 15-year old Stuart would need to be questioned about his suicidal thoughts and plans. When he is confronted about suicidal text messages, he claims to be just kidding. Yet, we already know he has talked about suicide several times in the past—and not just when he is angry, or emotionally upset. In cases like this, it's time to take the conversation further towards the eternal consequences involved. So, what do we say about heaven and hell? For Christians, one temptation is to tell teenagers that if they commit suicide, they will go to hell. But does God's Word bear this out? Even though it is true that the taking of one's own life is a sin, Scripture does not teach or give any example of suicide as sending a person to hell. Relatedly, it is also a broad generalization to conceive of all people who commit suicide as unbelievers. Christians can have suicidal thoughts and even attempt or commit suicide. If salvation is truly accomplished by grace through faith in the accomplished work of Christ, then nothing can separate the believer from God—not even suicide (Rom. 8:28-29).

Now, here's where we must be very careful. While it is true that the person who commits suicide is not automatically destined for hell, it is also true that he or she is not automatically destined for heaven either. Promising a professing Christian like Stuart that he will still go to heaven even if he commits suicide is never a good idea. Satan can use the truth that heaven is a free gift of God's grace to convince people to disobey and rebel against God in all sorts of ways, including by committing suicide. The better approach to eternal questions begin with statements and questions like: 'If you are having suicidal thoughts, you need to reflect on your relationship with Christ.' 'If you have put your faith in Jesus, you must also have faith to continue to live the life God has given you.' 'You may think you know Christ, but why risk your life on it?' 'If you kill yourself, you can't change your mind.' So while it is wrong to threaten a suicidal teen with hell, it is also wrong to promise him or her eternity in heaven. The issue here is whether the teenager will act in obedience and in faith, or give in to the lies and deception of the evil one.

Other options

Some teenagers are either actively planning, or have attempted to commit, suicide. Qwan, a 17-year old, tried to shoot himself after being arrested for drunk driving. The motivating force for this desperate act was the knowledge that his third arrest would certainly mean jail time. In Qwan's mind, the only available option to him was killing himself, thereby avoiding prison. In this extreme case, there realistically may not be many options available. And, yet, it is essential that Qwan be challenged to look at other possibilities. If jail time is required, how much time? Will there be opportunities for early release or parole? Can he finish his high school education or receive some sort of job training while in prison? The point is that the teenager needs to see how there are not just two options: impossible pain or death. While it is understandable for a teen like Qwan to think that way, he needs to be encouraged to consider all possible scenarios. Is death really better than time in prison? Does someone who goes to prison automatically have a life that is ruined forever? In order to not act on emotions and the stressors of the moment, a teen who is contemplating suicide will need help to think clearly.

A Scripture passage to apply in this case is found in 1 Corinthians 10: 'No temptation has overtaken you that is not common to man. God is faithful, and he will not let you be tempted beyond your ability, but with the temptation he will also provide the way of escape, that you may be able to endure it' (1 Cor. 10:13). The connected emphases here are that God is faithful, God does not allow us to be tempted beyond our capacity, and that God will make a way of escape. The believer is not alone in a seemingly desperate situation! So, it is essential to ask the teenager about 'ways of escape' that God can provide, out of His faithfulness and love. Sometimes, God provides people and relationships that can help the teen escape from suicidal thoughts. Other times, clear thinking allows the teen to contemplate better plans to solve the current problem. Suicide must never be seen as the only option for the Christian, even in the most severe cases. Helping a teenager walk through each and every scenario may allow him or her to move forward Biblically.

Support system

Even though many teenagers who contemplate suicide tend to push people away, break friendships, and withdraw from relationships, a support system is mandatory to be able to emerge from that dark place. Riley refuses to go to youth group anymore, and has cut off her closest friends. Even so, hopefully, there are parents and other family members who can be the foundation of her support through this time. The reality is, teenage peers may not be the best support for a teen who is suicidal. They can more easily judge, criticize, and gossip—or simply become immobilized by fear and anxiety. Wise and mature parents, and other adults, are needed to bring calm and encouragement into the teenager's life. Teens like Riley, Qwan, and Stuart should never feel that they are alone in their struggles. Unfortunately, some teenagers only seek the help of their peers and not parents or youth ministry workers. Again, if the signs of suicide are there, adults need to offer a support system for the troubled teen.

So, practically speaking, how do those family members and friends who want to help actually provide support? Initially, depending on the situation, the support system should be very intensive. Ensuring the teenager is watched twenty-four hours a day, every day for a time, may be necessary. After the initial crisis period wanes, parents, friends, and family members should continue the conversations and establish accountability. One important caution here is to take care not to bring greater shame or humiliation into the teen's heart and mind.

It is easy to turn the teenager into a child, putting him or her under some sort of house arrest. Again, fear and panic cannot rule the day, even though this is clearly a stressful time. A loving support system does more than simply watch, trying to prevent a successful suicide. All involved should be praying for and with the teenager, providing Biblical counsel, and walking with him or her all along the way. In this way, they will fulfill the law of love by bearing the great burden of the suicidal teenagers (Gal. 6:2).

Make a covenant

If it is determined that a teenager is truly thinking about attempting suicide, or even has a plan in place, it is time to make a contract, or covenant, with him or her. The term 'covenant' is preferred since it is a rich, theological term—as well as highly relational in nature. Using 'contract' terminology makes things seem more business-like and clinical rather than spiritual and connectional. Parents or youth ministry workers can start with a verbal covenant, and move to a signed, written one if necessary. Basically, the covenant should say that the teenager concurs to not commit suicide for a 24-hour (or any agreed upon) period of time. It should also include language about what the teenager agrees to do if he or she is tempted to harm self in any way. On the other side of the covenant, the parent or youth ministry promises to keep the teen accountable, and provide counseling and care when needed. Again, the covenant can be verbally attested—but preferably signed—to make it more formal and binding. Then, make sure to lead the teen in a covenant prayer to our covenant-keeping God, since the covenant is ultimately made to Him.

Some may ask: What good does a covenant promise do for the suicidal teenage? Wouldn't the teenager just say what has to be said, and then do what he or she is planning to do? Certainly, there are teens, especially those who are unbelievers, who will deceive parents or youth ministry workers. Or, some teens may have good intentions, but still break the covenant and commit suicide. Yet, in many cases, a covenant or contract actually becomes binding on the conscience, and can be used by the Holy Spirit to restrain sinful impulses. There is a certain power in commitment, as well as the fact that God's power comes to rest in our hearts as we covenant with Him. So this is no mere formality or some sort of useless activity to make all parties feel better. A teenager who is willing to make a covenant for even a day or two will have better motivation to keep from committing suicide beyond that. Again, this covenant connects the teenager to a support system as well as to the Lord God Himself, allowing change and growth to happen rather than continuing the sinful downward spiral.

Emergency hospitalization

In the most extreme cases, a teenager may need more intervention than a parent or Biblical counselor can offer. Laws and procedures concerning emergency 'lockdown' hospitalization vary from state to state in the United States, as well as other countries. In some states, a teenager who is assessed to be a harm to himself can be involuntarily admitted to a hospital or psychiatric unit for 48 hours to as much as 72 hours. In other places, commitment is for a much shorter amount of time. Sometimes, parents can have their teenager hospitalized; other times, a medical or psychiatric diagnosis is required. In some places, even the county coroner can ask for an emergency hospitalization. If you aren't familiar with your state or national laws and procedures, a good place to start is with your family doctor. When hospitalization is required because of a failed suicide attempt (like in Qwan's case), then a psychiatric evaluation will become mandatory. There will be important choices to make about future medical or psychiatric care in the coming days; the emergency hospitalization is meant to get through the all-important first 24-48 hours of the crisis.

An emergency hospitalization also affords the opportunity for the teenagers to have a complete medical checkup. It would be very helpful to find out if there are any physiological problems in the life of the teen. Since Riley has battled depression and anxiety for the past year, ruling out any physical problems would be required. When medical doctors or psychiatric workers get involved, that doesn't mean parents and youth ministry workers step aside and disappear. Suicidal thoughts or attempts are spiritual problems even if there are body problems present. Be careful not to communicate to the teenager that his or her suicidal ideations are solely a chemical or hormonal issue that cannot be helped, unless there are true physiological issues present. So, while the hospital may be necessary as a short-term respite and intervention, Biblical counseling and the Christian community will provide the long-term solution.

Underlying problems

Depending on the situation, the problem of suicidal thoughts and attempts can put a family and a church into an instant state of crisis. Yet, it is important not to simply treat it as a problem that quickly passes if the actual suicide doesn't happen. Teenagers who are having suicidal thoughts in the present will potentially have them again in the future. Unfortunately, a singular suicide attempt may not be the last one. So, once the initial crisis has dissipated, the next stage of Biblical counseling work must begin. As has already been discussed in other chapters, problems of anger, bitterness, guilt, shame, depression, and anxiety are issues that need to be addressed. Biblical counseling is always about getting to the heart of the matter, exposing root issues that need to be solved, by the work of the Spirit. In that sense, the suicidal thoughts in a teen serve to illuminate other problems that may have been more hidden and secretive. Idols of the heart will also come to the surface as a full examination into the teen's emotional and mental state is accomplished.

Most importantly, any thoughts of suicide point to the need for the teen to think about his or her view of God, and his or her relationship to Him. Questions such as the following can be asked: 'Do you believe God loves you?' 'Do you believe God is sovereign and active in your life?' 'Do you believe God has a plan for your life?' 'Do you believe

God is punishing you or not caring for you in some way?' Exposing the teenager's relationship to God allows for further gospel conversations about the nature of true Christianity. A teenager may come to the realization that he or she is not a Christian in the first place. Or, he or she may simply be struggling with the assurance of salvation. Maybe there are particular sins that the teen is hiding, or doesn't believe God will forgive. Whatever the case, the underlying spiritual problem needs to be addressed, and solutions sought. Since suicide is truly a matter of life and death, this is the time for a laser-like focus on the teen's beliefs about God, human beings, and salvation.

Choose life

In the end, Qwan, Riley, and Stuart—as well as all the teenagers like them—have a critical decision to make: either they will choose life, or choose death. But, Christians know that the stakes are higher than simply physical life or death. Teenagers who are struggling with suicidal thoughts need to hear the gospel as recorded by the apostle John: 'And this is the testimony, that God gave us eternal life, and this life is in his Son. Whoever has the Son has life; whoever does not have the Son of God does not have life' (1 John 5:11-12). Life is not found in our possessions, our activities, our human relationships, or our circumstances—but in Christ Himself. If Qwan truly believes his life is his to take, then he may never have had eternal life in the first place. Riley too may fail to see that, as a Christian, she has been bought with a price, and her life is no longer hers. Stuart may be idolizing someone else's life rather than resting in the eternal life Christ has given him. Guiding our teens to choose life over death is a call to choose Christ over self—to enjoy his grace, instead of being enslaved to sin and death!

Wisdom POINTERS

The following are some 'do's and don'ts' to remind you to remain gospel-centered and Biblically grounded as you deal with the problem of suicide:

- Do promote a Biblical view of life and death.
- Don't miss the teen's behaviors and attitudes that point to suicide.
- Do understand that many signs of suicide can be missed.
- Don't just seek to stop a teen from committing suicide.
- Do speak the truth about heaven and hell.
- Don't act out of fear and anxiety.
- Do encourage the community of saints to get involved.
- Don't fail to make a covenant.
- Do seek outside medical help and hospitalization, when necessary.
- Don't forget to help the teenager to look at other options.
- Do deal with underlying issues, especially spiritual ones.

Don't forget to proclaim the gospel of life in Christ.

17.
Technology and Media

Every generation of teenagers in these modern times has new technological innovations that have a way of improving life and, at the same time, making it more challenging. Moving from the wonder of radio to the miracle of television adjusted how teenagers spent some of their free time. When video games entered the home, subsequent generations became less physically active and more sedentary. The emergence of the internet, smartphones, and social media has transformed how teens learn, acquire knowledge, communicate, and relate. With each new innovation, adults vary in how they respond to new technology and media practices—with some embracing it, some being more passive and unresponsive, and others anxiously overreacting. Often times, adults are one (or many) steps behind what teenagers are doing and experiencing, regularly trying their best to catch up and understand. Responding well to the problems that are connected to the misuse of technology and media is essential for a teen's pursuit of wisdom in Christ.

Opening PORTRAITS

- Terry, a 13-year old, has very few interests other than video games. When his parents tell him to take a 'technology break,' he either sulks, or becomes agitated. All he can talk about is the latest online game.

- Uma, a 15-year old, lives on social media. She posts selfies multiple times a day. Uma is rarely without her smartphone in her hand. She gets angry and/or depressed when she doesn't get enough 'likes' for her pictures or comments.

- 17-year old Victor lives in front of his computer. He is either binge-watching his favorite shows, getting into online theological debates, or reading political commentary. He wants to be a computer science major in college, and then go to seminary.

Typical *PROBLEMS*

Each type of technology and entertainment media that is available to our teenagers has potential benefits as well as inherent risks. Some can be more addictive in nature, others are simply time-wasters, and still others deliver harmful content. So common problems will be delineated according to major technology and media types:

1. Internet-related problems

Teenagers use the internet for education, research, shopping, gaming, video watching, and socializing. The main problem for many teens is internet pornography. Yet, there is much non-porn content that is also unhealthy and dangerous. On top of that, the internet can simply be a great waster of teenage time, as well as the purveyor of useless and false information.

2. Entertainment media-related problems

From television, to movies, to video clips, to music, the access to entertainment is at extreme levels. Sexual, violent, and profane content are the top concern. The ability to waste an extreme amount of time binge-watching shows is also on the list. With the rise of personal media devices, teens can become isolated and individualistic in their choices of entertainment.

3. Social media-related problems

A significant amount of teenage relating occurs via social media, which can become a problem on many levels. 'Self' problems can be either produced by social media habits or exacerbated by them. Teenagers are also prone to be 'cyberbullied' or enter into inappropriate relationships as well. Social media can also be one of the greatest forms of time wasters, as well as a poor way to gain news and information.

4. Smartphone-related problems

Cell phone addiction tops the list of problems related to today's smartphones. As they connect teens to the internet and social media, online porn and inappropriate relationships are also major issues. The texting habits of teenagers can also be a concern, as well as the habit of 'sexting' (texting illicit photographs or using sexual language).

5. Video game-related problems

Ever since video games became a staple of home entertainment, they have become the activity of choice for many teens, especially young males. Violent content has always been an issue, as well as their addictive nature. Video games can not only waste a lot of time, but have a unique way of shaping identity when played in excess.

Evaluation PERSONALIZATION

If your teen has problems related to or fueled by unhealthy technology and media practices, there are important questions that need to be answered:

Overall patterns

1. What are the teen's entertainment habits?
2. What are the teen's social media habits?

3. What freedoms does the teen have regarding their use of technology?
4. What are the specific problems?

Physical factors

1. What is the current state of the teen's physical health?
2. Does the teen have any physical disabilities?
3. Is the teen physically active, or more inactive?

Relational issues

1. What is the state of your teen's friendships?
2. Is the teen being cyberbullied in any way?
3. Is the teen dating or in a serious relationship?
4. Is the teen isolated or withdrawn?
5. How does social media impact his relationships?

Media habits

1. How much time is spent on entertainment technology and media?
2. What content is the teen viewing or listening to?
3. Is the teenager viewing pornography?

Marriage and family

1. Are there significant family problems that are contributing to the issues?
2. What is the teen's relationship with his or her mother? Father?
3. What is the general nature of parenting?
4. Does the teenager have too much freedom?

Relationship with God

1. What is the teen's basic understanding of God? Of sin?
2. What about his or her devotional life? Prayer and Bible study?

3. How does the teen describe his or her relationship to Jesus Christ?
4. What about the role of the Holy Spirit in spiritual maturity?
5. Are media practices taking away from the teen's spiritual life?

Other related problems

1. Is there significant stress in the teen's life?
2. Is the teen angry, anxious, or depressed?
3. What other problems are possibly connected?

Biblical PRINCIPLES

Modern technology and media play such a major role in most people's lives, and that is especially true with teenagers. Compared to other problems, the goal is not simply to eliminate all forms of technology and media (if that were even possible), but solving the problems associated with their mishandling. Seeking Biblical principles to guide our counseling is always essential, even when it appears that God's Word doesn't speak directly to these types of problems. After all, television, movies, the internet, and social media didn't exist in the times of Moses, Isaiah, Jesus, or Paul! Yet, the human heart has not changed, even if the circumstances of the day create different patterns of sin and suffering. How our teenagers handle today's technology and media, as well as what innovations will be coming right around the corner, will deeply connect to their spiritual, mental, emotional, and relational health. Parents and youth ministry workers are responsible to help teenagers navigate through the potential minefields related to media and technology.

Understanding the culture

For several generations, it has been a challenge for adults to fully grasp the behaviors and preferred activities of teenagers. It is often tempting for parents to think: 'I was a teenager. Times aren't that different today. I know what my teenager is going through.' Sentiments like these are only partially true. Yes, parents were teenagers, and the hearts of teenagers are no different today than in the past. But the times are always changing, which means the experiences of teenagers change regularly as well. The one outstanding quality of today's culture is how fast things change! To keep up with every technological innovation and advancement (or degradation) in media is nearly impossible, unless the parent or youth ministry worker is just naturally tuned in to those things. So, a starting point is to recognize that youth culture is different than it was when the parent was a teenager. And, it will continue to change at a light-speed sort of pace. These facts make understanding the culture a necessary component of Biblical counseling.

Another aspect that contributes to problems in this area is the reality that popular culture tends to market itself primarily to teenagers. Even the so called 'mature' television shows and movies are consumed by teenagers, becoming part of the youth culture. It wasn't that long ago that cell phones were a technological tool relegated to adulthood; now, teenagers and even children are consumers as well, attracted to everything about the phone except the phone itself. The intensity of video gaming has always been within youth culture, and is even more so today. The internet is used by all ages, yet teens have grown up immersed in it. Finally, social media is certainly used by adults, but it is teens who drive each succeeding iteration of it, as well as the darker, sexier, and more bullying aspects as well. As consumers, even Christian teenagers are willing to experiment and use just about any new aspect of technology, with few filters to avoid what is most destructive.

So, while each teenager is different in his or her consumption and usage of technology and entertainment media, an understanding of the culture at large is the starting place. Unless the teenager lives some sort of technological monastic-style existence, he or she is not only impacted by the popular culture, but will have to learn how to deal with it. Teens need to learn what parts need to be avoided, which ones can be enjoyed, and which must be transformed. As Paul writes in Romans 12:2, our teens are not to be conformed to this world but transformed by the renewing of their mind. We live in the culture of our time. In some ways, we are a product of our cultural moment. Yet, Christians must engage the culture with the mindset that they belong to the Kingdom of God, not the kingdom of this world. So, a big part of the effort to help our teens with technology and media issues is pointing them to pursue wisdom regarding what the culture is teaching them. If they are blindly accepting and enjoying everything that is new and inviting, then they are more susceptible to negative influences.

Understanding the teen

To help our teens navigate through the complexities of the popular culture, it is essential to understand and take into account what is unique about these formative years. Teenagers are not children anymore; and, they are not adults yet. It can certainly be argued that Scripture doesn't 'think' in terms of a category other than adult and children, yet the modern mind does. When it comes to the more dangerous forms of technology and entertainment media, it is much simpler to just shield and protect our children from them. What two-year old has her own smartphone, or is sitting up late at night consuming R-rated movies? But we err if we just treat teenagers like they are taller children, blocking them from most technology and media. They are more mature than toddlers, even if they don't act like it sometimes. They do have minds that are able to think rationally, even if they are often driven by their emotions and passions.

A comprehensive description of the mind, motivations, and attitudes of the teenager is beyond the scope of this book. What is most important—specifically related to the use of technology and media—is to understand the teen's mixed impulses toward adulthood. The average teen is not just steadily maturing to adulthood, taking on responsibility and making wise decisions all the time. Mixed into the maturation process is the sinful pull to remain as a foolish child. This manifests in the demands for more privileges, without an equal desire to take on the required responsibilities of adulthood. So, depending on the teenager, there will be times of foolish behavior and times of wisdom. There will be the longing to do all the things an adult can do, watch all the things adults watch, while not being fully capable to act and think in the right ways about what is being experienced. Since teens are effectively targeted by the popular culture, why wouldn't they want to experience just about everything offered? Adults should not be surprised that teens become consumed with all things technological and entertainment-oriented. The path from childhood to adulthood is a challenging road, with teens caught between maturity and immaturity.

Harmful content

When children are young, Christian parents tend to be fairly vigilant about what is being watched and listened to in the entertainment media or on the internet. Teenagers are often given more freedom regarding content, even to the point where parents know very little about what is being viewed. Seventeen-year old Victor is one of those teens who binge watches many shows, and confesses he has watched a lot of trash. Some of his favorites TV series often include scenes of soft-porn or excessive violence. He is feeling convicted that this is not pleasing to God—especially with his desire to go to seminary; yet he really loves the stories and characters. This scenario should be pretty easy to counsel, right? Victor can be encouraged to follow the conviction of the Spirit and resist the desires of the flesh (Gal. 5:16-18). He needs to make wise choices about what TV shows to avoid, and ones that still can be salvaged. Acknowledging that content can bring harm into our minds and hearts—leading to spiritual destruction—is an important step in the process.

But what if Victor comes to you about a problem with something else—like depression or anxiety or anger? When asked about his entertainment practices, Victor doesn't think those have anything to do with his problem. But in reality, do they? Can watching television shows and movies fuel anxiety, anger, or depression? Too many teenagers wrongly believe that what is put into their minds will not have any impact on their mental, emotional, or spiritual life. Or, they know it does have an impact, but resist giving up the shows that they love. Victor needs to learn how what is put into his mind either helps to renew his mind, or ends up corrupting his mind. What may just seem to be mindless entertainment is potentially influencing the way he is thinking and even how he feels. While every teen is different when it comes to what sorts of content can be handled, there are dangerous boundaries that should never be crossed. It's not that avoiding harmful content in and of itself makes our teens more holy; yet the binging of impure content can certainly inhibit the holiness to which God calls our teens.

Misuse of time

The apostle Paul instructs us: 'Look carefully then how you walk, not as unwise but as wise, making the best use of the time, because the days are evil' (Eph. 5:15-16). When it comes to the teen's use of technology and entertainment media, the question must be asked: 'Is this the best use of my time?' The reality is that much of what our teens watch on television or on the internet is designed to take up a lot of time, especially when it can be accessed any time, all the time. Even if Victor gives up shows that are too violent or sexual, his binge-watching habits—by definition—use up a lot of time. So, when is your teen spending too much time on entertainment, social media, gaming, or other technological practices? This is a spiritual issue of self-discipline, not simply a place for legalistic limits. A wise Biblical counselor should help the teen to evaluate his or her use of time, and where changes should be made. Our time is important to God, and it is essential for our spiritual growth in these evil days.

Terry, your 13-year old, consumes all of his free time with video games. Getting him to 'unplug' and do something else, exposes how much his life revolves around electronic gaming. On one level, Terry needs help disciplining his time, just like Victor. But, he also needs to consider if the activity itself is worth his time. When it comes to a proper use of time, it's not just about spending only a prescribed amount of time on the things we like, but asking ourselves what God wants regarding our free time. In other words, there is nothing necessarily wrong with Terry spending some recreational time on his video games, but are there better activities he could be doing instead or in addition to? His parents asking for a 'technology break' is one way to help Terry to do other things with his time. He may need to be counseled on what other activities are available to him, and why those things would be beneficial to him. Teenagers need to be trained to use time wisely and consider which activities would help them grow mentally, emotionally, spiritually, relationally, and physically.

Addiction and idolatry

A related issue to time usage is how easily technology and media can become an addiction. The problem of porn addiction, the most prolific of all media addictions, has been covered in a previous chapter. Terry, our 13-year old gamer, certainly appears to be addicted to video games, especially online games. Other teens can become addicted to their smartphones, social media, or just about any other form of technology. Addiction is the natural consequence of the sinful nature. Human beings, including teenagers, have a way of being controlled by that which they think they control. Whatever becomes the central behavior or activity in the life of the teenager easily becomes an idolatrous addiction. Even if the content isn't itself sinful—unlike pornography—it is a problem whenever a teen allows an activity or behavior to have too much power in his or her life. Terry's sulking and agitation when not allowed to play video games demonstrates how he has ceded control of his life over to gaming. Our technology can easily become idols that appear to be bringing all of the joy and peace into our lives.

Fifteen-year old Uma is clearly on the verge of making social media an idol, combined with her personal smartphone. Just like Terry, the key indicator of her idolatry is the way her moods change when she doesn't get the right responses to 'selfies' or to what she chooses to post on social media. Through these technological vehicles, Uma is also allowing other people to control her. Ultimately, the basic heart issue of self-idolatry is simply manifesting in her use of modern social media. So, what happens if a parent or youth ministry worker challenges Uma, telling her that she is enslaved to an idol? If she is a Christian, she may not admit to the worship of a false god in her life. Hopefully, talking through why she gets so angry or depressed will help reveal her heart and mind. She needs to take to heart these verses from the apostle Paul: "'All things are lawful,' but not all things are helpful. 'All things are lawful,' but not all things build up. Let no one seek his own good, but the good of his neighbor' (1 Cor 10:23-24). When a teen's use of technology and social media tears down rather than builds up, and seeks his or her own good rather than the good of other people, there is a problem. Helping teens assess whether something that is 'lawful' has become a source of addiction and idolatry is a big part of spiritual growth and wisdom.

Privacy and self-centeredness

This may sound overly nostalgic, but there was a time when entertainment technology actually brought people—including teenagers—together. Going to the movies was a highly anticipated social event for the community. The living room was a place for the entire family to enjoy the same television show together. The telephone was actually a tool to connect two people in a conversation. Yes, these communal activities still exist today—but often to a lesser extent than in the past. Changing technology and media delivery has put the focus on 'my playlist,' 'my queue' of shows or movies, and my personal media device. More teens experience the entertainment world all on their own, with total liberty of choice, genre, and extent. Turning much of entertainment into a private, personal affair has given teens the potential to live in their own technological world for seemingly endless

PURSUING A HEART OF WISDOM

hours a day. If a teenager desires to be isolated, or doesn't want to take the risk of relationship, then he or she has the opportunity to do so. Being alone with our modern technology opens up the possibility of all sorts of sinful behavior, not to mention the problem of loneliness.

Even if a teen is not engaging in anything explicitly sinful, the private, solitary nature of much of our entertainment technology adds to the temptation towards self-centeredness. What 'I' want in my media choices becomes more important than sacrificing desires for the interests of others. Since many of our teenagers are already self-centered, the ability to make their own self-driven entertainment choices is only adding fuel to the fire. So one of the problems of technology and media is that they contribute to a variety of 'self' issues—including self-love and self-image problems. Terry, Uma, or Victor may not see themselves as having self-centered lifestyles, but they certainly don't appear to be other-centered, or even Christ-centered in their behavior. Addressing how technology and media play a part in their mental, emotional, and spiritual development is essential if they are to mature in Christ. As mentioned earlier, it is not about getting rid of all technology or rejecting all entertainment media. Teenagers need to recognize that self is becoming more dominant when God calls them to die to self and love others.

Friendships and communication

Modern technology has changed the way teenagers make and maintain friendships with other teens. A teenager who doesn't have a smartphone or a social media account will potentially claim that he or she is on the outside of all human relationships. Certainly, there are those who don't care about having friends or being a friend. Yet, teenage development tends to include a longing to make friends with peers, to be understood, and even to be loved. Many parents end up giving teens the tools to stay connected with friends, as well as the ability to connect to people they only know through social media. Here again, Biblical counsel is required to help a teenager make wise decisions.

A teen like Uma needs to be compassionately rebuked for believing that other teens are only true friends if they approve of her photos or posts. Teenagers who are isolated, only relying on social media to maintain friendships, need to understand what being a true friend is all about. Adults probably won't be able to change how teens currently relate to one another; but parents and youth ministry workers must advocate positive ways to seek and grow Christian friendships.

Show up at a typical youth ministry gathering and you would probably see teenagers text messaging each other more than actually speaking to each other. Now, that may be an exaggeration, but the fact is that our technological advancements have also changed how we communicate with each other. Communication—even among adults—has degenerated from phone calls and letters, to email, to texts, and even to expressive icons, pictures and video clips. Certainly, humans have always communicated with more than mere words. But, is it even arguable that each generation is finding personal communication more challenging due mainly to our changing technology? Connected to how we use our time, teens are engaging in less and less face-to-face conversation than the previous generations. So, how is this general problem manifesting in the life of the teenager you are raising or counseling? Does your teen need help in learning to communicate with others, or is he on his own? Encouraging better means of communication. as well as time for real heart-to-heart conversation, is one of the solutions to the problems of our modern technology.

Distorting sexuality

It should go without saying that most of what comes out of the entertainment industry does not present a Biblical depiction of human sexuality. Teenagers who immerse themselves in movies and television shows will be presented with the basest and even vilest of sexual experiences. They will inevitably learn that sex outside of marriage is a good thing, homosexuality is equivalent (or even superior) to heterosexuality, and 'hooking up' with many partners is what the good life is all about. Thankfully, all of these media lies give parents and youth ministry workers ample illustrations to use to teach what is true. Unfortunately, some teenagers only show up in counseling when they have become sexually active, are already experimenting in homosexual behaviors, or are deeply addicted to pornography. In these cases, Biblical counseling is more focused on repentance, reformation, and re-training. It is tragic that much of the entertainment media only feeds our teen's sinful sexual desires rather than teaching what is true and virtuous. But, that's where the church and the Word of God must speak louder and more passionately about sexuality, purity, and Biblical love.

What if the problem is sexual interaction between teenagers? The sending of nude or semi-nude photos by text message or via social media has become popular even with Christian teens. While much of pornography is fantasy-based, teens are often making it a reality in their opposite-sex relationships. Even if it is obvious to parents or youth ministry workers that 'sexting' is sinful and outside the bounds of Biblical sexuality, teenagers often need some convincing. They need to see that this is a distortion of sexuality as well as destructive to relationships. It is beyond flirtation and even seduction, to the wanton abuse of our bodies. Again, advocating for purity and chastity may be difficult in a highly sexualized world. But the voices of wisdom and Biblical sanity must speak into the lives of our teens who profess faith in Christ. Whether your teen is the sender of sexual material, or the receiver, he or she must be protected and rebuked at the same time. The Bible is clear that the lust of the eyes and the lust of the flesh is not from the Father, but of this fallen world (1 John 2:16).

Cyber bullying and stalking

The ability for our technology to connect human beings to one another 24 hours a day has led to other problems for our teenagers. More and more teens report being harassed and bullied on social media, by texts, and on the internet. While bullying has always been a part of the teenage years, the access and ability has increased exponentially because of smartphones and other electronic devices. If your teenager is the one engaging in cyber bullying, then your counsel is pretty straightforward. There is no place for a teen to attempt to destroy another teen, even if it is out of revenge or pain. When your teenager is on the receiving end of bullying, the task is much more difficult. How do you love your enemy in this case (Luke 6:27-36)? How does a parent or youth ministry worker protect and defend? Bullying must be addressed for many reasons, but certainly because there is often an increased risk of suicide. Bullying is a form of violence our teens cannot handle on their own. Often, a teenager keeps quiet about the bullying for far too long. As was discussed in the chapter on suicide, adults must read the signs and intervene Biblically.

Even more dangerous and criminal is the problem of cyber stalking. If your teen is using social media or his smartphone to pursue a girl, what happens if it moves to aggressive and unwanted pursuit? Again, this may be the result of a wrong understanding of relationships and a misuse of technology. Teaching a teenage boy to honor and respect women is essential. Dealing with their normal sexual desires and built-in male aggression is vital as well. The parent or Biblical counselor should confront any form of cyber stalking firmly. On the other side of the issue, what do we do if our teenage girl is being stalked? Certainly, civil authorities and adult protectors can be brought in to help. The bigger task is giving wise counsel on how to deal with it mentally and emotionally, as well as ensuring safety in the process. The social media world of the teenager can be a violent place, and can be used to expose, intimidate, and humiliate others. As Christians, we not only need to help our teens navigate this world, but rise above it and stand for righteousness in the midst of it.

Glorifying God vs. amusing self

Much of what is presented to our teens as entertainment is mindless and meaningless. Yet, there is also much that is evil, disgusting, and denigrating to God and humanity. While it is human to laugh and be amused, many teens can become preoccupied with self-entertainment. We have the capacity to be consumed with our amusements, prioritizing our pleasure over loving and glorifying God. Terry, Uma, and Victor all need help in learning what it means to do all things to the glory of God (1 Cor. 10:31). They require assistance in balancing the pursuit of entertaining things alongside the more productive activities of work, study, service, and worship. If joy only comes in the context of entertainment media, then everything else will become boring and lifeless. Even worse for the teen's heart and mind, entertainment media can become the sole way to escape from the pain and suffering in this life. Keeping a God-centered holiness is what we desire to see in our teens as they grow up. Managing the impact of technology and media is an essential part of the sanctifying process.

Wisdom POINTERS

The following are some 'do's and don'ts' to remind you to remain gospel-centered and Biblically sound as you deal with problems related to technology and media:

- Do promote a Biblical worldview of technology and media.
- Don't ignore how teenagers experience the world differently today.
- Do understand the content teenagers are consuming.
- Don't just seek to control what teens are able to do, as if they were still children.
- Do talk about time and its importance.
- Don't miss the addiction and idolatry.
- Do encourage better friendships and relationships.

- Don't fail to address problems of stalking and bullying in a firm way.
- Do protect your teen from dangerous content and relational influences.
- Don't avoid confronting the distortions of sex and sexuality.
- Do deal with underlying issues, especially spiritual ones.
- Don't forget to direct the teen to glorify God in all things.

18.
Unmotivated Teens

Our final problem category is easy to observe, yet often challenging to change: the problem of the unmotivated teenager. As human beings, we often tend to lack motivation to do the things that do not interest us, or that are too difficult for us. There is really no such teenager problem of lacking total motivation for absolutely everything! So, motivation, in this sense, is defined as simply the desire or willingness to do something. The same teenager who is unmotivated in his schoolwork can be highly motivated to play video games. Another teen who is unwilling to go to church can be highly motivated to go to other social activities. In contrast to many of our other issues, a teenager may not see this as much of a problem as do parents or other adults. Yet, if a teenager is going to mature in wisdom, then a lack of motivation requires attention—even if the teen is unmotivated to solve it.

Opening PORTRAITS

- William, a 15-year old, has always been lazy. He procrastinates in his schoolwork. He stays up late playing video games, and sleeps in as long as possible. His parents are at a loss of what will motivate him.
- Xander, a 16-year old, shows no interest in church, the youth group, the Bible, or having a daily quiet time. His parents have

tried to force him to do all these things for a couple of years. His only interest seems to be working out at the gym.

- 17-year old Zoe is about to graduate from high school. She has never enjoyed school. All of her friends are going to college in the fall, but Zoe is not sure if she is college material. She is not quite certain what she wants to do with her life.

Typical PROBLEMS

Teenagers can lack the motivation to do just about anything, depending on the circumstances—even things that they used to enjoy. So, what are the most common areas that will justify the label of an 'unmotivated' teen? To put it another way: What problems will cause parents and other adults who are in the life of the teenager the most dissatisfaction? Here is the short list:

1. Academic education

Some teenagers lack motivation in all academic subject areas—the classic 'underachiever.' Others are just disinterested in one or two subjects, unwilling to put the time and energy into them. Still others are unmotivated to go any further than a high school education, when they have the ability to pursue a post-high school degree.

2. Work

Many teenagers are adverse to hard work, some to any real work at all. For some teens, work is acceptable if there is a paycheck involved, but lack willingness to do any basic chores around the house.

3. Spiritual pursuits

Teens who are professing Christians should not lack the motivation to read the Bible, pray, and go to church—but some do. Others are seemingly unmotivated to go beyond just a surface level of religion.

4. Relationships

Making friends is a challenge for many teens. Yet, some teenagers lack the motivation to not only seek out friendships but to do the work to maintain those friendships. Other teens are unmotivated to connect to other people in general, including parents and siblings.

Evaluation PERSONALIZATION

If your teen has problems with motivation, there are some other questions that need to be answered:

Overall patterns

1. In what areas is the teenager unmotivated?
2. In what areas is the teenager motivated?
3. How long has the teenager lacked motivation?

Physical factors

1. What is the current state of the teen's physical health?
2. Does the teen have any physical disabilities?
3. Is a medical check-up necessary?

Relational issues

1. What is the state of your teen's friendships?
2. Is the teen isolated or withdrawn?
3. Does the teen lack motivation to maintain his relationships?

Media habits

1. How much time is spent on entertainment technology and media?
2. What are the teenager's viewing/listening habits?
3. Is the teenager viewing pornography?

Marriage and family

1. Are there significant family problems that are contributing to the issues?
2. What is the teen's relationship with his or her mother? Father?
3. What do parents expect/require of the teenager?
4. Does the teenager have too much freedom?

Relationship with God

1. What is the teen's basic understanding of God? Of sin?
2. What about his or her devotional life? Prayer and Bible study?
3. How does the teen describe his or her relationship to Jesus Christ?
4. Is the teenager regularly attending church/youth ministry?

Other related problems

1. Is there significant stress in the teen's life?
2. Is the teenager depressed or anxious?
3. What other problems may be connected?

Biblical *PRINCIPLES*

You will probably not have a teenager plop down in the chair if front of you and say, 'Please help me! I'm an unmotivated teenager.' Yet, at the same time, your teen may see some of the consequences of his or her lack of motivation, and actually be frustrated about the inability to change. Recognizing the motives of the heart and what keeps us from doing what we ought to do is a challenge even for adults. So, here is yet another problem which not only requires a Biblical approach, but parents and mature youth ministry workers to properly assess and intervene. In a world that, in many ways, expects teenagers to only be motivated by their own interests and pleasures, God's Word demands much more. It clearly speaks to the heart of the matter—even to the motivations of our hearts! Move beyond simply the goal of the teenager being a responsible, hard-working, motivated citizen—to the higher goal of having a heart of wisdom in pursuit of God's Kingdom. As with all other problems, parents and youth ministry workers should be seeking God's wisdom and resisting the wisdom of this world.

Internal and external

God's Word gives us many pictures and instructions regarding what motivates us as human beings. A right Biblical anthropology begins with the fact that, outside of Christ, we are driven by our sinful hearts—even when we do right things. As Jesus taught His disciples, it is out of the internal human heart that flows all sorts of sinful desires and actions that drive us to unrighteous, external behavior (Mark 7:21-23). Not one of us is righteous, or acts from purely righteous and good motives. At best, our willingness to do anything good comes from mixed motives, tainted by our sin and weakness. For example, a teenager may actually be highly motivated to get good grades in school; yet, the real underlying motivation is not just to glorify God, but also to reap the praise of men. Another teenager may be motivated to serve and worship God, but secretly is hoping it will make God love him more. The motives of our heart are tricky because of the deceitfulness of the heart. Even with the work of the Holy Spirit, motivation may be lacking, or grounded in more self-centeredness than holiness.

When thinking about motivation, it is common to distinguish between intrinsic and extrinsic motivation—that which comes from within, and that which pulls on us from without. When children are young, parents tend to focus primarily on external motivation in order to get them to do what is right. Various punishments are used to move the child to obedience, as well as to provide consequences for disobedience. Positive reinforcements and rewards are often employed to motivate children to complete chores, do well in school, or even have good attitudes. Yet, external motivation is not the ultimate goal, or we end up with teenagers who only do what is good and right if there is some external threat or reward. Therefore, extrinsic motivation is less than desirable with teens, since our goal is to see them pursuing a heart of wisdom. Parents should evaluate if they have become too reliant on external motivation techniques to help the unmotivated teenagers. At some point, this effort will lack effectiveness. And, even when it does 'work,' it will only be temporary.

So, an initial Biblical principle regarding the unmotivated teenager is that we want to see more intrinsic motivation in his or her life. Parents and youth ministry workers can help a teen like William, our 15-year old who his underachieving in school, by listening to his heart. Why is he procrastinating in his schoolwork? Is it really simple laziness? Even though his parents are at a loss for what motivates him, that may be because they have relied primarily on external motivation: 'No more video games until you finish your homework.' 'If you get A's and B's on your next report card, then I'll buy you a new gaming system.' An approach that focuses more on internal motivation would press William on his fears, anxieties, or apathy. It might reveal that he is enslaved to comfort; or, that he is simply not challenged enough in school—or in life. Again, you need to hear his heart and interpret his thoughts and emotions—which is a challenge in itself. Even if it is hard to find out what is going on in the heart and mind of a 15-year old, we need to keep moving to internal motivation and resist relying solely on external sources of motivation.

Parental expectations

Every parent has certain expectations for his or her child. For some, it's a particular academic achievement (straight A's, high standardized test scores, etc.). Others expect to have a star athlete or a skilled musician in the family. Still others communicate the expectation of a college degree or a certain high-paying profession. In some cases, there are even parents who expect their children to become eminently godly and righteous! As a child reaches the teen years, the pressure to begin to achieve those parental goals often escalates. While some teens internalize those expectations and pursue them, others resist them— thereby demonstrating a lack of motivation. So the first question to ask is: How realistic are the parental expectations? Getting good grades is important; but, what if the parent expects his or her teenager to be the top student in the class? Being a member of a sports team can be a good desire for a teen, but will it all be a disappointment to parents if he or she doesn't make the all-star team? An important part of the counseling process is distinguishing between what is a normal, healthy expectation and what is abnormal and potentially harmful.

Two related aspects to the expectation itself is how parents communicate it to their teenager—as well as respond when the expectation is not being met. Parents who are very verbal about what they expect from their teenagers, without much love or grace, can end up demotivating them. Others, who may not be as communicative with words, yet show their disappointment in critical ways, can have the equal result. Then, when the teenager fails to meet the expectation, what happens next? Does parental fear and anxiety go through the roof? Will the teenager reap the wrath of mom or dad? Some parents employ threats, while others resort to tears or bribes. In the end, it's essential that parents examine themselves to see if they are contributing to the teen's lack of motivation. Living under the pressure of either overly high expectations, or the humiliation of letting down parents can take its toll. Some teens will become over-achievers, and others end up under-achieving. While there are many other factors to look at, changing parental expectations can move toward real solution.

Performance pressure

Lest we forget, God's Word is replete with expectations, commands, laws, and standards for those who live by faith in Christ Jesus. To put it in the vernacular, Christians do have a responsibility to 'perform' in ways consistent with their love for God. Accordingly, we are right to expect our teenagers to understand that God demands holiness, righteousness, hard work, and excellence in all areas of conduct. Therefore, William is certainly disobeying God in his laziness and procrastination in his schoolwork. Xander, our 16-year old, is not glorifying God by refusing to pray, read his Bible, or worship with God's people. Other teens who are unmotivated may also end up disobeying God, not just frustrating parental expectations. If teenagers perceive there is too much pressure to perform as Christians, then they will miss the grace of God. With the call to obey always comes the grace to obey—and grace and forgiveness when we do not obey. As John wrote, 'For this is the love of God, that we keep His commandments. And His commandments are not burdensome' (1 John 5:3). God cannot be blamed for demanding too much, thereby somehow causing the teen to have a lack of motivation.

On the other hand, the adults in the teenager's life may be sinfully applying performance pressure, effectively creating or adding to a lack of motivation. So, how does this typically manifest? In Zoe's case, she is often compared to her older sisters by her parents, grandparents, and even her friends. Her lack of desire to go to college is not because she is academically weak, but an over-reaction to being expected to perform. After all, she better not be the first child to not succeed in college! Similar to the pressure of expectation, being measured by performance can disable a teen in many ways. If not coupled by love, compassion, and grace, it should not surprise us to see some lack of motivation to perform. Again, we must be careful here to not communicate to teenagers that there is absolutely no pressure to perform, or that performance doesn't matter. What must be embraced is that we are called to 'perform' for God, for the glory of God, by the grace of God, and by faith in God. Teenagers who lack motivation because of a rebellion against performing for God or parents are not glorifying God or helping themselves.

Fighting Laziness

The unmotivated teenager may be enslaved to the sin habit of laziness. Written to young men, the Book of Proverbs is filled with harsh truths about laziness, or slothfulness. 'The hand of the diligent will rule, while the slothful will be put to forced labor' (Prov. 12:24). 'Slothfulness casts into a deep sleep, and an idle person will suffer hunger' (Prov. 19:15). 'The sluggard buries his hand in the dish; it wears him out to bring it back to his mouth' (Prov. 26:15). Over and over again, laziness is shown to not only be connected to foolishness, but to bring with it some devastating consequences. Laziness, described in Scripture also as idleness, should have no place in the life of the believer. So when laziness is seen as the root cause or a contributing factor to a teen's lack of confidence, it must be addressed. Even though we understand how easy it is to become lazy in any area of life, it should not be simply tolerated in the life of a teenager.

So, what Biblical counsel do we give a teen like William who professes to being lazy most of his life? Even though laziness is a sinful habit, it will probably not be effective to just tell him to stop being so lazy. Like other long-term behaviors, it takes time to learn and practice a better habit. William's late-night video game habit will have to change in order to effectively counteract his laziness. His sleep habits will also need to be adjusted since they are also potentially feeding his laziness. Putting off the bad habits that contribute to laziness, or result from a lazy heart and mind, must be followed by putting on new habits that better reflect a godly work ethic. But, beyond behavioral change, what is going on in the teen's heart? What makes laziness attractive and comfortable—other than the fact that it often feels better than doing hard work? Laziness in our teens can often be driven by the idol of comfort, or the idol of pleasure. As will be discussed further, laziness can also be a cover-up for fear, depression, or other sins of the heart as well. And, in some cases, some teenagers can either excuse laziness as just a part of their personality and even revel in their laziness. In the end, laziness should be confessed and repented of, with the help of the Holy Spirit.

Fear factor

One of the most immobilizing forces in our lives is the emotion of fear. Fear can typically cause us to either flee or fight; yet it can just as easily freeze a person into inaction. So, when you have a teenager who is unmotivated in a particular area of his or her life, look for possible underlying fear. A student like Zoe who fears the future may lack motivation to work hard in school. 'What's the point? I'll probably fail anyway,' she says. When you spend more time with Xander, you discover that his lack of spiritual motivation partly has to do with his fear of the youth group. He has been rejected by so many of his peers that he has no interest in making friends or being around Christians. It is safer to be by himself in the gym. Another teenager may lack motivation to play sports or compete in an activity because of deep insecurity and fear of failure. Since fear is the opposite of love (1 John 4:18), it makes sense that fear takes away passion and motivation. Teenagers who are generally anxious will often underachieve and isolate rather than be driven to work harder and succeed.

So, what is the best way to help the teenager when his or her fear is causing a lack of motivation? Simply saying, 'There is nothing to be afraid of; just trust God.' may be a true statement, yet may not be well-received. Teenagers initially need to receive some level of empathy and understanding from parents and youth ministry workers. It's normal that Zoe would be afraid of the future. Xander's fears of getting hurt by peers is also understandable. What our teenagers need to learn is that they are not alone in life. Fear communicates that there is no one who can protect, or no one who can deliver me from my situation. Teens need to believe in the God who is always present—Immanuel, who is God with us! They also need mature adults in their lives who will calm fears by their presence as well. Too many teens are left to navigate through a scary world as spiritual and emotional orphans. Why wouldn't they be afraid if they are left to themselves? Yet, in Christ, they can act in faith instead of fear, taking risks and seeing what God will do as a result.

Depression result

One of the most obvious consequences of depressed feelings in the life of a teenager is the lack of desire to do things he or she enjoyed in the past. Depression takes away energy—as well as interest—especially for the more difficult or mundane things in life. Just as fear immobilizes, depression is also a great de-motivator. So even though depression can be seen as a symptom of other heart problems, it can also be a primary cause of decreased motivation. Why would a teenager in the depths of despair want to do the hard work of maintaining relationships, working at academics, or excelling in athletics? Teens who are depressed will also lack interest in spiritual things, such as prayer, Bible reading, worship, and Christian fellowship. Unfortunately, a lack of motivation is not only a possible result of depression, but can end up making the depression worse. After all, an unmotivated teen will not be active or successful, which is often perceived as being even more depressing in the end.

If depression is fueling a lack of motivation in a teenager, what can we do about it? Clearly, telling a teen to do activities he has no interest in or motivation to do will not work. As was discussed in a previous chapter, we must ultimately get to the true root problem that is producing depressed feelings in the first place. Yet, also remember that the teenager needs to learn that he or she cannot rely on those negative emotions to drive his or her choices. If Zoe is depressed about all of her friends going to college, she cannot factor that reality into her own decision about her future. Satan is using her grief to tell her lies about herself and fuel her insecurities. Xander may be depressed about his lack of relationships, but that cannot be allowed to motivate him to stay away from church. In other words, teenagers need to recognize the power of emotions to control and motivate—especially negative ones. After all, when we are excited or happy, it is so much easier to do things that are mundane or even hard. Rather than allow fleeting, changing emotions to be our motivators, it must be a renewed mind and a wise heart that pushes us to action.

Feeling overwhelmed

Ever since the entrance of sin into the world, life has become an overwhelming enterprise. Once filled with peace and love, marriage and family is now burdened with conflict, competition, pain, jealousy, and envy (Gen. 3:12, 16; 4:5-8). Our daily work is no longer effortless, but difficult and exhausting—covered in blood, sweat, and tears (Gen. 3:17-19). Sin has made all relationships a struggle, and the world is a place filled with temptation, destruction, and death. Therefore, it should not be a surprise that our teens also find this life overwhelming at times. To be overwhelmed is to literally be submerged, or under water. This experience of being overwhelmed may either be self-inflicted, or just a result of the circumstances of life. While some teenagers may be more motivated to rise above the water; others will believe they are about to drown at any time. For this latter type of teenager, they lack motivation until the burden is lifted, and they are rescued from the depths of the sea.

A teenager who is overwhelmed needs comfort and encouragement. They need to gain courage by the strength of the Lord in order to do the hard things in this life. Yet, they also may require help to do a thorough analysis of their activities and responsibilities. While Xander seems to only spend the majority of his time working out at the gym, a more thorough investigation indicates that he is actually overcommitted. He has a part-time job, is in several extra-curricular clubs and teams, is in a serious dating relationship, and is even taking a couple of advanced placement classes. So, part of his lack of motivation to do anything church-related is because he is already overwhelmed with his current commitments. His time in the gym is a way of escape from everything that is too hard, including spiritual things. It is easy for many parents to needlessly allow their teenagers to keep exceedingly busy, in some misguided effort to keep them out of trouble. Even if a teen looks like he or she is handling everything that is 'on their plate,' a lack of motivation can be caused by feeling overwhelmed in other areas. Forcing a teenager just to do more will possibly only decrease motivation.

Adolescent apathy

Unmotivated teenagers often appear apathetic. Apathy is that state of heart that is indifferent at best, and uncaring at worst. It is first a spiritual problem, since it is rooted in a lack of love for God and/or other people. Speaking of unbelievers, the apostle Paul well describes the problem of apathy: 'They are darkened in their understanding, alienated from the life of God because of the ignorance that is in them, due to their hardness of heart. They have become callous and have given themselves up to sensuality, greedy to practice every kind of impurity' (Eph. 4:18-19). A hardened, apathetic heart not only produces a lack of motivation to do what is right, but also creates an attraction to do what is wrong or useless. William's apathy about his schoolwork is coupled with a passion for video games. Xander's apathy about anything spiritual or church-related is also connected to his zeal for working out. Again, the apathetic teenager is not only passion-less about important, essential things, but is usually more consumed emotionally and passionately with an imitation, or worthless substitute.

So, how do you create passion in the heart of a teenager who is apathetic? The short answer is: You can't. You aren't the Holy Spirit, so you cannot change your teen's heart. But, before getting there, it's essential to properly qualify the apathy. Is the teenager really apathetic, or is it just a cover? William may actually still care about his grades, but he is just pretending not to care, for some reason. Or, maybe the apathy is really a passion-filled act of defiance. Xander refuses to be like his parents and older siblings, just dutifully going to church and obeying the rules. Apathy could also just be a defense, as it may be in Zoe's case. Being indifferent about college is rooted in the belief that she may fail in college. Thus, it is easier just not to care. Finally, as can be the case for many teenagers, apathy can arise from cynicism. Our young people can look around them, become deeply confused and frustrated, and simply find it safer to live in a place of cynical apathy. Talk about a de-motivator! So, make sure to have an understanding of the type of apathy as you counsel your teen. Again, you can't give them passion for Christ, or grades, or work, or their future—but you can help them face their current apathy.

Lack of maturity

To the Church at Philippi, Paul writes: 'I press on toward the goal for the prize of the upward call of God in Christ Jesus. Let those of us who are mature think this way, and if in anything you think otherwise, God will reveal that also to you' (Phil. 3:14-15). One of the signs of Christian maturity is the focus and diligence to press on in our calling in Christ Jesus. In relation to this discussion, an unmotivated teenager lacks the dedication, commitment and singular focus that defines true maturity. In other words, when our teenagers lack motivation in a particular area in their lives, then they are being immature in their thinking. William's procrastination and lack of focus on his schoolwork demonstrates immaturity. Xander's preoccupation with his physical body to the neglect of his soul is also a sign of immaturity. A teenager's lack of motivation can simply be rooted in his or her desire to be a child, rather than move on to adulthood.

A certain level of immaturity is to be expected in our teenagers. After all, they aren't adults yet! If your teen isn't a Christian, then no real spiritual maturity will occur. For those teenagers who are professing Christians, they are able to become more mature at some point. Therefore, when parents and youth ministry workers are counseling a teen who claims to be a Christian, it is essential to direct him or her to understand how to grow as a Christian. In the Parable of the Sower, Jesus points the way: 'And as for what fell among the thorns, they are those who hear, but as they go on their way they are choked by the cares and riches and pleasures of life, and their fruit does not mature' (Luke 8:14). Teenagers who get overwhelmed by the cares of this world, or become preoccupied with the wasteful pleasures of this life, will not mature very well. Only by feeding on God's Word and stoking a passion for Christ and His Kingdom will true maturity occur. The Spirit brings growth to all who are in Christ. When that maturity emerges, then your teen will be more motivated in all aspects of life.

Prayer and patience

This last principle not only belongs at the end of this chapter, but as the final word for all those helping teenagers with their problems: pray and be patient. As frustrating as it may be to deal with an unmotivated teenager, a parent or youth ministry worker should not operate from a place of impatience. Remember, we are seeking intrinsic motivation for our teenagers, not simply looking for more external ways to motivate! Biblical patience comes from a love for the teenagers as well as a love for and trust in the Lord. Our dependence on the Holy Spirit for real heart change must be reflected in our patient, persistent prayer life as well. At some point, a Biblical counselor may have less to say to a teenager who is unmotivated, and more to say to Jesus, the teen's mediator. Prayer and patience are not signs of hopelessness or resignation, but actually point to the hope that is only found in the powerful, gracious work of the Spirit. Again, whatever problems teenagers are experiencing, the adults in their lives must exude plenty of patience, bowing the knee before the throne of grace on a daily basis.

Wisdom POINTERS

The following are some 'do's and don'ts' to remind you to remain gospel-centered and Biblically sound as you counsel unmotivated teenagers:

- Do understand what motivates teenagers.
- Don't rely solely on external motivation techniques.
- Do recognize the impact of parental expectations.
- Don't underestimate the impact of performance pressure.
- Do factor in how fear decreases motivation.

- Don't miss underlying depressive feelings.
- Do challenge the teenager regarding laziness.
- Don't fail to address the spiritual problem of apathy.
- Do look for where the teenager is overwhelmed.
- Don't forget to show grace and mercy, coupled with exhortation and rebuke.
- Do recognize the problem of immaturity.
- Don't neglect constant prayer and patience.

Closing Remarks

On the one hand, mishandled problems during the teenage years can set an individual on a course that is difficult to dramatically alter in the future. On the other hand, God's grace and power are so great that He can redeem and rescue our teenagers from their sins and errors to such an extent that He can give them an amazing future. Those dual realities are intended to give parents and youth ministry workers a sense of urgency, as well as a deeper sense of peace and confidence. God calls mature adults to enter into the lives of teens and call them out of their problems, and into Biblical solutions. At the same time, this counsel must be given from a place of rest in God's sovereign work in the lives of our teenagers. Parents and youth ministry workers are certainly essential tools that God uses to shape, form, and mold teenagers more into the image of Christ. Yet, adults are never to think of themselves as the ultimate saviors or rescuers of troubled teens. Striking the balance between rest and work, peace and urgency, will allow Biblical counselors to be in the right frame of heart and mind to truly help.

Even though the reality is that the teenage years are a relatively short time in the typical human lifespan, they can often feel like eons when significant problems are present. Parents, understandably, can give in to the fatigue and frustration of these years, believing they will never end. Those laboring in youth ministry can also quickly burn out, partly due to the overwhelming nature of teenage problems. So, an essential aspect of counseling teens Biblically is staying the course, running the race, a race that ends in Christian maturity and wisdom. Our teenagers need to have adults in their lives who persevere with them—even when they tend to push people away. This is only possible when Biblical counselors are operating in the strength of the Lord, and not their own power. Handling any and all of these problems may wear you out and make you feel weak at times. But, that should not deter you from your mission and ministry to your teenagers. Again, they need to know they are not alone, and their problems are not hopeless.

Parents and youth ministry workers must want far more than just well-adjusted teenagers, or young people devoid of significant problems. Following the example of Paul's epistles, we should desire growth in faith, in hope, and in love—as our teens pursue hearts of wisdom (1 Cor. 13:13). Only if our teenagers put their faith in Christ alone will anything else in life matter. Only when that saving faith grows into a Christ-centered hope for their future will they gain a right view of their problems and solutions. And, above all, when our teens love the Lord with all their hearts, and their neighbors as themselves, will they have a wise and righteous perspective and focus. Faith, hope, and love are the summary virtues of the Christian life—the qualities that our teenagers should exude. A heart of wisdom is a heart of faith, a heart of love, and a heart of hope. How amazing it is to see our teenagers growing in grace! Ultimately, solving all of these teenage problems is subservient to their salvation and sanctification.

In the end, teenagers who are resting in Christ for their salvation are the adopted children of our Heavenly Father. He has them safely in the palm of His hand, and their lives are hidden in Jesus Christ (Col. 3:3). In Christ, they are able to grow, mature, and enjoy real heart change— moving gradually from foolishness to wisdom. These teens can hear and receive Biblical counsel, as their spiritual eyes and ears have and are being opened by the Spirit. Yet, the reality is, there will also be teenagers in Christian homes and in our churches who are not believers in Jesus Christ. They may be in outright rebellion, running from the Lord, or just confused and lost at the moment. These teenagers also need Biblical counseling, in order to see their need of Christ and their inability to change without Christ. Whatever the state of the teenage heart, the gospel must remain in the center, with Christ lifted up as King. Pursuing a heart of wisdom can only be accomplished in the fear of the Lord and the reliance on the Spirit of wisdom!

Helpful Resources

Anger and Bitterness

Jones, Robert D. *Uprooting Anger: Biblical help for a common problem.* Phillipsburg, NJ: P&R Publishing, 2005.

Powlison, David. *Good and Angry: Redeeming anger, irritation, complaining, and bitterness.* Greensboro, NC: New Growth Press, 2016.

Priolo, Lou. *The Heart of Anger: Practical help for prevention and cure of anger in children.* Amityville, NY: Calvary Press, 1988.

Welch, Edward T. *A Small Book about a Big Problem: Meditations on anger, patience, and peace.* Greensboro, NC: New Growth Press, 2017.

Anxiety, Fear, and Worry

Kellemen, Robert W. *Anxiety: Anatomy and Cure.* Phillipsburg, NJ: P&R Publishing, 2012.

Lane, Timothy. *Living without Worry.* Epsom, UK: The Good Book Company, 2015.

Powlison, David. *Worry: Relief for worried people.* Greensboro, NC: New Growth Press, 2012.

Welch, Edward T. *Running Scared: Fear, worry, and the God of rest.* Greensboro, NC: New Growth Press, 2007.

Depression

Eswine, Zack. *Spurgeon's Sorrows: Realistic hope for those who suffer from depression.* Scotland, UK: Christian Focus, 2015.

Lloyd-Jones, D. Martyn. *Spiritual Depression: Its causes and cures.* Grand Rapids, MI: Wm. B. Eerdmans Publishing Company, 1965.

Piper, John. *When the Darkness Will Not Lift: Doing what we can while we wait for God—and joy.* Wheaton, IL: Crossway, 2006.

Welch, Edward T. *Depression: Looking up from the stubborn darkness.* Greensboro, NC: New Growth Press, 2011.

Drugs and Alcohol

Powlison, David. *Breaking the Addictive Cycle: Deadly obsessions or sinful pleasures?* Greensboro, NC: New Growth Press, 2010.

Welch, Edward T. *Addictions: Banquet in the Grave.* Phillipsburg, NJ: P&R Publishing, 2001.

Eating Disorders

Fitzpatrick, Elyse. *Love to Eat, Hate to Eat: Breaking the bondage of destructive eating habits.* Eugene, OR: Harvest House Publishers, 2004.

Notcheva, Marie. *Redeemed from the Pit: Biblical repentance and restoration from the bondage of eating disorders.* Amityville, NY: Calvary Press, 2011.

Guilt and Shame

Lane, Timothy S. *Freedom from Guilt: Finding release from your burdens.* Greensboro, NC: New Growth Press, 2008.

Nelson, Heather Davis. *Unashamed: Healing our brokenness and finding freedom from shame.* Wheaton, IL: Crossway, 2016.

Welch, Edward T. *Shame, Interrupted: How God lifts the pain of worthlessness and rejection.* Greensboro, NC: New Growth Press, 2012.

Homosexuality and SSA

Allberry, Sam. *Is God Anti-gay?* Epsom, UK: The Good Book Company, 2013.

Black, R. Nicholas. *Homosexuality and the Bible: Outdated advice or words of life.* Greensboro, NC: New Growth Press, 2017.

Burk, Denny and Lambert, Heath. *Transforming Homosexuality: What the Bible says about sexual orientation and change.* Phillipsburg, NJ: P&R Publishing, 2015.

DeYoung, Kevin. *What Does the Bible Really Teach About Homosexuality.* Wheaton, IL: Crossway, 2015.

Marshall, Ben. *Help! My Teen Struggles with Same-sex Attractions.* Wapwallopen, PA: Shepherd Press, 2014.

Identity, Gender, and Self Problems

Geiger, Tim. *Explaining LGBTQ+ identity to your child: Biblical guidance and wisdom.* Greensboro, NC: New Growth Press, 2018.

Hatton, Kristen. *Face time: Your identity in a selfie world.* Greensboro, NC: New Growth Press, 2017.

Pornography

Challies, Tim: *Sexual Detox: A guide for guys who are sick of porn.* Hudson, OH: Cruciform Press, 2010.

Lambert, Heath. *Finally Free: Fighting for purity with the power of grace.* Grand Rapids, MI: Zondervan, 2013.

Reju, Deepak. *Pornography: Fighting for purity.* Phillipsburg, NJ: P&R Publishing, 2018.

Premarital Sex

Lane, Timothy S. *Sex Before Marriage: How far is too far?* Greensboro, NC: New Growth Press, 2009.

Pinson, Cooper. *Alive: Gospel Sexuality for Students.* Greensboro, NC: New Growth Press, 2018.

Tripp, Paul David. *Teens and Sex: How should we trust them?* Phillipsburg, NJ: P&R Publishing, 2002.

Rebellion

Coats, Dave and Coats, Judi. *Help! My Teen is Rebellious.* Wapwallopen, PA: Shepherd Press, 2014.

Juliani, Barbara. *Dealing with the Rebellious Teenager: Help for worried parents.* Greensboro, NC: New Growth Press, 2018.

Self-Harm and Cutting

Lelek, Jeremy. *Cutting: A healing response.* Phillipsburg, NJ: P&R Publishing, 2012.

Welch, Edward T. *Hurts so Good: Exposing the lies of self-injury.* Greensboro, NC: New Growth Press, 2004.

Suicide

Black, Jeffrey. *Suicide: Understanding and intervening.* Phillipsburg, NJ: P&R Publishing, 2003.

Powlison, David. *I Just Want to Die: Replacing suicidal thoughts with hope.* Greensboro, NC: New Growth Press, 2010.

Technology and Media

Huie, Eliza. *Raising Kids in a Screen-Saturated World.* Youngstown, OH: 10Publishing, 2018.

Mueller, Walt. *Youth Culture 101.* Grand Rapids: Zondervan Publishing, 2007

Reinke, Tony. *Twelve Ways Your Phone is Changing You.* Wheaton, IL: Crossway, 2017.

Unmotivated Teens

Horne, Rick. *Get Outta My Face!: How to reach angry, unmotivated teens with Biblical counsel.* Wapwallopen, PA: Shepherd Press, 2009.

Scripture Index

Also available from Christian Focus Publications...

JOHN PERRITT

INSECURE

**FIGHTING OUR LESSER FEARS
WITH A GREATER ONE**

978-1-5271-0330-6

Insecure

Fighting our Lesser Fears with a Greater One

JOHN PERRITT

It's there when you look in the mirror. You'll find it roaming the halls of your school or workplace. It tucks you in at night and greets you as you roll out of bed. You'll read it in text messages & tweets. See it on Facebook and Instagram. It's in our conversations and is always rattling around in our minds.

What is it? Insecurity.

Insecurity is something all humans struggle with. Young and old, male and female, across the globe—insecurity has no boundaries. While it is a commonality among humanity, it doesn't mean it's something you have to live with.

Insecurity is painful for many, but there is a greater fear to drown out this lesser one. Scripture tells us that the fear of the Lord is the beginning of wisdom. It is in this greater fear, that we learn how to grow, live, and, possibly defeat, our insecurity.

John is such a good guide for this common struggle. It turns out that we can do more than simply live with our insecurities and hope to hide them. Instead, we can listen to God, take a stand against them, and grow in wisdom.

Edward T. Welch
Counselor & Faculty at Christian Counseling and Educational Foundation

As a father trying to tackle these issues on a daily basis, I simply can't wait to give John's book to my own kids. It's readable, relevant and real.

Daniel Strange
College Director, Oak Hill Theological College, London

Reformed Youth Ministries (RYM) exists to reach students for Christ and equip them to serve. Passing the faith on to the next generation has been RYM's passion since it began. In 1972 three youth workers who shared a passion for biblical teaching to youth surveyed the landscape of youth ministry conferences. What they found was an emphasis on fun and games, not God's Word. Therefore, they started a conference that focused on the preaching and teaching of God's Word. Over the years RYM has grown beyond conferences into three areas of ministry: conferences, training, and resources.

- **Conferences:** RYM's youth conferences take place in the summer at a variety of locations across the United States and are continuing to expand. We also host parenting conferences throughout the year at local churches.
- **Training:** RYM launched an annual Youth Leader Training (YLT) conference in 2008. YLT has grown steadily through the years and is offered in multiple locations. RYM also offers a Church Internship Program in partnering local churches as well as youth leader coaching and youth ministry consulting.
- **Resources:** RYM offers a variety of resources for leaders, parents, and students. Several Bible studies are offered as free downloads with more titles regularly being added to their catalogue. RYM hosts multiple podcasts: *Parenting Today*, *The Local Youth Worker*, & *The RYM Student Podcast* – all of

which can be downloaded on multiple formats. There are many additional ministry tools available for download on the website.

If you are passionate for passing the faith on to the next generation, please visit www.rym.org to learn more about Reformed Youth Ministries. If you are interested in partnering with us in ministry, please visit www.rym.org/donate.

Christian Focus Publications

Our mission statement –

STAYING FAITHFUL

In dependence upon God we seek to impact the world through literature faithful to His infallible Word, the Bible. Our aim is to ensure that the Lord Jesus Christ is presented as the only hope to obtain forgiveness of sin, live a useful life and look forward to heaven with Him.

Our books are published in four imprints:

CHRISTIAN
FOCUS

Popular works including biographies, commentaries, basic doctrine and Christian living.

CHRISTIAN
HERITAGE

Books representing some of the best material from the rich heritage of the church.

MENTOR

Books written at a level suitable for Bible College and seminary students, pastors, and other serious readers. The imprint includes commentaries, doctrinal studies, examination of current issues and church history.

CF4·K

Children's books for quality Bible teaching and for all age groups: Sunday school curriculum, puzzle and activity books; personal and family devotional titles, biographies and inspirational stories – because you are never too young to know Jesus!

Christian Focus Publications Ltd,
Geanies House, Fearn, Ross-shire,
IV20 1TW, Scotland, United Kingdom.
www.christianfocus.com
blog.christianfocus.com